Religious believers understand the meaning of their lives
and of the world in terms of the way these are related to
God. How, Vincent Brümmer inquires, does the model of
love apply to this relationship? He shows that most views
of love take it to be an attitude rather than a relationship:
exclusive attention (Ortega y Gasset), ecstatic union
(nuptial mysticism), passionate suffering (courtly love),
need-love (Plato, Augustine), and gift-love (Nygren). In
discussing the pertinent issues, Brümmer inquires whether
these attitudes have a role to play in the love-relationship,
and so develops a relational concept of love which can
serve as a key model in theology.

THE MODEL OF LOVE

THE MODEL OF LOVE

A study in philosophical theology

VINCENT BRÜMMER

*Professor in the Philosophy of Religion,
University of Utrecht*

CAMBRIDGE
UNIVERSITY PRESS

Published by the Press Syndicate of the University of Cambridge
The Pitt Building, Trumpington Street, Cambridge CB2 1RP
40 West 20th Street, New York, NY 10011-4211, USA
10 Stamford Road, Oakleigh, Melbourne 3166, Australia

First published 1993

Printed in Great Britain at the University Press, Cambridge

A catalogue record for this book is available from the British Library

Library of Congress cataloguing in publication data

Brümmer, Vincent.
The model of love: a study in philosophical theology / Vincent Brümmer.
p.   cm.
Includes index.
ISBN 0 521 44463 2 (hardback). ISBN 0 521 44909 X (paperback).
1. Love. 1. Title.
BD436.B78   1993
128'.4–dc20   92-42300 CIP

ISBN 0 521 44463 2 hardback
ISBN 0 521 44909 X paperback

For Jean,
from whom through the years I have learnt the meaning of loving
fellowship.

Contents

ix

Preface

I have been working on this book off and on for a number of years now, and there are many friends and colleagues whom I would like to thank for the assistance, advice, and comments with which they have helped me both to get it finished and to eliminate many mistakes which I would otherwise have overlooked. I would also like to thank the president and fellows of Wolfson College, Cambridge, for electing me visiting fellow in 1982. Their hospitality enabled me to start collecting material on love and thus to get this project started. Furthermore, I would like to thank my students in Utrecht to whom I have lectured on this material for many years. Their comments and questions, as well as their need for clarity and relevance, have not been without effect on the final form of the book. I am especially grateful to the Department of Theology in the University of Durham for its hospitality during my term as Richardson Fellow in 1991. It was during that delightful stay that I was able to finish the greater part of the book. Among the friends I made in Durham, I am most grateful to David Brown, Carol Harrison, Margaret Harvey, Ann Loades, and Alan Suggate for reading and commenting on various parts of my manuscript, and especially to Ann Loades for so graciously allowing me to use her room in Abbey house as a workplace during my stay in Durham. Finally, I would like to thank Gerbrandt van Santen for his invaluable assistance in preparing the manuscript and making the index. Previous versions of chapters 1, 3, and 6 were published in article form in various journals. I wish therefore to acknowledge the use I have been able to make of material taken from the following papers:

'Metaphorical thinking and systematic theology' in *Nederlands Theologisch Tijdschrift* 43 (1989), 'God and the union of love' in *Bijdragen* 52 (1991) and 'Atonement and reconciliation' in *Religious Studies* 28 (1992).

PART I

Choosing a model

CHAPTER I

Models and metaphors

My dear friends, let us love one another, because the source of love is God. Everyone who loves is a child of God and knows God, but the unloving know nothing of God, for God is love. This is how he showed his love among us: he sent his only Son into the world that we might have life through him ... Thus we have come to know and believe in the love which God has for us. God is love; he who dwells in love is dwelling in God, and God in him.

(1 John 4: 7–9, 16)

This passage suggests that in the Christian faith, love is not merely an aspect of God's relation to us humans and to the world in which we live, but rather the very key to understanding what this relation is all about. Of course, our relation to God is very complex, involving as it does many other aspects, like God's power, authority, justice, wisdom, knowledge, goodness, steadfastness, presence, etc. However, God's love is in some sense central to our understanding of his relation to us and hence, presumably, to the way we are to understand all these other aspects of the relation as well.

In the context of systematic theology, this would suggest that 'love' is an obvious candidate for the role of key conceptual model for structuring the way we conceive of our relation to God. What would be the implications of this suggestion for theology in general and for our concept of God in particular? That depends of course on what we mean by 'love' and how we understand the role of conceptual models in theology. The chapters that follow will be devoted on the one hand to an inquiry into the nature of love as a personal relationship and of the various attitudes involved in this relationship, and on the

3

other hand to exploring the implications for Christian theology of using this as a conceptual model for talking about the relationship between God and human persons. This first chapter will deal with the preliminary methodological issues: in what sense is all human thinking metaphorical[1] and what does this entail for the use of conceptual models in scientific inquiry, religious belief, and systematic theology? How should the systematic theologian set about testing the adequacy of 'love' as a key conceptual model for theology?

I.I METAPHORICAL THINKING

Comparisons are odious, as the saying goes. And this is quite true, of course, since we all resent being compared to other people. I want my own individuality to be acknowledged, since in my own eyes I am myself and not like everybody else. Comparisons are odious because they tend to ignore our individuality. Furthermore, this is true of all things and not only of people. Every thing is itself and not another thing. By comparing any thing to something else, we ignore its individuality and look upon it as an instance of some general characteristic shared by many things. In this way we forget that every individual thing *is not* like any other thing.

On the other hand, all human thought and experience would

---

[1] The recent literature on metaphor is immense. The following small sample includes a number of important works on the metaphorical nature of religious thought: Ian Barbour, *Myths, Models and Paradigms* (London 1974); Max Black, *Models and Metaphors* (Ithaca 1962); M. Gerhart and A. Russell, *Metaphoric Process. The Creation of Scientific and Religious Understanding* (Fort Worth 1985); Mary B. Hesse, *Models and Analogies in Science* (London 1963); Earl R. MacCormac, *Metaphor and Myth in Science and Religion* (Durham NC 1976) and *A Cognitive Theory of Metaphor* (Cambridge Mass. 1985); Sallie McFague, *Metaphorical Theology* (London 1983) and *Models of God* (London 1987); Andrew Ortony (ed.), *Metaphor and Thought* (Cambridge 1979); Ian T. Ramsey, *Models and Mystery* (Oxford 1964); Paul Ricoeur, *The Rule of Metaphor* (Toronto 1977); Sheldon Sacks (ed.), *On Metaphor* (Chicago 1979); W. A. Shibles, *Metaphor. An Annotated Bibliography and History* (Whitewater Wiss. 1971); Janet Martin Soskice, *Metaphor and Religious Language* (Oxford 1985); T. Wright, *Theology and Literature* (Oxford 1987), especially chapter 4 which provides a useful introduction to the subject. For an interesting attempt to apply these developments in metaphor theory to an analysis of the doctrine of atonement, see Colin E. Gunton, *The Actuality of Atonement* (Edinburgh 1988). See also chapter 2 of my *Speaking of a Personal God* (Cambridge 1992).

become impossible if we refused to compare things to each other. Thus one of the most basic conceptual activities which are characteristic of human thinking is that in which we classify entities according to the characteristics which they have in common. In a variety of circumstances we do this deliberately – for example in botany, zoology, and populations surveys. More important, however, is the intuitive or unconscious classification in which we bring order to our experience.[2] Thus all perception involves a classificatory organization of the data perceived. On this point Kant is correct in his view that our perception and cognition of the world around us are not merely a passive registration of sensory impressions but an active ordering of such sensory data. If we wish to get a hold on the chaos of sensory impressions we receive in perception, we must recognize the similarities and differences between the things we perceive and classify them according to these similarities and differences. In perceiving the world we do not merely register chaotic sensory impressions, nor do we perceive random undefined objects. We always perceive objects as belonging to a kind (people, chairs, tables, houses, trees, etc.) and therefore as having recognizable characteristics in common and differing in recognizable ways from other objects. In this sense all experience is 'experience as ... '[3] which involves comparing things. Without making comparisons we would not be able to experience anything at all.

This classificatory organization of experience constitutes our horizon for understanding the world: we seek to understand things by comparing them to similar things with which we are already familiar. I try to understand how A works or what value I should attach to A by comparing it with B whose workings or value I already understand. We understand one thing in terms of another. For this reason understanding the world around us would become impossible if we refused to compare things to one another.

---

[2] D. E. Cooper points out the metaphorical nature of such classification in *Metaphor* (Oxford 1986), 139. See also the examples in G. Lakoff and M. Johnson, *Metaphors We Live By* (Chicago 1980).

[3] For this term, see John Hick, *God and the Universe of Faiths* (London 1973), chapter 3.

Clearly, then, human thought and human experience require that we assert of every individual thing that it *is* like other things. And yet, even while saying this we have the suspicion that it *is not*.[4] Comparisons may be unavoidable; they are odious nevertheless. We remain in two minds about the way we classify things and bring order to the world of our experience. Let us take a closer look at the process of classification in order to find the reason for our uneasiness.

Classification[5] is the division of entities into classes according to the characteristics which they have in common. The same set of entities may be classified in an infinite variety of ways, depending on which characteristic or set of characteristics we adopt as a basis for the classification. We could classify in such a way that any two random entities fall in the same class, since any two entities will always have some characteristic in common (if only the characteristic that we are now thinking of them). We could also classify in such a way that any two random entities fall in different classes, since there will always be one or more characteristics which they do not have in common – otherwise they would not be *distinct* entities.

Three points are important for our understanding of classification. First, the similarities and differences between things are given to us in experience. We do not produce them ourselves. When doing a population survey, we will have to find out how many people share which characteristics; we cannot think this up for ourselves. Secondly, which characteristics are to serve as a basis for classification is a matter of choice on the part of the classifier – a choice made on pragmatic grounds in the light of the latter's aims, interests, concerns, etc. Thus we could divide up the same group of people in widely different ways, according to the various ends our classification is to serve. Consider for instance the different classifications of persons in a population register, a police register, a medical aid fund register, a school register, a church register, a textbook on cultural anthropology, etc. Thirdly, we are only able to divide things into classes if we

---

[4] See Ricoeur, *The Rule of Metaphor*, 224.
[5] For a more extended discussion of these features of classification, see my *Theology and Philosophical Inquiry* (London 1981), chapter 3.

have developed the skill to recognize the similarities and differences on which our classification is based. We are not born with this ability but have to acquire it like all our other conceptual skills, if not on our mother's knee or in the nursery school, then in some other way in the course of our dealings with the world in which we live.

These features of the activity of classification apply also to the way in which we intuitively organize our experience of the world. Thus the characteristics which things have in common and in which they differ are *given* to us in experience. Although we are the organizers of our experience, we are not its creators. Secondly, we intuitively choose and apply certain similarities as principles of order. There is, however, nothing sacrosanct about this selection. It is also possible to take other similarities as principles of order. In different cultures and historical situations, people organize their experience in different ways, depending on their interests, concerns, and the requirements of their social, cultural, and physical environment.[6] To put it differently: the hermeneutical horizon in terms of which we interpret our experience is not timeless and immutable, but subject to cultural variation and historical change. Thirdly, we are not born with these principles of order, but must acquire the ability to apply them to our experience. This is done in the process of socialization[7] in which society imparts its cultural standards to us as we grow up. This can happen at a conscious level through education and training, but also unconsciously through the language we learn to speak. The language in which we talk about our experience expresses the ways in which we organize it conceptually.[8]

It is now clear why we always have a lingering suspicion that our comparisons are odious, even though they are unavoidable. Every classification is one-sided, since it only takes certain similarities into account while others are ignored. When

---

[6] For some good examples, see Paul Henle (ed.), *Language, Thought and Culture* (Ann Arbor 1966), chapter 1.

[7] See Denis Nineham, *The Use and Abuse of the Bible* (London 1976), 35f.

[8] On this point see Henle, *Language, Thought and Culture*, chapter 1; Nineham, *The Use and Abuse of the Bible*, chapter 1; and my *Theology and Philosophical Inquiry*, chapter 3.

including things in the same class, we take note only of those similarities in terms of which we group them together and ignore their differences or further similarities as irrelevant. More generally, this also applies to the horizon of understanding in terms of which we interpret our experience of the world around us. When we understand A in terms of B, we know deep down that it is also in many respects unlike B.

What we have been describing so far is in fact the fundamentally *metaphorical* nature of all human thought and experience.[9] The term 'metaphor' does not only refer to a figure of speech distinguished from literal language (as is usual in literary theory), but can also be used to refer to a basic characteristic of all our thinking. In this sense Sallie McFague defines metaphor as

seeing one thing *as* something else, pretending 'this' is 'that' because we do not know how to think or talk about 'this', so we use 'that' as a way of saying something about it. Thinking metaphorically means spotting a thread of similarity between two dissimilar objects, events, or whatever, one of which is better known than the other, and using the better-known one as a way of speaking about the lesser known.[10]

McFague also stresses the openness and relativity of all such metaphorical understanding: metaphorical statements 'always contain the whisper, "it is *and it is not.*"'.[11]

An ever-present danger, however, is that we shall fail to hear this whisper. We become so used to looking on A as B that we fail to notice the differences between them. When we become accustomed to a specific classificatory organization of our experience, we become sensitive to and observant of the similarities between things on which it is based, and both insensitive to and unobservant of the differences which are ignored by it. The psychologists Bruner and Goodman show how this process can lead to a form of conceptual blindness or

---

[9] On this connection between classification and metaphor, see Mary Hesse, 'The cognitive claims of metaphor', *The Journal of Speculative Philosophy* 2 (1988), 1–16. See also M. A. Arbib and M. B. Hesse, *The Construction of Reality* (Cambridge 1986), chapter 10, and J. Van Brakel and J. P. M. Geurts, 'Pragmatic identity of meaning and metaphor', *International Studies in the Philosophy of Science* 2 (1988), 205–26.

[10] McFague, *Metaphorical Theology*, 15.   [11] Ibid., 13.

'mental set' in which 'subjects can be conditioned to see and hear things in much the same way as they can be conditioned to perform such overt acts as knee jerking, eye blinking or salivating'.[12]

Language is an important conditioning factor in this connection. Class words or descriptive terms are the instruments by means of which we explicitly exercise our classificatory skills. Since all of us acquire a specific vocabulary, we have words only for the exercise of *certain* classification concepts, and find it hard to organize our experience differently since we lack the instruments to do so. 'General words tend to *fossilize* our conception of the ever-changing, infinitely varied world of things to make us conceive the world as being composed of static *types* rather than of different things, each of which are similar enough to each other to be given the same name.'[13] Our language and our forms of thought or concepts determine each other mutually. On the one hand, our cultural interests and concerns determine what classificatory organization we need to give to our experience, and hence which classification words we require. On the other hand, the words we have (in the language we have learned) determine which classification concepts we can apply and hence how we organize our experience of the world. This in turn reinforces our cultural interests and concerns.

This circle becomes vicious and dangerous when the circumstances of our lives change in ways which make it essential for us to notice those features of the world which we have become conditioned to overlook. If, under such circumstances, we view our conceptualization of experience as absolute or as 'expressing the essential nature of reality', our thought forms become irrelevant[14] and we become unable to cope conceptually with the new circumstances in which we have to live. In brief, when our metaphors die and become literalized so that we fail to hear in them the whispered 'and it is not', the comparisons they express become not only odious but positively dangerous.

[12] Quoted by Henle, *Language, Thought and Culture*, 6.
[13] John Hospers, *An Introduction to Philosophical Analysis* (London 1967; 2nd edn.), 44.
[14] On the danger of irrelevance, see McFague, *Metaphorical Theology*, chapter 1.

When this happens we need new 'iconoclastic'[15] metaphors which make us experience the shock of recognition needed to break down our mental set and thus enable us to see those features of the world which we have been conditioned to overlook.

1.2 MODELS IN SCIENCE

The metaphorical nature of human thought is fundamental to scientific discovery and explanation. Thus scientific discoveries very often consist in the shock of recognition by which an imaginative scientist suddenly notices a significant similarity between two very different things or situations. The similarity had up to then gone unnoticed because in the generally accepted conceptual structuring of experience the things in question were quite unrelated. Such discoveries are in fact iconoclastic 'breakthroughs' since they break down the mental set which prevented people from noticing what was there all along before their eyes. Arthur Koestler[16] provides many examples of such discoveries in which similarities are seen which had previously been blocked. The classical example is of course that of Archimedes in his bathtub. Another is that of Newton who discovered a property of the moon by noticing that it behaved like the apple falling from the tree beside him: like the apple, the moon was subject to gravity.

One of the fundamental procedures of scientific inquiry consists in turning certain metaphorical comparisons into *conceptual models*, i.e. 'sustained and systematic metaphors'.[17] The scientist does not merely look on A as B (the moon as an apple) but does so in a sustained and systematic manner in order to see how far the analogy goes.[18] Of course not all metaphors can be fruitfully developed as conceptual models.

[15] For this term, see ibid., chapter 1.

[16] Arthur Koestler, *The Act of Creation* (New York 1964), 119–21. According to Colin Gunton, metaphor serves as 'the vehicle of discovery': *The Actuality of Atonement*, 31. On this point see also Richard Boyd, 'Metaphor and theory change: what is "metaphor" a metaphor for?', in Ortony (ed.), *Metaphor and Thought*.

[17] Black, *Models and Metaphors*, 236.

[18] Mary Hesse argues that these analogies examined in science could be positive, negative or neutral. See Hesse, *Models and Analogies in Science*.

The analogy between the moon and an apple may have been very significant for Newton, since it enabled him to make a momentous discovery about the functioning of the moon. Nevertheless, it remains a very limited analogy which does not lend itself to sustained and systematic development in the form of a scientific theory. Other metaphors prove to be more fruitful in theory formation. The nature and workings of A can be fruitfully explored and explained by comparing it systematically to B. Thus the behaviour of gases can be fruitfully explained by comparing it systematically with the behaviour of billiard balls, and the behaviour of light rays can be fruitfully explained by comparing it systematically with the behaviour of waves or of moving particles.[19]

The use of conceptual models is not only characteristic of scientific inquiry but of human thinking in general. Thus, in the words of Sallie McFague, 'just as individuals model themselves after others, so entire cultures seek and achieve defining metaphors that provide ways of organizing and speaking intelligibly about a vast array of details which, without the models and metaphors, would be chaos'.[20] In the context of scientific inquiry, such conceptual models function as grids which enable us to organize the way in which to proceed, to decide on the avenues to explore, and to determine the sorts of questions to be asked. When we look upon gas molecules as upon billiard balls, we ask the sorts of questions about the molecules which are familiar to us in connection with billiard balls, and we try to apply the mathematical calculations to the molecules which we usually apply to the billiard balls impinging on each other on a billiard table. When we interpret light rays in terms of waves or of moving particles, we ask the sorts of questions about the behaviour of light which we would otherwise ask about the behaviour of waves or of particles. In this way conceptual models are indispensable for scientific inquiry. Without them we would not know how to set about it. On the other hand, a conceptual model can be very dangerous

---

[19] See Barbour, *Myths, Models and Paradigms*, 30 (on the billiard ball model) and 71f. (on the wave and particle models in light theory).

[20] McFague, *Metaphorical Theology*, 68.

since it can turn into a mental strait-jacket, forcing our thinking
into a fixed pattern. It is well to heed R. B. Braithwaite's
warning that 'the price of the employment of models is eternal
vigilance'.[21]

This vigilance is essential on two counts. First of all, since
models are themselves metaphors, they carry with them the
whisper 'and it is not'. As the similarities suggested in a model
are developed in a sustained and systematic way, the danger is
even greater that the whisper will be silenced and the analogies
interpreted as identities.[22] It may be useful and enlightening to
look on gas molecules in the way we look upon billiard balls, but
it is equally important to remember that they are in many
respects not like billiard balls. That they are similar remains a
hypothesis which it is fruitful to explore, but should never
become a necessary assumption which needs no further systematic testing. Secondly, although conceptual models help us
to formulate illuminating questions, they also act as filters
which prevent us from asking other questions. Max Black
explains this point with the following example:

Suppose I am set the task of describing a battle in words drawn as
largely as possible from the vocabulary of chess. These latter terms
determine a system of implications which will proceed to control my
description of the battle. The enforced choice of the chess vocabulary
will lead some aspects of the battle to be emphasized, others to be
neglected, and all to be organized in a way that would cause much
more strain in other modes of description. The chess vocabulary filters
and transforms: it not only selects, it brings forward aspects of the
battle that might not be seen at all through another medium.[23]

The conceptual model enables us to discover features of the
world which we would otherwise have overlooked. However, it
also filters out other aspects and prevents us from seeing them.
For this reason it is essential that we should guard against

---

[21] R. B. Braithwaite, *Scientific Explanation* (Cambridge 1953), 93.
[22] Earl MacCormac shows how myths originate when metaphors are taken to be
absolute reality. According to him this also applies when scientific theories are made
absolute: 'To claim finality for a tentative scientific theory is to create a myth, and
that act of myth-making is no different from believing that the gods really did create
the world by hacking the body of a fallen warrior into pieces.' McCormac, *Metaphor
and Myth in Science and Religion*, 102.   [23] Black, *Models and Metaphors*, 41–2.

making our models absolute and considering the way they enable us to look at the world as the one and only way in which the world should be looked at. Often we need complementary models which allow us to see things which we would be prevented from seeing if we used only one model. Thus in the theory of light we need both the wave model and the particle model because each of these enable us to say things about light which the other model would filter out. Sallie McFague summarizes this point neatly as follows:

Models are necessary... for they give us something to think about when we do not know what to think, a way of talking when we do not know how to talk. But they are also dangerous, for they exclude other ways of thinking and talking, and in so doing they can easily become literalized, that is, identified as *the* one and only way of understanding a subject. This danger is more prevalent with models than with metaphors because models have a wider range and are more permanent; they also tend to object to competition in ways that metaphors do not.[24]

1.3 MODELS IN RELIGION

As in the case of science, metaphor plays an essential role in religion and in theology. Much of what we have argued above therefore also applies to religion and to views of life in general. However, the metaphorical comparisons of religion fulfil a very different function in human life and thought than do those of science. Religion is not an alternative for science nor science for religion.[25] Imagine a medical officer filling in a death certificate and specifying the cause of death as follows: 'This person was a sinner and the wages of sin is death (Romans 6: 23).' This could not be described as merely an unsatisfactory causal explanation, since in fact it is not a causal explanation at all. Wittgenstein might say: 'For a blunder, that's too big.'[26] Religious metaphors are not intended to help us discover or explain how

---

[24] McFague, *Metaphorical Theology*, 24.

[25] For a more extended analysis of the difference between the language games of science and religion, see my introductory chapter to Vincent Brümmer (ed.), *Interpreting the Universe as Creation* (Kampen 1991).

[26] Ludwig Wittgenstein, *Lectures and Conversations on Aesthetics, Psychology and Religious Belief* (Oxford 1966), 62.

physical phenomena work, but rather to help us understand the *meaning*[27] or sense of our lives and of the world in which we live and in relation to which we act. In this way they determine the way we should act and the attitudes we should adopt in life. Different religious traditions and views of life provide their adherents with a fund of conceptual models in terms of which life and the world can be meaningfully understood, and which are definitive for the religions or views of life in question.

As in the case of scientific inquiry, some metaphors in religion are also developed in a sustained and systematic way as conceptual models. Thus in the Christian tradition God is sometimes called a rock (or a 'rock of ages') in order to express his eternal dependability and trustworthiness. However, since the analogy between God and a rock does not go much further than that, the rock metaphor does not lend itself for systematic development as a theological model.[28] In contrast, God is also talked of as a person, addressed as a person, etc. The analogy between God and human persons is so rich that it has been developed as the most fundamental and characteristic conceptual model in theistic god-talk. A personalist theology is feasible. A 'rock' theology is not.

Like all conceptual models, those in theology remain metaphors and therefore what they assert is always accompanied by the whisper 'and it is not'. The fruitfulness of personalist models for talking about God should therefore never make us deaf to the whisper that God is not like other people.[29] In the history of Christian theology it has often been a lack of sensitivity for the limits of conceptual models which has given rise to heresy. A good example of this is Arius, of whom Bethune-Baker writes as follows:

Arius seems, in part at least, to have been misled by a wrong use of analogy, and by mistaking description for definition. All attempts to explain the nature and relations of the Deity must largely depend on

---

[27] For an extended analysis of this concept of 'meaning', see my *Theology and Philosophical Inquiry*, chapter 9.

[28] See Terence E. Fretheim, *The Suffering of God* (Philadelphia 1984), 10–12.

[29] In a recent article Keith Ward has given voice to this whisper: 'Is God a person?', in Gijsbert van den Brink, Luco J. van den Brom and Marcel Sarot (eds.), *Christian Faith and Philosophical Theology* (Kampen 1992), 259–66.

metaphor, and no one metaphor can exhaust those relations. Each metaphor can only describe one aspect of the nature or being of the Deity, and the inferences which can be drawn from it have their limits when they conflict with the inferences which can be truly drawn from other metaphors describing other aspects. From one point of view Sonship is a true description of the inner relations of the Godhead: from another point of view the title Logos describes them best. Each metaphor must be limited by the other. The title Son may obviously imply later origin and a distinction amounting to ditheism. It is balanced by the other title Logos, which implies co-eternity and inseparable union. Neither title exhausts the relations. Neither may be pressed so far as to exclude the other.[30]

It is the task of systematic theology to explore which inferences may be validly drawn from the conceptual models of a religious tradition.

Wittgenstein makes a useful point in this connection when he argues that, in order to participate in religious belief, one has to be trained in the technique of using the appropriate picture or pictures.[31] Acquiring this technique involves learning which inferences may be drawn from the picture and which not. In discussing this point in Wittgenstein, W. D. Hudson distinguishes two sets of inferences which believers must learn to draw.[32] First of all, they must learn to see how the expressions used in the 'picture' both resemble and differ from their use in other non-religious contexts. Thus, if we use personal models in talking about God and his relations with human persons, we must determine the limits of the models: how is the relation between God and ourselves like, and how unlike, human relations? Here we have to sort out which implications of personal relation concepts, as these are used with reference to human relations, do and which do not carry over to the way we are to understand the relationship between God and ourselves. Secondly, believers must come to see what implications the metaphors and models have for their actions and attitudes when

[30] J. F. Bethune-Baker, *An Introduction to the Early History of Christian Doctrine* (London 1958), 160. Recent scholarship casts some doubt on Bethune-Baker's interpretation of Arius. However, this does not affect the point illustrated by this example.

[31] Wittgenstein, *Lectures and Conversations*, 53f.

[32] W. D. Hudson, 'Some remarks on Wittgenstein's account of religious language', in G. N. A. Vesey (ed.), *Talk of God* (London 1969), 38f.

they interpret their life and experience of the world in terms of
these. Sorting out these two kinds of implications in a systematic
way is one of the important tasks of theological inquiry. Thus
Sallie McFague argues that 'the central role of models in
theology is to provide grids or screens for interpreting this
relation between the divine and the human... In order to
interpret this relationship, conceptual clarity and precision is
necessary: the structure implied in the relationship must be
sorted out and its implications for personal, historical, social
and political life made manifest.'[33]

Religious models determine the actions and attitudes to
which believers commit themselves, in two main ways. First, in
coming to understand themselves and their own lives in terms of
the conceptual models derived from their religious tradition,
believers discover the role they have to play in their lives and
actions. As Iris Murdoch puts it,[34] 'man is a creature who makes
pictures of himself and then comes to resemble the picture'.
Secondly, by interpreting their experience of the world in terms
of such models, believers come to see which actions and attitudes
are called for in relation to the world and in the various
situations in which they have to act. These two points could be
illustrated with reference to the Christian faith.

First of all, Christians look on their own lives as lives lived
coram Deo – in the presence of God. Their role in life is
determined by the way their lives are related to God, and thus
by the conceptual models in terms of which they understand this
relation. To the extent that they interpret this relation in
personal terms, they will see their role in life as one of personal
fellowship with God and commit themselves to actions aimed at
realizing God's intentions with their lives. Secondly, Christians
also interpret their experience of the world in terms of the way
it is related to God. The way they cope with their experience
and act in relation to their environment therefore depends on
the conceptual models in terms of which they understand the
relation between God and the world. To the extent that they

---

[33] McFague, *Metaphorical Theology*, 125.
[34] Iris Murdoch, 'Metaphysics and ethics', in D. F. Pears (ed.), *The Nature of
Metaphysics* (London 1962), 122.

understand this relation in personal terms, believers interpret the world in terms of the intentional agency of God. This entails that much of what they experience in the world is for them an object of praise and thanksgiving to the God who brings it about. In this sense J. Neville Ward claims that thanksgiving is 'the essential Christian posture before experience'.[35] On the other hand, much else that Christians encounter in the world is understood as contrary to God's purposes and therefore to be opposed and changed. This is a task which believers are called upon to perform in fellowship with God.[36] In these ways the models and metaphors in terms of which believers understand themselves and the world in which they live, have a *commissive* force, since, in accepting the interpretation, they commit themselves to specific attitudes and forms of action.

Do these models also have a *constative* force? Are they also claimed to be *factually true*? Or are they merely useful fictions in terms of which believers bring order to their lives, without claiming them to be factually true in any sense?[37] According to a philosopher like R. B. Braithwaite,[38] religious beliefs are stories in terms of which religious believers express their attitudes and moral commitments, and which also inspire them to adopt these attitudes and these commitments. However, the stories do not have to be believed to be factually true in order to fulfil these functions for the believer. Similarly, W. D. Hudson points out that what Wittgenstein seems 'at times to have come near to suggesting is that, because religious beliefs have commissive force, that somehow entitles us to by-pass the troublesome problem of their constative force'.[39] The trouble with this sort of view is that the actions and attitudes to which believers commit themselves when understanding their lives in terms of their beliefs become incoherent if they reject the factual

[35] J. Neville Ward, *The Use of Praying* (London 1967), 20.

[36] On the relation between divine and human agency, see chapter 5 of my *Speaking of a Personal God*.

[37] Similar questions also arise with reference to the use of models in scientific inquiry, and realists differ from instrumentalists as to the answers. See Barbour, *Myths, Models and Paradigms*, chapter 3.

[38] R. B. Braithwaite, 'An empiricist's view of the nature of religious belief', in J. Hick (ed.), *The Existence of God* (New York 1964), 229–52.

[39] Hudson, in *Talk of God*, 44.

claims involved in the beliefs. It would be incoherent to live my life as a life in the presence of God if I were to deny that there really is a God in whose presence I live. Since the truth of the belief is a constitutive presupposition of the way of life, the latter would be incoherent if the former is denied.[40] R. W. Hepburn provides a good illustration of this point:

If I say 'the Lord is my strength and shield', and if I am a believer, I may experience feelings of exultation and be confirmed in an attitude of quiet confidence. If, however, I tell myself that the arousal of such feelings and confirming of attitude is *the* function of the sentence, that despite appearances it does not refer to a state of affairs, then the more I reflect on this the less I shall exult and the less appropriate my attitude will seem. For there was no magic in the sentence by virtue of which it mediated feelings and confirmed attitudes: these were *responses* to the kind of Being to whom, I trusted, the sentence referred: and response is possible only so long as that exists to which or to whom the response is made.[41]

Truth claims cannot be eliminated from religion. Yet, such claims differ from those in science by being logically related to the religious way of life: religious truth claims are made with reference to the factual presuppositions which are constitutive for the way of life. For this reason they are 'existential' in a way that the truth claims of science are not. It might make sense to say: 'It is true that the planet Jupiter exists and is the largest planet of our solar system, but I don't really care much about that.' It is however absurd to say: 'It is true that God exists and is the personal creator of the universe, but I don't really care much about that.' Here too Wittgenstein might comment: 'For a blunder, that's too big.'[42]

The points we have raised so far concerning the metaphorical nature of religious belief can be briefly summarized as follows:

[40] On the role of such constitutive presuppositions, see chapter 1 of my *Interpreting the Universe as Creation*.

[41] R. W. Hepburn, 'Poetry and religious belief', in A. MacIntyre (ed.), *Metaphysical Beliefs* (London 1957), 148.

[42] Wittgenstein, *Lectures and Conversations*, 62. Elsewhere I have also argued that the existential nature of religious belief does not exclude factual claims but in fact entails them. See *Theology and Philosophical Inquiry*, chapters 17–19; *What Are We Doing When We Pray?* (London 1984), chapter 2; *Interpreting the Universe as Creation*, chapter 1; *Speaking of a Personal God*, chapter 2; 'Has the theism – atheism debate a future?', *Theology* 97 (1994).

remain metaphors which are accompanied by the
and it is not'. This whisper should always remind
limits of their undertaking. Instead of overlooking
ariety of models and metaphors provided by the
ystematic theologians should inquire whether these
natural (non-contrived) interpretation which makes
ement rather than contradict the key model which
ians propose to develop. Since this inquiry is never
the need for sensitivity and 'eternal vigilance' never
n end. Systematic theologians may never claim to
uced the final conceptual form for the faith. The
' which they produce are never more than suggested
the faith which have to prove their worth in the lives
thful. Secondly, the choice of a metaphor to be
as key model should be well considered rather than
adequately argued rather than uncritical. Systematic
s should look before they leap. The problem is: how
o look and what criteria should they use in deciding
etaphor is the most adequate candidate for devel-
s comprehensive theological key model? There are at
criteria which are relevant here. All of these are
and none of them are sufficient. These are consonance
lition; comprehensive coherence; adequacy for the
of life; and personal authenticity. Let us examine
re closely.

e with tradition. Systematic theologians do not create
or God.[50] They derive them from the religious tradition
they stand. For Christians the Bible is the classic text[51]
radition and as such the classic source of metaphors and
n terms of which they understand the meaning of their
the world. In the tradition of the Christian faith, these

th quoting McFague on this point: 'No one, of course, can create images of
igious symbols are born and die in a culture for complex reasons. At most one
o attend carefully to the images in the culture and church which appear to
rging and to experiment imaginatively with them, reflecting on their
ions for life with God and with others.' *Models of God*, 20.
concept of a 'classic' see David Tracy, *The Analogical Imagination* (London
hapter 3.

(1) Theistic believers are people who understand their lives and
their experience of the world in terms of the way these are
related to God. Their lives are lived *coram Deo*, in the presence
of God. (2) Thus interpreting life and experience in terms of
faith does not explain anything in the sense in which this is done
through scientific inquiry. Instead it determines the meaning or
sense or significance of life and experience. In other words, for
believers the meaning of life and the world is determined by the
way these are related to God, and hence by the conceptual
models in terms of which they try to express this relation.
(3) Understanding the meaning of life and the world in terms of
such theistic models presupposes belief in the factual truth of
these models. Conceptual models fail to provide the understanding sought for in religion if they are taken to be merely
useful fictions and not in some sense 'reality depicting'.[43] In
other words, religious faith entails some form of critical realism[44]
regarding the ontological status of religious models.

What kind of relation, then, do believers presuppose to exist
between God and themselves, and how does systematic theology
develop conceptual models with which to express this relation in
a comprehensive and coherent way?

1.4 MODELS IN SYSTEMATIC THEOLOGY

As we have argued above, beliefs about the nature of God are
existential in the sense that they are always directly connected
with the ways in which we relate to God. For this reason all the
metaphors and models employed in God-talk are primarily
relational: they are intended to indicate the ways in which we
are to relate to God. If we call God a rock, this is meant
primarily to indicate the way in which we can depend upon
God and only in a secondary, implied sense to make the factual
statement about God, that he is the kind of Being on whom we
can depend in this way. Since the ways in which believers relate
to God are varied and complex, and in fact comprise their whole
way of life, it is not surprising that a large variety of metaphors

[43] For this term see Soskice, *Metaphor and Religious Language*, chapter 7.
[44] On critical realism, see Barbour, *Myths, Models and Paradigms*, chapter 3.

is needed in order to indicate all the various aspects of this relation. Relating to God is like relating to a father, a king, a mother, a judge, a mountain, a rock, an ocean, a lover, a friend, a shepherd, a liberator, a protector, etc., etc.[45] The Christian tradition provides countless metaphors for this purpose, none of which is adequate for expressing all aspects of the relation and each of which requires others to support and supplement it.

To the extent that believers need to bring coherence to their life in the presence of God, they cannot rest content with expressing it by means of a myriad of disconnected metaphors. Some of these metaphors will have to be developed systematically into coherent and more or less comprehensive conceptual models. Of course, not all metaphors are developed into models and not all models are developed to the same degree of comprehensiveness. Each model requires to be supplemented and supported by other models and metaphors: The latter either express aspects of the relation to God which are overlooked or 'filtered out' by the former, or they provide emphasis for certain aspects which are implied but not specially emphasized by the former. Thus the rock metaphor lends a special emphasis to the dependability and trustworthiness of God implied in the conceptual model of God as a friend. In this way conceptual models complement each other and bring some systematic order among the many metaphors which support them.

Systematic theology tries to go a step further by seeking to develop a 'root metaphor'[46] or comprehensive *key model* which

[45] The following verse from the hymn 'How sweet the name of Jesus sounds' provides a good example of such multiplication of metaphor:

> Jesus! my Shepherd, Husband, Friend,
> My Prophet, Priest and King,
> My Lord, my Life, my Way, my End,
> Accept the praise I bring.

[46] This term was introduced by Stephen C. Pepper, *World Hypotheses* (Berkeley 1942), and has been taken over since by many authors (e.g. David Tracy and Sally MacFague). Unlike them, I will avoid this term, since I am not using it in precisely the same sense as Pepper. For a useful discussion of the differences between Pepper's use of this term and that of MacFague, see James Moulder, 'Metaphors and models in religion and theology', *South African Journal of Philosophy* 6 (1987), 29–34. Moulder, like McFague, also uses the term 'dominant metaphor' which sounds rather loaded and negative. I prefer the more neutral term 'key model' which I shall therefore use.

can coherently integrate thi
world in relation to God, as
kind provides coherence for
theology, it will have implica
Different key models will t
logies' which express differe
the world in relation to God.
a Father as our key model,
theology and way of understa
key model of God as a Kin
theology and an hierarchica
world.[48] A deterministic theo
generated by a key model whic
and the world in purely caus
merit could result from a k
relation between God and the
rights and duties.[49] From th
although all these relational
cannot be eliminated from Chr
them into a theological key mo
sided theology in which many
Christian understanding of life a
out and ignored.

The danger of one-sidedness
metaphors and models increases
hensively developed. This has tw
quences for systematic theologia
prehensive coherence. First of all,
the price of the employment of r
especially relevant for systematic
always be sensitive to the fact that t

[47] Ferré points out that theology differs from s
of theological concepts with respect to un
models, is to help construct a completely comp
every possible event can be interpreted as ex
models and religion', *Soundings* 51 (1968), 34
[48] On the use of these two key models in theolog
and *Models of God*.
[49] On the use of these two key models in theology
Pray?, chapter 6, and *Speaking of a Personal God*

to develop
whispered '
them of the
the great
tradition, s
allow for a
them supp
the theolo
completed
comes to
have prod
'theologie
designs for
of the fai
developed
intuitive,
theologia
are they
which m
opment a
least fou
necessary
with trac
demands
these mo

Consonan
models f
in which
of their t
models i
lives and

[50] It is wo
God; re
can try
be eme
implica
[51] For th
1981),

metaphors and models have been actualized, interpreted, reinterpreted, developed, and amended in many ways throughout the ages, and handed down in many ways from person to person and generation to generation. In this sense Wilfred Cantwell Smith emphasizes the *cumulative* character of every religious tradition.[52]

There are two important reasons why systematic theologians should derive the metaphors which they develop as key models, from the cumulative tradition in which they stand. First of all, like science, religion is not an individual but a co-operative enterprise.[53] Like scientists, religious believers therefore interpret experience within a communal tradition. In the case of science, this entails that the paradigm of the community of scientists sets limits to the range of acceptable models within that community. In religion it is the cumulative tradition which determines the range of models which are acceptable within the community of believers. Of course this does not prevent theologians from being innovative and suggesting reinterpretations of the faith and new ways of developing the models of the Christian tradition. However, if these innovations are too far removed from the cumulative tradition from which the community derives its faith, they become unrecognizable for others and therefore make co-operation impossible. Richard Hare makes a similar point with reference to speaking and dancing:

> What makes co-operation possible in both these activities is that the speaker or dancer should not do things which make the other people say 'We don't know what to make of this.' That is to say, he must not do things which cannot be easily related to the unformulated rules of speaking and dancing which everybody knows who has learned to perform these activities.[54]

In brief, the search for community, which Stanley Cavell equates with the search for reason,[55] requires that systematic theologians derive the key models of their theology from the

[52] See Wilfred Cantwell Smith, *The Meaning and End of Religion* (London 1978), chapter 6.   [53] See Barbour, *Myths, Models and Paradigms*, 147f.
[54] R. M. Hare, *Essays on Philosophical Method* (London 1971), 33.
[55] Stanley Cavell, *The Claim of Reason. Wittgenstein, Skepticism, Morality, and Tragedy* (Oxford 1979), 20.

cumulative tradition of the religious community to which they address themselves. A second reason for looking to the cumulative tradition is that this enables theologians to learn from the efforts and the mistakes of their predecessors. A religious tradition is also a theological tradition in which theologians through the ages have tried to develop many metaphors systematically into models and key models for their theologies. In this tradition it has become clear which conceptual models have proved their staying power and systematic potential and have gained recognition as viable alternatives within the community of faith.

In these two ways the cumulative tradition of the faith sets the limits on the range of models which have proved to be acceptable to the community of faith and viable candidates for development as key models for theology. Although this limits the range of options open to systematic theologians, it nevertheless does not determine their choices. Within the same Christian tradition many theologies remain possible, each of which is systematically structured by a different key model.[56] The unity of the Christian faith is not given in an identity of doctrine leaving only one option open, but in the continuity of a cumulative tradition encompassing a range of options. In the words of John Cobb: 'The unity of Christianity is the unity of an historical movement. That does not depend on any self-identity of doctrine, vision of reality, structure of existence, or style of life. It does depend on demonstrable continuities, the appropriateness of creative changes, and the self-identification of people in relation to a particular history.'[57] Although the criterion of 'consonance with tradition' is necessary, it is clearly not sufficient for determining the choice of a key model for theology. Further criteria are needed as well.

---

[56] On this point McFague writes as follows: 'If one reflects on the contrasts between the theologies of Paul, Augustine, Luther, Schleiermacher and Barth (just to take a sampling of the tradition) as to their basic images, root metaphors, concepts and assumptions about reality, one has to acknowledge an enormous variety, all of it, however, capable of being accommodated within the Christian paradigm.' *Models of God*, 21.

[57] John Cobb, 'Feminist and process thought: A two-way relationship', in Sheila Greeve Davaney (ed.), *Feminism and Process Thought* (New York 1981), 42.

Comprehensive coherence. We have seen that conceptual models are selective: They highlight certain features of the faith and overlook or filter out others.[58] There is a conceptual price-tag attached to each theological model, and to a large extent the task of systematic theology has to do with calculating the cost of our models in order to determine whether we are willing and able to pay the price. The more comprehensively a model is developed, the greater the price and the more complex the calculation required. In order to carry out this calculation, a systematic theologian is required to develop a suggested theological key model derived from the cumulative tradition,[59] coherently and comprehensively, in order to see what it entails for the whole conceptual scheme of the faith: which elements of the tradition will be highlighted and which will be filtered out or overlooked? To what extent can its weaknesses be compensated by means of supporting metaphors and complementary models? Can these allow for coherent development in a way which supplements and does not contradict the key model? A conceptual inquiry of this kind reveals the consequences which a suggested key model would have for the conceptual scheme of the faith. It does not, however, determine whether these consequences are acceptable, but leaves open the choice between accepting the model at the calculated price, or deciding that the price is too high to pay and hence rejecting the model. The only possibility which they exclude is that we should accept the model and refuse to pay the conceptual price. Although criteria of logical coherence in this way provide a further limitation to our conceptual options, they do not force conclusions. In the words of Antony Flew:

Every sound argument 'forces', in the sense that it limits the available options even though no argument can ever be 'completely com-

---

[58] For a useful discussion of the way this takes place, see Lakoff and Johnson, *Metaphors We Live By*, 10–13.

[59] Colin Gunton correctly warns against the tendency to deal with theological metaphors in abstraction from the tradition from which they are derived. 'Such abstraction carries the danger that certain expectations or presuppositions will be taken into the discussion and prevent the theological meaning from speaking for itself.' *The Actuality of Atonement*, 48.

pulsive', if by that were to be meant – what never is meant – that it blocks up literally every alternative to accepting its conclusions. For ... any valid deductive argument can as such be either a proof of its conclusions or a disproof of one of its premisses.[60]

The criterion of 'comprehensive coherence', although necessary, is not by itself sufficient for deciding which of the models that are consonant with tradition, should be accepted as key model for theology. Further criteria are needed as well.

Adequacy for the demands of life. In section 1.1 above we pointed out the danger of thinking that our conceptualization of experience is absolute and expresses 'the essential nature of reality'. If we consider our thought forms to be immutable in this way, they can become irrelevant to the changing demands of life and consequently fail to help us cope with these demands conceptually. Because of changes in the demands of life, our conceptual forms cannot remain eternally adequate. Wittgenstein explains this point as follows:

Earlier physicists are said to have found suddenly that they had too little mathematical understanding to cope with physics; and in almost the same way young people today can be said to be in a situation where ordinary common sense no longer suffices to meet the strange demands life makes. Everything has become so intricate that mastering it would require an exceptional intellect. Because skill at playing the game is no longer enough, the question that keeps coming up is: can this game be played at all now and what would be the right game to play?[61]

This has profound implications for the way in which systematic theology tries to conceptualize the faith. Changes in the demands of life bring about changes in the aspects of faith which are relevant and necessary in order to make sense of life and cope meaningfully with our experience of the world. At different times and in different cultural situations, systematic theology therefore requires different conceptual models in order to highlight those aspects of the faith which are relevant to the

[60] Antony Flew, *An Introduction to Western Philosophy* (London 1971), 24.
[61] Ludwig Wittgenstein, *Culture and Value* (Oxford 1980), 27.

cultural and historical situation and to filter out those aspects which are not relevant to the current demands of life. Sallie McFague provides a good example to illustrate this point:

> In an era when evil powers were understood to be palpable principalities in contest with God for control of human beings and the cosmos, the metaphor of Christ as the victorious king and lord, crushing the evil spirits and thereby freeing the world from their control, was indeed a powerful one. In our situation, however, to envision evil as separate from human beings rather than as the outcome of human decisions and actions, and to see the solution of evil as totally a divine responsibility, would be not only irrelevant to our time and its needs but harmful to them, for that would run counter to one of the central insights of the new sensibility: the need for human responsibility in a nuclear age. In other words, in order to do theology, one must in each epoch do it differently. To refuse this task is to settle for a theology appropriate to some other time than one's own.[62]

In order to calculate the conceptual cost of theological models and key models, systematic theologians have to apply the logical criterion of comprehensive coherence. In order to decide whether this price can be paid, however, they will have to look to the demands of life in their historical and cultural situation and see whether the model or key model under consideration enables them to cope adequately with these demands. But even this criterion is not sufficient to force conclusions. In the final analysis every systematic theologian will have to apply a further criterion in order to come to a decision.

Personal authenticity. The demands of life are subject to cultural variation and historical change, and the adequacy of theological models and key models with respect to these demands varies accordingly. However, even within the same historical and cultural situation, not everybody will necessarily cope in the same way with these demands. Theological models which are adequate for some people are not necessarily experienced as such by everybody. Even when believers agree in their diagnosis of the demands of life, it does not follow that they will necessarily

---

[62] McFague, *Models of God*, 29–30.

respond to these demands in the same way in the light of their
faith. In the final analysis, all faith is truly personal. In the
words of Wilfred Cantwell Smith: 'My faith is an act that *I*
make, myself, naked before God.'[63] Of course this does not
exclude the possibility that others might share my personal faith
by recognizing it as similar to their own. In fact all believers
desire that their own personal faith might correspond to that of
others in the community of believers, for only then will they be
able to identify with the community without sacrificing their
own personal integrity in order to do so. Nevertheless, whether
somebody approves of a theological model or key model and
can agree with the 'theology' developed from it, will finally
depend on whether he or she can personally accept these with
integrity. This kind of 'person-relativity'[64] applies not only to
religious faith, but to all the beliefs which people hold. In this
sense Augustine was right in pointing out that, however much a
pupil can learn from his teacher, there is one thing he must
always discover for himself, i.e., that what his teacher tells him
is true, because no one can discern this truth for him in his
stead.[65] In brief, although personal integrity is not the only
criterion, it remains the final court of appeal in deciding what
we are able to believe. This is also true in the case of systematic
theologians having to decide which theological models to
develop as the key model for their theology.

As we have argued above, systematic theology should never
aim at producing the final conceptual form for the faith, since
the faith can never have such a final form. On the contrary,
systematic theology can do no more than suggest possible
conceptual designs for the faith and inquire into their coherence
and adequacy. The sort of questions raised in systematic

---

[63] Smith, *The Meaning and End of Religion*, 191.

[64] On 'person-relativity', see George I. Mavrodes, *Belief in God* (New York 1970),
chapter 2.

[65] 'If my hearer sees these things himself with his inward eye, he comes to know what
I say, not as a result of my words but as a result of his own contemplation. Even when
I speak what is true, it is not I who teach him. He is taught not by my words but by
the things themselves which inwardly God has made manifest to him.' Augustine, *De
Magistro*, 12.40, in J. H. S. Burleigh (ed.), *Augustine: Earlier Writings* (Philadelphia
1953), 96–7. See also Etienne Gilson, *The Christian Philosophy of Saint Augustine*
(London 1961), 70.

theology could be expressed in the following form: 'Imagine what it would be like if we expressed our faith thus… ' In this respect systematic theology is exactly like conceptual inquiry in philosophy.[66] Thus for example the Socratic dialogues dealt with such questions as: 'Imagine what it would be like if knowing were the same as perceiving', and: 'Imagine what it would be like if piety were the same as being approved by the gods.' Similarly Wittgenstein's *Philosophical Investigations* abounds with passages introduced by the words: '(Let us) imagine', and Husserl tells us that philosophy is an exercise in imagination. In a similar sense systematic theology is not only a highly imaginative enterprise, but also a highly theoretical discipline conducting thought experiments with reference to the conceptual form of the faith in terms of which believers try to make sense of their lives and their experience of the world.

On the other hand, systematic theology as we have described it is also an eminently *practical* undertaking, since it tries to produce conceptual expressions for the faith of the community of believers which would enable its members to achieve coherence or wholeness in their lives, to cope adequately with what Wittgenstein calls the 'strange demands of life', and to live authentically in the light of their faith. In the end, the conceptual designs produced by systematic theology have to prove their worth in the lives of the community of believers.

1.5 THE MODEL OF LOVE

What would be the conceptual price for taking the love of God as a key model in theology? This depends of course on what we mean by 'love', and in the history of western thought the use of this term has been far from unambiguous. Even if we were to limit ourselves to the cumulative tradition of the Christian faith, we are still confronted by a wide variety of concepts of love, used not only with reference to human relations but also for the relation between God and human persons. Each of these would generate a different 'theology' if it were developed as theo-

---

[66] For an extended discussion of the relation between systematic theology and philosophical inquiry, see chapter 1 and the Epilogue of my *Speaking of a Personal God*.

logical key model. How then are we to decide which concept of love to develop as such?

One way in which this problem is often approached is that proposed by a kind of 'biblical theology' which seeks a biblical concept of love through exegetical study of the way the word love and its cognates are used in the Bible. This approach acknowledges the variety of views within the Christian tradition which claim to represent the biblical concept of love. However, since these views cannot all be correct, their claims should be tested in the light of an exegetical search for the true biblical concept of love. Only the latter can be a valid candidate for development as key model for theology.

This approach is valid in one important respect. As we have argued above, the Bible is the classic or paradigmatic text within the Christian tradition. If, therefore, we want to develop a key theological model of love which is to be consonant with this tradition, we will have to show that it is consonant with the notions of love presented to us in the Bible. However, this approach will not do as it stands, for it is based on a number of doubtful presuppositions.

One of these presuppositions has to do with the claim that a biblical concept of love can be found merely by looking at the way the word love is used in the Bible. This claim mistakenly supposes that the concept of love is expressed only by means of the word 'love' and its cognates. In the Bible this happens in many other ways as well, including many narratives in which love both human and divine is described, reported or depicted without the word 'love' necessarily being used at all. This difficulty might be overcome by using a more sophisticated method of exegesis which is not merely limited to word studies.

A second, more problematic supposition is that the same word in the Bible always expresses the same concept. There may be a family resemblance between the concepts expressed by the same word when used by different authors and in different contexts. In no way, however, are these concepts identical, let alone do they always have the same implications and presuppositions. Although the biblical authors use the *word* love in many contexts, they never provide a systematic development of the

Nietzsche and Max Scheler. In part IV we will develop a relational concept of love and show how the various attitudes discussed in parts II and III are all involved in this relationship. While analysing the various aspects of the concept of love in the chapters that follow, we will at the same time try to explore the implications for the doctrine of God of using this concept as a model for talking about the relationship between God and human persons. What is the conceptual price of looking on God as a God of love?

PART II

Romantic love

CHAPTER 2

Exclusive attention

2.1 INTRODUCTION: ROMANTIC LOVE

'Love is an Austro-Hungarian Empire uniting all sorts of feelings, behaviours, and attitudes, sometimes having little in common, under the rubric of "love".'[1] Where, then, shall we start to look for a coherent concept of love which can serve as a model for thinking about our relations with God? When we talk of love, most people in our culture think first of romantic love, the sort of love which a lover has for his or her beloved.[2] Since this kind of love is inextricably tied up with sexuality, it might at first sight seem inappropriate for our purpose. Some people might even consider it blasphemous to think of our relations with God in erotic terms. However, there are at least three reasons why romantic love, including its erotic aspects, is an illuminating point of departure for developing a conceptual model for the love of God.

First of all, even if we do not go as far as to claim that 'God

---

[1] Bernard I. Murstein, 'A taxonomy of love', in Robert J. Sternberg and Michael L. Barnes (eds.), *The Psychology of Love* (London 1988), 33.

[2] It is clear that we are not using the term 'romantic love' in the technical sense denoting a *view* on the nature of love defended in nineteenth-century romanticism, but rather in the more general sense denoting the *kind* of exclusive love which a lover has for his or her beloved as distinct from brotherly love or neighbourly love which is inclusive and directed toward other people in general. In this sense romantic love is a phenomenon of all ages and not merely of the nineteenth century. In part II we will discuss various views on the nature of romantic love in this general sense, and in part III some views on love directed to other people in general. For an extended analysis of the views on love defended in romanticism, see Irving Singer, *The Nature of Love* (Chicago 1984), II.

is a sexual God',[3] we cannot deny that erotic images have often been used in the Bible (e.g. in the Song of Songs) and in the Christian tradition (e.g. in nuptial mysticism) in order to express our relation with God. Thus the Spanish essayist and philosopher José Ortega y Gasset (1883–1955) remarks on the 'profound similarity between falling in love and mysticism ... in view of the remarkable coincidence with which the mystic employs erotic words and images to express himself.'[4]

Secondly, if we develop the concept of romantic love into a conceptual model, it does not necessarily follow that the erotic aspects of this kind of love have to be carried over when applying the model to our relations with God. But then we will have to sort out what other aspects are characteristic of romantic love, how these are related to sexuality and whether they can be meaningfully divorced from the latter. In other words, if we are to hold that love of God is not erotic, we will have to show in what way it differs from erotic love. An analysis of the various characteristics of romantic love will enable us to do this.

Thirdly, Sartre argues that the sexual attitude is the primary form of behaviour toward the other, and not a mere contingent extra to human life. Although he does not claim that all attitudes toward the other are reducible to sexual attitudes, he does hold the latter to be as it were the paradigm or 'skeleton' upon which all human relationships are constructed.[5] If Sartre is correct, an analysis of romantic love should provide us with clues to a number of characteristic features of all forms of love and even of human relations as such.

In what follows we will concentrate on three such features which are especially important for all human love relations, and which have important implications when carried over to our talk of God's love. First of all, romantic love is exclusive. It

---

[3] 'There is – and always has been – a heavenly "sexuality" of which all earthly sexuality is, in some degree, a reflection ... God is a sexual God. If the "big bang" started the universe, as most astro-physicists now claim, then I believe that it may be described, without irreverence or salaciousness, as God's mighty ejaculation.' Murdoch Dahl, *Daughter of Love* (Worthing 1989), 280.

[4] José Ortega y Gasset, *On Love. Aspects of a Single Theme* (London 1959), 50. (References to Ortega in the text of this chapter are all from this work).

[5] Jean-Paul Sartre, *Being and Nothingness* (New York 1956), 406–7.

considers the beloved as the one and only object of love with the exclusion of all others. In this chapter we will discuss this feature of romantic love in the light of Ortega y Gasset's view that love is a form of exclusive attention to the beloved. Secondly, romantic love is a desire to be united with the beloved. In chapter 3 we will discuss this feature in the light of those forms of mystic love which aim at achieving the *unio mystica* with the divine. Thirdly, romantic love entails forms of passionate suffering on account of the distance which is maintained between the lover and the beloved. This feature plays a central role in courtly love and in Simone Weil's views on the love of God, and will therefore be discussed in chapter 4 in the light of these views.

According to Ortega, '"falling in love" is a phenomenon of attention' (40). We will discuss this view as follows. After seeing what Ortega means by 'attention' and in what sense he considers falling in love to be a form of attention (section 2.2), we will examine three important aspects of his view more closely: can we freely choose to fall in love? (section 2.3); does falling in love provide the lover with knowledge or with illusions regarding the beloved? (section 2.4); what is the relation between love and sexuality? (section 2.5). In conclusion (section 2.6) we will see to what extent the love of God can be understood in terms of this concept of love.

2.2 LOVE AND ATTENTION

What does Ortega mean by 'attention'? He argues that the world surrounding us is composed of a very large number of objects – many more than we can possibly attend to sim-ultaneously. All these objects struggle to gain our attention. Since our 'attentive consciousness can be regarded as the very space of our personalities', we could as well say that we are attentive of something as that it 'dislodges a certain space in our personalities' (40). By occupying this space, something gains for us a 'greater reality' or a 'more vigorous existence' than those things on which we do not focus our attention, and which form 'an anaemic and almost phantasmic background which lurks on the periphery of our minds'. When in this way something has a greater reality for us, 'it of course achieves greater esteem, merit and importance and compensates for the obscured remainder of the universe' (41).

This struggle for our attention is an unequal one, since it is determined by the innate system of preferences and dislikes which each of us bears within himself. The values which constitute the basis of our character, determine the preferences of our attention. 'Thanks to this, we are exceedingly wise about situations in which our preferred values are brought into play, and blind about others in which different, whether equal or superior, values exist which are alien to our sensibilities' (68). In this way our attention reveals our basic character and personality. 'Tell me where your attention lies, and I will tell you who you are' (42).

Normally things fail to occupy this privileged centre of attention for more than a few moments at a time, and are soon driven out by something else. Thus our attention shifts from one object to another, remaining briefly or at length fixed upon each in accordance with its vital importance to us. When, however, attention is fixed upon an object for a greater length of time or with greater frequency than normal, we speak of 'mania'. A maniac is somebody with an abnormal attention-span. According to Ortega, 'almost all great men have been maniacs, except that the consequences of their mania, of their "fixed idea", seem useful or commendable to us' (41). Thus when Newton was asked how he came to discover his mechanical system of the universe, he replied: 'Nocte dieque incubando' (by thinking about it day and night). This, says Ortega, is 'a declaration of obsession' (42).

Thus it sometimes happens that something can lay claim to our attention for an extraordinary long time. This can even take on the form of an abnormal obsession. According to Ortega this also applies to falling in love, which he describes as 'an abnormal state of attention in a normal man' (42). Normally the attention of every person shifts indifferently from one member of the opposite sex to another. One day, however, this equal division of attention ceases. One's attention of itself seems to become abnormally fastened upon one person, and it soon requires an effort to dismiss that person from one's thoughts in order to pay attention to something else. 'The attention remains paralysed: it does not advance from one thing to another' (43). In this way falling in love brings about a contraction of consciousness whereby things which formerly absorbed us are progressively eliminated from our attention. Nevertheless, the lover has the impression that the life of his consciousness is very rich. His reduced world is more concentrated.

This convergence of attention not only 'gives a false aspect of superlative intensity to his existence', but at the same time 'endows the favoured object with portentous qualities' (44). Here Ortega is not referring to imaginary perfections, as is the case in Stendhal's theory of crystallization which we will discuss below. What he has in mind is that our consciousness, by overwhelming an object with attention, 'endows it with an incomparable force of reality. It exists for us at every moment; it is ever present, there alongside us, more real than anything else' (44). 'Actually what happens is that the world does not exist for the lover. His beloved has dislodged and replaced it' (45).

Ortega points out that, if the beloved knows how to utilize his or her privileged position, it becomes possible to nourish the attention of the lover, as is done by 'conquistadors' of both sexes:

Once a woman's attention is fixed upon a man, it is very easy for him to dominate her thought completely. A simple game of blowing hot and cold, of solicitousness and disdain, of presence and absence is all that is required. The rhythm of that technique acts upon a woman's attention like a pneumatic machine and ends by emptying her of all the rest of the world ... Most 'love affairs' are reduced to this mechanical play of the beloved upon the lover's attention. (47)

The only way in which the lover can be freed from this captivity of love, is some shock from outside which forces him or her to pay attention to some other object and thus to break the exclusive position which the beloved occupies in his or her consciousness. In this way absence or long journeys are considered a good cure for lovers, since these starve their attention for the beloved and prevents anything from rekindling it.

This analysis seems to suggest that love is a kind of mechanical fixation which is imposed on us from outside. It is not a matter of choice, but something that happens to us. On the other hand, Ortega also argues that love is something voluntary which we enter into because we want to. In what way is this to be understood?

2.3 LOVE AND FREEDOM

According to Ortega, there is a radical difference between falling in love as a fixation of attention upon another person, and the hold which pressing political or economic affairs sometimes take on our attention. In the latter case the fixation of attention is forced upon us against our inclination, whereas 'there is no such imposition upon the person who falls in love, for his attention is voluntarily given to the beloved' (48). In a similar way love, which is a normal phenomenon, can be distinguished from obsession, which is a pathological state. We can say that 'whoever falls in love does so because he wants to fall in love', whereas an obsession presents itself to the mind 'in the form of a tenacious external imposition, which emanates from some anonymous, non-existent "other one"' (48). In this respect Ortega compares love with hate since both of these involve a 'kind of activity, or, almost effort... in contrast to passive emotions like happiness or sadness... (which) are, in effect, states and not efforts or acts' (17. cf. 15–6, 38 and 48).[6]

It would seem as though Ortega's views involve a contradiction at this point. On the one hand he claims that falling in love is a paralysis of attention 'which does not leave us any freedom of movement' (46), and which can be brought about in the lover 'with irremissible mechanism' (43). On the other

---

[6] Contrary to Ortega, many contemporary emotion theorists maintain that *all* emotions are active in the sense that they involve judgments or evaluations of the object of emotion. See e.g. Robert C. Solomon, *The Passions* (Garden City NY 1976), William Lyons *Emotion* (Cambridge 1980), and Robert C. Roberts, 'What an emotion is: a sketch', *The Philosophical Review* 97 (1988), 183–209.

hand, however, he argues that love is not a passive state but an activity which we voluntarily perform and which is not imposed on us from outside like an obsession. This contradiction could be eliminated if we interpret Ortega's view in the light of the distinction between freedom of *consent* (i.e. acting freely in the sense of doing something willingly) and freedom of *choice* (i.e. acting freely in the sense of doing something by choice).[7] Since choice is always between alternative courses of action, doing something out of choice entails the two-way ability to do both what one chooses to do and to act otherwise as well. For this reason freedom of choice is incompatible with determinism: one cannot choose to do the unavoidable since the unavoidable leaves us no alternative but to do it. Freedom of consent is not in this way incompatible with determinism since one could gladly and willingly consent to do the unavoidable. In this light we could interpret Ortega as arguing on the one hand that, since love is a paralysis of attention which does not leave us any freedom of movement, we do not *choose* to fall in love. On the other hand we do voluntarily *consent* to falling in love, since love is not forced upon us against our inclination. In fact, we fall in love because we want to.

The apparent contradiction in Ortega's views could also be dealt with in terms of his distinction between liking and loving. By *liking* Ortega refers to 'the attraction which almost every woman exerts upon a man and which amounts to a sort of instinctual call to the profound core of our personality'. This call is 'usually not followed by any response, or only by a negative response' (75). By *loving* Ortega refers to the positive response which occurs 'when we are not only attracted, but we show interest'. This interest 'acts upon the innumerable attractions which are experienced, eliminating most of them

---

[7] The rather confusing terms which are usually employed for these two concepts of freedom are the 'liberty of spontaneity' and the 'liberty of indifference'. For a useful discussion of this distinction, see chapter 7 of Anthony Kenny, *Will, Freedom and Power* (Oxford 1975), and chapter 2 of Kenny's *Freewill and Responsibility* (London 1978). Kenny correctly argues that these two concepts presuppose each other. For this reason they should be taken as specifying two necessary conditions for an adequate concept of moral freedom. It is therefore wrong to view them as alternative complete concepts of freedom, as is usually done.

and focusing only upon one' (76). Loving is a freely chosen reaction. In this way it is as different from liking 'as being dragged is from moving voluntarily' (76). In terms of the distinction we introduced above, it now appears that for Ortega loving differs from liking in being free not only in the sense of consent but also in the sense of choice. 'Love, then, in its very essence, is choice' (76).

Although the choice of love is free, it is not arbitrary. According to Ortega 'the selective principles which determine it are at the same time the most intimate and mysterious preferences which form our individual character' (76). For this reason Ortega maintains that

we can find in love the most decisive symptom of what a person is. All other acts and appearances can deceive us with regard to his true nature, but his love affairs reveal to us the carefully concealed secret of his being. This is especially true in the choice of the beloved. In no other action do we reveal our innermost character as we do in erotic choice. (146)

In this way 'love is an impulse which springs from the most profound depths of our beings, and upon reaching the visible surface of life carries with it an alluvium of shells and seaweed from the inner abyss. A skilled naturalist, by filing these materials, can reconstruct the oceanic depth from which they have been uprooted' (70). This elaborate metaphor suggests that Ortega is using a rather attenuated concept of 'choosing' when he claims that love is a matter of choice. In fact, he states explicitly 'that there is choice in love – a choice which is more real than many which are made consciously and deliberately – and that this choice is not free but, rather, depends upon the individual's basic character' (89). The lover's basic character does not provide *reasons* for choosing from among real alternatives which person he is to love. It is rather the *determining cause* of his falling in love, and it does not leave him any alternatives at all. In all this 'the intervention of will over character is practically nil' (71). Clearly, then, Ortega's claim that love is voluntary amounts to no more than that love is a form of willing consent to the unavoidable. Only in this sense can he hold that 'whoever falls in love does so because he wants to fall in love'

(48). This rather deterministic concept of love is typically romantic. The question is, however, whether it is also an adequate concept of love. We will have to take up this question again in later chapters.

2.4 LOVE AND KNOWLEDGE

We fall in love, then, with someone who fulfils 'the most intimate and mysterious preferences which form our individual character'. Does this mean that the lover *knows* that the beloved measures up to these preferences, or that the lover *imagines* (correctly or incorrectly) that this is the case? Is love based on knowledge or on fantasy? When the world says of the lover 'We do not know what he sees in her', is this because his love has opened his eyes to perfections in his beloved for which the world is blind, or because his love has provided him with illusions about his beloved which the world does not share?

Love is sometimes taken to be an exercise in fantasy which generates illusions about the beloved. Stendhal's theory of crystallization could be seen as the standard example of this view. He describes this as follows: 'What I have called crystallization is a mental process which draws from everything that happens new proofs of the perfection of the loved one ... No sooner do you think of a virtue than you detect it in your beloved.'[8] In this way the imagination of the lover can transform an ordinary person into a glittering idol. Stendhal derives the term from what happens when

at the salt mines of Salzburg, they throw a leafless wintry bough into one of the abandoned workings. Two or three months later they haul it out covered with a shining deposit of crystals. The smallest twig, no bigger than a tom-tit's claw, is studded with a galaxy of scintillating diamonds. The original branch is no longer recognizable. (45)

A good example of this phenomenon is the description which Rousseau gives in his *Confessions* of how he fell in love with the very ordinary Madame d'Houdetot: 'Before long I had no eyes for anyone but Madame d'Houdetot, but reclothed her with all

---

[8] Stendhal (Marie-Henri Beyle), *Love* (Penguin Classics edition, London 1984), 45–6.

the perfections with which I had come to adorn the idol of my heart.'[9]

According to Stendhal, love can only survive as long as the process of crystallization is kept alive. Love dies when the lover does not need to fantasize about his beloved. For this reason the lover should always remain uncertain about his beloved. Certainty confronts him with the real and removes the need for fantasy. 'The moral of Stendhal's scientific treatise is that only love resting on imagined pleasures can be constant. If love is directed to a real object, it is bound to become satiated, for once the object is possessed, love necessarily dies.'[10] In this sense Stendhal's lover is in fact a solipsist. His love is not directed to a real person, but only to the products of his own fantasy. His love creates its own object. In the words of Stendhal: 'Love is the only passion which rewards itself in a coin of its own manufacture.'[11] Since Stendhal's lover does not relate to the real, his love cannot provide him with knowledge of the real. On the contrary, it can only enclose him in his own fantasies. His beloved is in fact not the object of his love, but only the occasion for his crystallizations. She 'serves him only as a mannequin to wear his fantasies'.[12]

According to Ortega, the theory of crystallization does contain a germ of truth, but only in the limited sense in which it applies to all human experience, and not only to the way a lover looks upon a beloved. 'The projection of imaginary qualities upon a real object is a constant phenomenon. In man, to see things – moreover, to appreciate them – always means to complete them' (34). In this sense all experience involves interpretation, and 'no one sees things in their naked reality' (35). This does not mean, however, that all experience is pure illusion. Although our experience of the world is fallible, it is not therefore also invariably false. In this respect love does not differ from experience in general. 'The lover's valuation is no more illusory than that of the political partisan, the artist, the

---

[9] Quoted by Gregory Vlastos in 'Plato: the individual as object of love', in Ted Honderich (ed.), *Philosophy through Its Past* (London 1984), 31–2. Vlastos' comment on Rousseau is: 'She served him only as a mannequin to wear his fantasies'.

[10] Shirley Robin Letwin, 'Romantic love and Christianity', *Philosophy* 52 (1977), 132.

[11] Stendhal, *Love*, 262.   [12] See note 9.

businessman, etc. One is more or less as perspicacious or obtuse in love as he ordinarily is in judging his fellow beings' (35). For Ortega, then, love does not merely endow the beloved with imaginary perfections, but is based rather on the real perfections which the lover perceives his beloved to have. 'Love is excited by certain real charms and qualities. It always has an object' (89). In this way 'falling in love consists in feeling oneself enchanted by something...and this something can cause enchantment only if it is or seems to be perfect. I do not mean that the loved one seems to be completely perfect...It is enough if there is some perfection in him' (31). Since, however, the lover's experience is no less fallible than that of anybody else, it is not a privileged source of knowledge about his beloved's perfections. On the other hand, the lover's love does provide the rest of the world with special knowledge about the lover himself, since the standards of perfection by which he judges his beloved are a manifestation of his innermost character. Thus 'we can find in love the most decisive symptom of what a person is' (146).

In one respect, however, Ortega does claim that love 'endows the favoured object with portentous qualities', although these are not non-existent imaginary perfections as Stendhal erroneously supposes. Rather, 'by overwhelming the object with attention and concentrating on it, the consciousness endows it with an incomparable force of reality...It is ever present... more real than anything else' (44).

What does Ortega mean by 'an incomparable force of reality'? At this point it might be illuminating to take note of Sartre's 'factual solipsist' who is in many respects the exact opposite of Ortega's lover. Instead of love, the solipsist adopts an attitude which Sartre calls 'indifference toward others', and instead of knowledge, the solipsist has 'a kind of blindness with respect to others':

Others are those forms which pass by in the street, those magic objects which are capable of acting at a distance and upon which I can act by means of determined conduct. I scarcely notice them; I act as if I were alone in the world. I brush against 'people' as I brush against a wall; I avoid them as I avoid obstacles...Those 'people' are functions: the ticket-collector is only the function of collecting tickets; the café waiter is nothing but the function of serving the patrons.[13]

If we were to interpret Ortega's views along these lines, then we could say that the 'incomparable force of reality' with which love endows the beloved is the reality of being a person rather than an object, and the kind of knowledge which love provides is knowledge of the other as a person rather than as an object. In this sense knowing a person can be said to involve loving that person. In Old Testament Hebrew the same word is used for knowing someone as for having sexual intercourse with that person. What kind of 'knowing' is involved here? We will return to this question in section 7.4 when we discuss the nature of personal relations.

2.5 LOVE AND SEXUALITY

'If it is an absurdity to say that a man's or woman's true love for one another has nothing sexual about it, it is another absurdity to believe that love can be equated with sexuality' (76). But how, then, are the two related? In order to unravel Ortega's views on this relation, we will have to take note of two distinctions which he makes.

First of all, Ortega distinguishes between love *sensu stricto* (i.e. abstracted from 'the total state of the person in love' (154)), and the various concrete ways in which love is expressed toward different objects. In this abstract sense, love is 'a pure sentimental activity' (38–9) toward an object. As a *sentimental* activity it is distinct from intellectual functions such as perception, consideration, thought, recall, imagination, etc., and also from desire, with which it is often confused. ('A glass of water is desired, but not loved, when one is thirsty.') As a sentimental *activity* it is distinct from inactive sentiments such as joy or sadness. Unlike hate, love is a *positive* sentimental activity. It is 'a cordial, affirmative interest' in which we 'exert ourselves on behalf of what we love' while hate is 'a terrible negative action, ideally destructive of the hated object'. Love can be directed toward any object, person or thing, 'toward a woman,

---

[13] Sartre, *Being and Nothingness*, 380–1.

a piece of land (one's country), a branch of human activity such as sports, science, etc.' As such love can take on a large variety of forms and be expressed in many ways appropriate to the various objects toward which it is directed. Sexuality is one of the many ways in which love is expressed when it is directed toward another person. Although it is not the only way this kind of love is expressed, Ortega considers it to be essential in the expression of love between persons: 'There is no love ... without sexual instinct. Love uses it like a brute force, as a brig uses the wind' (45–6).

A second distinction made by Ortega is that between sexual love and sexual instinct (32–3). While sexual instinct can be used as an expression of love, it can also occur by itself apart from love, in which case it degenerates into lust. As distinguished from love, 'pure voluptuousness – we could say pure impurity – exists prior to its object. One feels desire before knowing the person or situation which satisfies it. Consequently, anyone is able to satisfy it. Instinct does not show preferences when it is mere instinct.' In this way pure sexual instinct ignores the individuality of the other as well as the perfections which distinguish a beloved from everybody else.[14] In this respect sexual love is distinct from the sexual instinct in which it can be expressed. 'Instinct tends to amplify indefinitely the number of objects which satisfy it, whereas love tends toward exclusivism' (76). Instead of 'existing prior to its object', genuine sexual love 'is always born in response to a being who appears before us, and who, by virtue of some eminent quality which he possesses, stimulates the erotic process' (33).

According to Ortega, sexual love aims at a union with the beloved in which the latter's perfections are affirmed and perpetuated.

The lover experiences a strange urgency to dissolve his own in-dividuality in that of the other and vice versa, to absorb the individuality of his beloved into his own. A mysterious longing!

---

[14] 'It is a simple fact – anyone can observe it at a men's bathing place – that nudity emphasises common humanity and soft-pedals what is individual. In that way we are "more ourselves" when clothed. By nudity the lovers cease to be solely John and Mary; the universal He and She are emphasised.' C. S. Lewis, *The Four Loves* (London 1981), 96.

Whereas in every other situation in life nothing upsets us so much as
to see the frontiers of our individual existence trespassed upon by
another person, the rapture of love consists in feeling ourselves so
metaphysically porous to another person that only in the fusion of
both ... can it find fulfilment ... However, the longing for fusion does
not end with simple uncreative union. Love is complete when it
culminates in a more or less clear desire to leave, as testimony of the
union, a child in whom the perfections of the beloved are perpetuated
and affirmed. (33)

Here Ortega appeals to Plato's view that 'love is a desire to
generate in perfection' (34). In this respect, too, sexual love
differs from pure sexual instinct. While the latter may assure the
mere conservation of the species, sexual love aims at its
perfection.

2.6 LOVE AND GOD

A number of features of the attitude which Ortega's romantic
lover adopts toward his or her beloved apply also to the attitude
of a believer toward God. As Ortega tries to show, this is
especially true in the case of mysticism. Unfortunately Ortega
adopts a rather one-sided and negative view of mysticism.[15] In
the next chapter we will try to develop a more balanced view on
the nature of mystical love. Before doing that, however, we
should take note of a number of issues which arise when we
adopt Ortega's view of romantic love as model for the love of
God.

The most characteristic feature of the attitude which Ortega's
lover adopts toward his or her beloved is its *exclusiveness*. 'The
world does not exist for the lover. His beloved has dislodged and
replaced it' (45). Is the love which a believer has for God also
exclusive in this sense? It is often claimed to be so. Thus Ortega
points out that the mystic, like the romantic lover, is continually
aware of the presence of the Beloved, and has great difficulty in
paying attention to anything else. 'Every activity of the mystic's
day brings him into contact with God, makes him revert to his

---

[15] See Ortega, *On Love*, 50–60. A more perceptive comparison between romantic love
and mysticism can be found in Sharon Brehm's essay exploring the similarities
between Stendhal and St Teresa of Avila. See Sharon S. Brehm, 'Passionate love',
in Sternberg and Barnes, *The Psychology of Love*, 232–63.

idea' (44). St Augustine seems to go even further when he states that 'God then alone is to be loved; and all this world, that is, all sensible things, are to be despised.'[16] Everything else, besides the Beloved, is not only ignored, but should be despised. But did not Jesus declare: 'If anyone comes to me and does not hate his father and mother, wife and children, brothers and sisters, even his own life, he cannot be a disciple of mine' (Luke 14: 26)? Even if we were to adopt a less extreme position than these statements seem to suggest, it remains true that the love which a believer owes to God is exclusive and cannot be shared with anything or anybody else. This is well illustrated in the famous correspondence between Abelard and Heloise.[17] After having become a nun at Abelard's instigation, Heloise writes to him as follows: 'At every stage of my life up to now, as God knows, I have feared to offend you rather than God, and tried to please you more than him. It was your command, not love of God which made me take the veil' (134). To this Abelard replies that, although he used to be her lover and therefore the one who had an exclusive place in her life, she has now become the bride of Christ and that He should now assume the place in her life which Abelard previously had. 'It was a happy transfer of your married state, for you were previously the wife of a poor mortal and now you are raised to the bed of the King of kings' (138). Thus it would seem that if we love God we cannot love anybody else.

On the other hand, this claim seems to conflict with the injunction that we should love our neighbours and not ignore them (let alone despise or hate them). Is it not unacceptable from a Christian point of view to claim that our love of God should be exclusive in the way in which that of Ortega's romantic lover is exclusive? Furthermore, would it not be quite intolerable from a Christian point of view to say that God's love for human persons is exclusive in this sense? Does God's love only have room for favourites, or perhaps for only a single beloved, while all others are ignored (or despised or hated)? It

---

[16] St Augustine, *On the Morals of the Christian Church*, chapter 20. (St Augustine's view on love will be discussed fully in chapter 5).

[17] *The Letters of Abelard and Heloise* (Penguin Classics edition, London 1985).

would seem that in this respect Ortega's view of romantic love will not do as a conceptual model for the love of God. The question remains therefore: in what sense could we coherently claim that the love of God is exclusive? Are there other concepts of love which in this respect could serve as a more satisfactory conceptual model for the love of God?

A second important feature of Ortega's view on romantic love, is its *lack of freedom*. In a straightforward sense, we do not freely choose our beloved. On the contrary, whom we are to love is determined by the 'most intimate and mysterious preferences which form our individual character'. In the Christian tradition something similar is often claimed with regard to the love of God. Here, however, our fallen nature causes the 'most intimate and mysterious preferences which form our individual character' to be such that we do *not* naturally love God. It is only when through God's grace we are given a new nature, that the preferences of our individual character become such as to make us love God. 'I will give you a new heart and put a new spirit within you; I will take the heart of stone from your body and give you a heart of flesh. I will put my spirit into you and make you conform to my statutes, keep my laws and live by them' (Ezekiel 36: 27–8). When that happens to us, we cannot help but love God. In this sense, the love of God is claimed to be the effect of irresistible grace rather than the result of free choice.

Although this view has often been defended in the Christian tradition, it is not without its difficulties. If we are to account for the personal nature of the relation between God and human persons, we shall require a less deterministic view on the relation between grace and freedom than that entailed by this concept of love. Similar doubts arise with respect to God's love for us: is God free in his love for human persons, or is his love the inevitable and necessary effect of 'the most intimate and mysterious preferences which form his individual character' as for example Anders Nygren would seem to argue (see chapter 6)? We will have to inquire, then, whether this view is satisfactory, or whether we should seek another concept of love which in this respect provides a better conceptual model for the love of God.

A third important feature of the concept of love discussed above has to do with the relation between *love and knowledge*. The passage from the Johannine epistle which we quoted at the beginning of chapter 1, suggests that this relation is very relevant with regard to the love of God: 'Everyone who loves is a child of God and knows God, but the unloving know nothing of God' (1 John 4: 8). According to Ortega, love endows the beloved with an 'incomparable force of reality' for the lover. We suggested that this might be interpreted in personal terms in the sense that love entails recognizing the reality of the beloved as a person rather than an object and thus knowing the beloved as a person rather than as an object. In section 7.4 we will explore the nature of this kind of personal knowledge and see what is involved in the claim that knowledge of God is personal in this sense.

We also saw that, like Plato, Ortega holds that love entails recognizing (and thus knowing) the perfections of the beloved and striving to affirm and perpetuate these. Although this obviously also applies to the love of God, there is one fundamental difference between the way a believer recognizes the perfection of God and the way Ortega's romantic lover recognizes the perfections of his beloved. Ortega's lover judges the perfection of his beloved in the light of his own deepest character preferences. For this reason the choice of beloved is a manifestation of these preferences in the lover's character and in this way provides us with knowledge about the lover. In the case of God, however, it is not the believer's character preferences which determine whether God is to be acknowledged as perfect, but rather the Divine perfections which are the ultimate standard of value in the light of which the believer's preferences are to be judged. It is not the believer's character preferences which determine whether he should love God, but rather the love of God which in the end will remodel his character preferences.

A fourth feature of romantic love as viewed by Ortega, is that it involves in the lover 'a strange urgency to dissolve his own individuality in that of the other and, vice versa, to absorb the individuality of the beloved into his own' (33). Ortega points out that this also applies to the mystic's love of God. The mystic also tries to be united with God and to absorb God into himself. In this sense Ortega describes the mystic as 'a sponge of God' (59). In the next chapter we will discuss this feature of romantic love in the light of an examination of the mystic ideal of achieving the *unio mystica* with God.

A final feature of romantic love, which Ortega mentions briefly but does not discuss, is the fact that it involves *suffering*. 'Who doubts that the lover can find happiness in his beloved? But it is no less certain that love is sometimes sad, as sad as death – a supreme and mortal torment. It is more: true love best recognizes itself and, so to speak, measures and calculates itself by the pain and suffering of which it is capable' (12). In chapter 4 we will discuss this feature of romantic love in the light of an examination of courtly love. Before doing that, however, let us first turn to our discussion of mysticism.

CHAPTER 3

Ecstatic union

3.1 LOVE AS UNION WITH THE BELOVED

In the speech which Plato has him deliver in the *Symposium*, Aristophanes explains how Zeus split all human beings down the middle. Consequently every man or woman is only half a complete creature, and goes through life with a passionate longing to find his or her complement in order to be reunited with it. He then reports how Hephaestus, the smith of the gods, asks two lovers: 'Do you desire to be wholly one; always day and night in one another's company? for if this is what you desire, I am ready to melt and fuse you together, so that being two you shall become one.'[1] Although Aristophanes is not expressing Plato's own views, he is referring to a feature which in one form or another is characteristic for romantic love throughout all ages. This feature is especially prominent in romanticism[2] and in mysticism.

What is the nature of this union which romantic lovers desire

---

[1] *The Symposium* 190c. Taken from the fourth edition of the Jowett translation of *The Dialogues of Plato* (Oxford 1953).

[2] Compare for example the following lines from Shelley's poem on *Love's philosophy*:

> The fountains mingle with the river
> And the rivers with the ocean,
> The winds of heaven mix for ever
> With a sweet emotion;
> Nothing in the world is single,
> All things by a law divine
> In one another's being mingle –
> Why not I with thine?

For a discussion of this feature of romanticism, see Singer, *Nature of Love* II, chapter 9.

to achieve? In what sense do they wish to be 'melted and fused together' by Hephaestus? Does the lover 'experience a strange urgency to dissolve his own individuality in that of the other and, vice versa, to absorb the individuality of the beloved into his own', as Ortega y Gasset claims? And how should this kind of merging be understood? Or do lovers merely desire a kind of close relationship in which the individuality of each partner is preserved and left intact? And what sort of relationship could that be? Or, on the other hand, do the lovers merely desire some sort of ecstatic experience of union rather than a form of real ontological fusion? Let us deal with these questions in the light of the ways in which mystics try to achieve union with God. At the same time this will enable us to see what is entailed when we apply this aspect of the model of romantic love to talk about the relationship between the believer and God.

The aim of the mystic's life is to achieve the ecstasy of the *unio mystica*, the mystic union with God. To be united with God is what constitutes bliss and eternal happiness. There is, however, not much more than a family resemblance between the ways in which various mystics understand this ecstatic union and the ways in which they describe the various stages of the *via mystica* along which this union is to be achieved. Many mystics, especially in the Christian tradition, interpret the mystic way and its culmination in the mystic union in terms derived from romantic love, and very often they make use of erotic metaphors to describe their actions, attitudes and experiences. Thus for example St Bernard of Clairvaux developed a form of nuptial mysticism on the basis of his interpretation of the Song of Songs, and this was very influential in the works of a large number of Christian mystics since then. It is therefore not unreasonable to interpret much of mysticism as a form of romantic love in relation to God. In this chapter we will examine the ways in which these mystics view their lives and their relationship to the Divine in terms of romantic love. How do they describe the mystic union of love and the way in which it is to be achieved?

3.2 THE *VIA MYSTICA*

Evelyn Underhill describes how mystics frequently divide their journey to God into three stages.[3] This threefold division, which medieval mystics might have derived from neo-Platonism, occurs so often in the mystical tradition that it is probably the most adequate way of describing the mystical experience of the journey to God. Mystics differ with regard to the metaphors they use in describing these stages, and also in the relative weight the various stages are given in their lives. To some extent this accounts for the great differences between various forms of mysticism. Nevertheless, in one form or another this threefold division remains a thread of similarity running through the thought and experience of very many mystics and is therefore useful as a schema for describing their way to God. In accordance with Dionysius the Areopagite, these stages are often referred to as those of *purification* (or purgation), *illumination* (or enlightenment), and *ecstasy* (or union).[4] Let us examine these stages more closely. In doing so we shall concentrate on the way these are explained by St Bernard, since his mystical theology was paradigmatic for most nuptial mystics in the Christian tradition.[5]

The first stage of the *via mystica* is that of purification in which we learn repentance, self-denial and humility. In the previous chapter we pointed out that, unlike Ortega's romantic lover, it is not 'the most intimate and mysterious preferences which form

---

[3] Evelyn Underhill, *The Essentials of Mysticism and Other Essays* (London 1920), 7–11. This does not hold invariable, however. Thus for example, St Teresa of Avila distinguishes seven basic stages in the soul's progress toward God: the 'seven mansions of the interior castle'.

[4] 'Threefold is the way to God. The first is the way of purification, in which the mind is inclined to learn true wisdom. The second is the way of illumination, in which the mind by contemplation is kindled to the burning of love. The third is the way of union, in which the mind by understanding, reason and spirit is led up by God alone.' This celebrated passage from Dionysius is quoted by Underhill in *Essentials of Mysticism*, 11.

[5] St Bernard explains the stages of the mystic way in his *Sermons on the Song of Songs* and in his treatise *On the Twelve Steps of Humility*. Quotations from St Bernard are taken from the following editions: *On the Song of Songs*, 4 vols (Kalamazoo, 1971–80) and from *The Twelve Steps of Humility and Pride, and On Loving God* (London 1985). For an excellent exposition of his mystical theology, see Etienne Gilson, *The Mystical Theology of St Bernard* (London 1940).

our individual character' which determine whether the believer should love God. It is rather the love of God which will remodel his character preferences in the likeness of God. What is required is a thoroughgoing conversion in which we leave what St Bernard calls the *Regio dissimilitudinis* (land of unlikeness)[6] and regain the Divine likeness which we have lost through sin. For the mystic this remodelling of character is the essential first step on the way to God. 'False ways of feeling and thinking, established complexes which have acquired for us an almost sacred character, and governed though we knew it not all our reactions to life – these must be broken up.'[7] In order to achieve this kind of purification, we must come to know ourselves for what we really are. In this stage, as Dionysius says, 'the mind is inclined to learn true wisdom'. St Bernard explains how this wisdom or self-knowledge is imparted to us by 'the Son of God, who is the Word and Wisdom of the Father' who took hold of our intellectual faculty of reason

and in a most wonderful way he made it represent him. He then made it sit in judgment on itself so that by giving the correct reverence to the Word with whom it became linked it would act as its own prosecutor, witness and judge, and return the honest verdict of 'guilty' upon itself. Humility originates from this alliance between the Word and reason.[8]

In this respect St Bernard views the monastic life of poverty, chastity, and obedience as 'the apprenticeship of humility, that is to say a life in practical union with the life of Christ, who manifested himself as Humility Itself in his Incarnation'.[9] It is in this context that we must understand the role of asceticism in the life of the mystic. For the mystic asceticism is never more than a means to an end and, as Evelyn Underhill explains, it is often thrown aside when that end is attained. Its necessity is therefore a purely practical question. 'Fasting and watching may help one to dominate unruly instincts, and so attain a sharper and purer concentration on God; but make another so hungry and sleepy that he can think of nothing else.'[10] Thus all

---

[6] See Gilson, *Mystical Theology*, chapter 2.

[7] Underhill, *Essentials of Mysticism*, 12.   [8] *Twelve Steps of Humility*, chapter 7.

[9] Gilson, *Mystical Theology*, 98.   [10] Underhill, *Essentials of Mysticism*, 14.

things undertaken in the first stage of the mystic way are aimed solely at achieving humility before God. In his third sermon on the Song of Songs, dealing with the verse 'Let him kiss me with the kisses of his mouth' (Song of Songs 1: 2), St Bernard compares the three stages of the *via mystica* with three kisses. The first stage is called 'the kiss of the feet' with reference to Mary Magdalene kissing the feet of Jesus: 'It is up to you wretched sinner, to humble yourself as this happy penitent did so that you may be rid of your wretchedness. Prostrate yourself on the ground, take hold of his feet, soothe them with kisses, sprinkle them with your tears and so wash not them but yourself.'[11]

The second stage is that of illumination in which, as Dionysius states, 'the mind by contemplation is kindled to the burning of love'. St Bernard explains that the Word of God (Christ) informs our reason with self-knowledge in the first stage of the mystic way, whereas in the second stage the Spirit of God inflames our will with love. Thus

the Holy Spirit honoured the will by a personal visit, gently cleaning it, burning into it the warmth of affection and so making the will compassionate. Just as skin is made pliable with healing ointment on it, so the will, when it receives the ointment applied to it, is able to spread outward in love even toward its former enemies. Love is born of this second link-up between the Spirit of God and the will of man ... Reason has been taught by the Word and sprinkled with the hyssop of humility; the will has been inspired by the spirit of truth and set alight by the fire of love.[12]

In his seventh sermon on the Song of Songs, St Bernard compares this love of God, by which the soul of the mystic is set on fire, with the love which the bride has for the bridegroom. The attitude which the bride expresses in saying 'Let him kiss me with the kisses of his mouth' is that of the soul thirsting for God. This attitude is quite different from that of the slave who fears the face of his master, or the servant who looks for wages from his lord's hand, and it surpasses those of the disciple who merely is attentive to his teacher, or the son who is respectful to his father.[13]

---

[11] *Song of Songs*, Sermon 3.   [12] *Twelve Steps of Humility*, chapter 7.
[13] *Song of Songs*, Sermon 7. See also Sermon 83.

Three features are characteristic of this love: it is chaste, holy, and ardent.[14] It is *chaste* in the sense of being disinterested: it 'seeks the person whom she loves, and not other things of him'. This is what distinguishes the love of the bride from that of the servant who loves his master not for himself alone but for the sake of the wages he receives from him. It is *holy* in the sense of being spiritual rather than sensuous: it is 'the impulse of an upright spirit rather than of carnal desire'. For St Bernard the erotic metaphors have a purely spiritual meaning: what the mystic longs for is not a bodily union but a union of will with God. Finally, this love is *ardent* in the sense that the mystic approaches God with such unreserved candour that he overcomes all fear and reverence and has the audacity to aspire to union with the Divine. In the words of St Bernard:

It is an ardent love, blinded by its own excess to the majesty of the beloved. For what are the facts? He is the one at whose glance the earth trembles, and does she demand that he give her a kiss? Can she be possibly drunk? Absolutely drunk!... How great this power of love: what great confidence and freedom of spirit! What is more manifest than that fear is driven out by perfect love![15]

It is this ardent candour which distinguishes the love of the bride from the attitudes of the slave and the disciple and the son. In the second stage the mystic overcomes all the reticence toward God which is characteristic for the first stage. While St Bernard calls the first stage the kiss of the feet, he describes the second as that of being lifted up to kiss the hand of Christ.

First it must cleanse your stains, then it must raise you up. How raise you? By giving you the grace to dare to aspire. You wonder what this may be. I see it as the grace of the beauty of temperance and the fruits that befit repentance, the works of the religious man. These are the instruments that will lift you from the dunghill and cause your hopes to soar. On receiving such a grace then, you must kiss his hand, that is, you must give glory to his name, not to yourself.[16]

---

[14] Ibid., Sermon 7.

[15] Ibid., Sermon 7. Heinrich Suso expresses this ardent candour as follows: 'Now I begin to speak freely. I wish to talk with my Lord, with my husband, nobody can prevent me, I will fondle my beloved. That is what I long for with all my heart.' (Quoted by Friedrich Heiler, *Prayer* (Oxford 1932), 217).

[16] Ibid., Sermon 3.

At this point the mystic is prepared to enter the final stage of the mystic way, the ecstatic experience of *union with God*. While the second stage is characterized by *love* in the sense of an ardent desire for union with God, i.e. 'the hope of higher things', the third is characterized by *pure love* as the ecstatic enjoyment of this union. The ardent love of the second stage casts out fear. The pure love of the third casts out desire as well. Here there is no need for desire since there is perfect possession. St Bernard characterizes this as 'the kiss of the lips':

Having experienced these two kinds of kisses, as a double evidence of God's condescension, you may perhaps be bold enough to reach out still higher for more sacred things. For as you grow in grace and knock at the door with more assurance, you will seek for what is still lacking. In the first place, we fall at the feet of the Lord, and lament before him Who has made us the faults and sins which we ourselves have committed. In the second, we seek his helping hand to lift us up and to strengthen our feeble knees that we may stand upright. In the third, when we have, with many prayers and tears, obtained these two former graces, then at length we perhaps venture to lift our eyes to that countenance full of glory and majesty, for the purpose not only to adore, but (I say it with fear and trembling) to *kiss his lips*, because the Spirit before us is Christ the Lord, to whom being united in a holy kiss, we are by his marvellous condescension made to be one spirit with him.[17]

This third stage differs in an important respect from the other two: the soul has no part to play in achieving it. In the first two stages, according to St Bernard, the soul is led up to humility by Christ and to charity by the Holy Spirit. Someone who is led, moves by himself and co-operates with the one who leads. We therefore have to exert ourselves to acquire humility and charity under the guidance of the Son and the Spirit. The third stage, however, is like the third heaven to which St Paul refers in 2 Corinthians 12: 2, since something more than leading is required in order to reach it. Here the soul must be carried away or caught up (*raptus*) by God the Father. This stage is therefore literally an experience of rapture which God grants gratuitously

[17] Ibid., Sermon 3.

to whomever he pleases, when he pleases and as he pleases. St
Bernard uses an erotic metaphor to describe this experience of
ecstatic rapture:

> The soul can finally enter the king's chamber, longing for his love.
> After silence has been kept in heaven for a short time, maybe just half
> an hour, she rests at peace in the king's arms, asleep, yet with her
> inmost heart alert to the realm of secret truth (on whose memory she
> will feed when she awakens). But there in heaven she sees invisible
> things and hears unutterable things of which it is not right for man to
> speak.[18]

From this description it is clear that the experience of mystic
rapture is characterized by two features. On the one hand it is
a state of trance analogous to sleep or drunkenness which
Evelyn Underhill refers to as 'the suppression of the surface-
consciousness called ecstasy'.[19] On the other hand, the sleep is
by no means dreamless, but accompanied by indescribable
visions which enlighten the mind and inspire the will.[20] Gilson
distinguishes these two aspects of the mystic state as follows:

> First. The soul is freed from the use of the bodily senses; this constitutes
> ecstacy properly so called. In this sense it may be said that the first
> moment of this mystic slumber is *Extasis*... Second... The slumbering
> of the external senses is accompanied, in the mystic slumber, by an
> 'abduction' of the internal sense. By that must be understood that

---

[18] *Twelve Steps of Humility*, chapter 7. Gilson explains this passage from St Bernard as
   follows: 'The righteous soul, in which reason maintains silence for a short time, now
   reposes in the longed-for slumber of ecstasy. She sleeps; but her deepest sense, which
   is love, remains watchful within her, and gazes into the innermost recesses of truth,
   the memory of which will be her food when she returns to herself. There she sees the
   invisible, and hears secret words which man may not utter to man. But God may
   utter them to the soul, and we may speak them among the wise, giving our words a
   spiritual meaning to convey spiritual things.' Gilson, *Mystical Theology*, 105–6.
   Heinrich Suso writes in similar vein: 'The bedchamber is closed on our intimacy.
   Our love couch is bedecked with flowers. Come, O my beloved! Nothing remains
   now but for you to take me into the arms of Thy boundless love and let me fall into
   a blissful sleep.' (Quoted by Heiler, *Prayer*, 217).

[19] Underhill, *Essentials of Mysticism*, 22. Thus St Bernard also says of the bride that 'she
   was not drunk with wine, but in love' (*Song of Songs*, Sermon 49). Such an erotic
   metaphor suggests an analogy with coitus: 'For the mystic... coitus symbolizes a
   perfect union that earth does not afford' (Singer, *Nature of Love* I, 183).

[20] 'But holy contemplation has two forms of ecstasy, one in the intellect and one in the
   will. One is enlightened, and the other is fervent. One is knowledge, and the other is
   devotion.' St Bernard, *Song of Songs*, Sermon 49.

without falling asleep, but on the contrary remaining watchful, the internal sense is carried away by God, who illuminates it.[21]

St Bernard admits that, in an absolute sense, this ecstatic union with God is only possible in the next life when we are freed from the limitations of a mortal body. 'But this vision is not for the present life; it is reserved for the next … Neither sage nor saint nor prophet can or could ever see him as he is, while still in this mortal body; but whoever is found worthy will be able to do so when the body becomes immortal.'[22] However, in this life some mystics may receive the grace of experiencing what might be called brief glimpses of eternity. These moments of ecstasy are rare and of brief duration. The life of the mystic is therefore not one of continual ecstasy, but rather a life characterized by *vicissitude*: brief visits of the Beloved, followed by long periods of languor in which the soul longs for his return.

His heart's desire will be given to him, even while still a pilgrim on earth, though not in its fullness and only for a time, a short time. For when after vigils and prayers and a great shower of tears he who was sought presents himself, suddenly he is gone again, just when we think we hold him fast. But he will present himself anew to the soul that pursues him with tears, he will allow himself to be taken hold of but not detained, for suddenly a second time he flees from between our hands.[23]

In spite of the intensity of mystic love, its transitory character makes union in this life incomplete.

On the other hand, the vicissitude of the mystic's experience is not without purpose. It is aimed in the first place at purifying the love of the soul by making it live by faith alone. 'The lover flees from the arms of the bride and abides for some time far away to try her faithfulness; she, desperately unhappy about her isolation, mourns and sighs for the lost one, until finally he returns and the joys of love are renewed.'[24] Secondly, it is also aimed at filling the soul with love for others. Loving God entails

[21] Gilson, *Mystical Theology*, 105. [22] *Song of Songs*, Sermon 31.
[23] Ibid., Sermon 32.
[24] Heiler, *Prayer*, 215. There is an obvious analogy with Ortega's romantic lover who, as we saw in the previous chapter, 'feeds' the love of his or her beloved by 'a simple game of blowing hot and cold, of solicitousness and disdain, of presence and absence'.

loving all others not for their own sake but for the sake of God, and bringing them to love God as well.

It is characteristic of true and pure contemplation that when the mind is ardently aglow with God's love, it is sometimes so filled with zeal and the desire to gather to God those who will love him with equal abandon that it gladly forgoes contemplative leisure for the endeavour of preaching. And then, with its desire at least partially satisfied, it returns to its leisure with an eagerness proportionate to its successful interruption, until, refreshed again with the food of contemplation, it hastens to add to its conquests with renewed strength and experiences zeal.[25]

Here, according to Evelyn Underhill, is the test which enables us to distinguish between genuine mystic ecstasy and pathological states of trance: true mystical experience is known by its fruits. The real mystic is not a selfish visionary. He grows in vigour as he draws nearer and nearer to the sources of true life, and his goal is only reached when he participates in the creative energies of God. Here Underhill quotes Ruysbroeck: 'Then only is our life a *whole* when contemplation and work dwell in us side by side, and we are perfectly in both of them at once.'[26]

3.3 THE *UNIO MYSTICA*

The aim of the mystic's life is to achieve union with God. Having examined the way in which mystics like St Bernard try to reach this goal, we are now in a position to inquire after the nature of the desired union. At this point there is a great difference between various mystics, and even more between various ways in which mysticism is usually interpreted. Some-

---

[25] *Song of Songs*, Sermons 57, 58. Thomas Merton explains this point as follows: 'Indeed, the mystical marriage must bring forth children to the Spouse, that is, souls to the mystical life. But since the faculties cannot give themselves to the work of preaching and the care of souls when they are completely absorbed in the fruition of the highest graces of union, there must remain even in the mystical marriage some alternation between the pure love of God in himself and the love of God through our fellow men.' Jean Leclerq (ed.), *Thomas Merton on St Bernard* (Kalamazoo 1980), 218. This way of relating love of God to neighbourly love is very similar to that defended by St Augustine. We will return to this point below in our discussion of St Augustine's views on love.

[26] Underhill, *Essentials of Mysticism*, 23. For an interesting analysis of the relation between mysticism and ethics, see Grace M. Jantzen, 'Ethics and mysticism: friends or foes?', *Nederlands Theologisch Tijdschrift* 39 (1985), 314–26.

times the mystic union is taken to be a form of ontological merging; sometimes it is seen as merely an ecstatic experience of union; and sometimes it is interpreted as a close personal relationship in which the individual identity of the partners is preserved and left intact. There are two reasons which are especially important in explaining this diversity. The first is the highly metaphorical language in which mystics describe the mystic union. It is not always easy for interpreters to determine the exact point of these metaphors: are they intended to assert a form of merging with the Divine, or to express an ecstatic experience or to describe an intimate personal relationship? A second reason has to do with the variety of religious traditions from which various forms of mysticism derive. This applies even to the various forms of Christian mysticism, because, as Irving Singer points out, Christianity springs from divergent sources. From Hellenism it derives the tendency toward merging, suggested by Plato and enunciated by Plotinus, they themselves having possibly received it from Hinduism via the Orphic mysteries. From Judaism, Christianity takes the belief in separateness between finite man and the infinitely awesome God whose nature transcends everything tinged with mortality. 'As the offspring of such contrary parents, Christianity turns into a series of syntheses, each mixing more or less the same elements but in a different composition.'[27] The result is that in Christian mysticism descriptions of spiritual union arrange themselves in a spreading continuum in which statements at one extreme are vastly different from those at the other. At one end of the continuum we find mystics who characterize the union as a total and complete destruction of their individuality. In ways that are reminiscent of Plotinus, they speak of merging with the highest good. At the opposite extreme are those mystics who consider total merging with God to be either impossible or undesirable. For them the consummation of religious love preserves the identity of the lovers.[28] In the light of these considerations it is clearly unfruitful to try and find the 'real nature' of the *unio mystica*. Let us instead examine various

---

[27] Singer, *Nature of Love* I, 220.　　　　[28] Ibid., 216.

interpretations of mystic union more closely. What would be the implications if we were to interpret the goal of mystical love as merging with the Divine, or as an ecstatic experience, or as a close personal relationship with God?

Let us first examine the view of mystical love as a form of *merging*. The first difficulty we have to face here, is trying to form some idea of what this could mean. As Irving Singer points out, the notion that people can merge with one another is elusive and baffling. In everyday life, we realize that one person's experience may have something in common with another's, but we would not ordinarily speak of merging in our personalities, or of being or becoming one another. We are distinct individuals, each living his own life, each responsible for what he does.[29] The idea of merging is found especially in the works of those whom Steven Katz calls 'the unitive Christian mystics' such as Eckhart, Tauler, and Suso, who have been schooled in the strong neo-Platonic current in Christian intellectual history.[30]

Plotinus conceived of the universe as a double process. On the one hand, all things emanate from the One or the Absolute like water from an eternal fountain. On the other hand, all things strive to return to their origin and to merge again with the One from whom they proceeded in the first place. Neo-Platonic mysticism tries to express in abstract metaphysical terms this cosmic urge of all beings within the universe to return and be reabsorbed into the unity of the absolute Origin. We might think of our own creation as the gift of autonomous existence as individual beings outside of God in a way analogous to our birth, in which each of us receives an independent existence as an individual being outside and independent of our mother's womb. We could then try to think of neo-Platonic mysticism as an attempt to reverse this process: by laying down our autonomous existence as individuals, we return as it were to the 'cosmic womb' and are reabsorbed into the divine Origin whence we all came. In the words of Plotinus:

[29] Singer, *Nature of Love* II, 6.
[30] Steven T. Katz, 'Language, epistemology and mysticism', in Katz (ed.), *Mysticism and Philosophical Analysis* (London 1978), 42.

The man is changed, no longer himself nor self-belonging; he is merged with the Supreme, sunken into it, one with it: centre coincides with centre, for centres of circles, even here below, are one when they unite, and two when they separate...There were not two; beholder was one with beheld; it was not a vision compassed but a unity apprehended. The man formed by this mingling with the Supreme must...carry its image impressed upon him: he has become the Unity, nothing within him or without induces any diversity.[31]

Many Christian mystics describe the mystic union by means of metaphors which are, to say the least, reminiscent of this kind of neo-Platonic ideal of self-annihilating absorption into God. Thus for example Eckhart maintains that

where two are to become one, one of them must lose its being. So it is: if God and your soul are to become one, your soul must lose her being and her life. As far as anything remains, they would indeed be *united*, but for them to become *one*, the one must lose its identity and the other must keep its identity: then they are one.[32]

Elsewhere he writes that the ' I ' is reduced there to utter nought and nothing is left there but God and with God's all-penetrativeness she streams into the eternal Godhead, where in an eternal stream God is flowing into God.[33] Eckhart's pupil Henry Suso expresses this as follows: 'When a good and faithful servant enters into the joy of his Lord...he is quite dead to himself, and is entirely lost in God, has passed into him, and has become one spirit with him in all respects, just as a little drop of water that is poured into a large quantity of wine.'[34] St Teresa of Avila describes the mystic union by means of a similar metaphor:

It is like rain falling from the heavens into a river or a spring; there is nothing but water there and it is impossible to divide or separate the water belonging to the river from that which fell from the heavens. Or it is as if a tiny streamlet enters the sea, from which it will find no way of separating itself.[35]

[31] Plotinus, *The Enneads* (London 1957), 624.
[32] Meister Eckhart, *Sermons and Treatises* (3 vols, London 1979–87) I, 52.
[33] See Meister Eckhart, *Schriften* (Jena 1943), 170.
[34] Henry Suso, *The Little Book of Truth* (London 1953), 185.
[35] Teresa of Avila, *Interior Castle*, Seventh Mansion, chapter 2 (in *The Complete Works of St Teresa of Jesus* (London 1946), 335).

St Bernard states that 'anybody who has this experience, even if only rarely, or just once in his lifetime and then for only a moment, is indeed blessed by God and holy. So to forget yourself, that you do not exist, and be totally unconscious of yourself, to become nothing, is not a human feeling, it is a divine experience.'[36] And again:

A drop of water mixed with wine, disappears as it takes on the taste and colour of the wine. Molten iron in the furnace seems to lose its state to become like fire, just as air saturated in sunshine is more than 'lit up', it transforms into sunlight itself. Similarly all human love in the saint will mysteriously melt away to be transformed into the will of God.[37]

If we interpret the mystical ideal as a form of merging with the Divine, then three serious objections can be raised against it. In the first place, this ideal seems to involve a kind of pantheism which directly contradicts that other important strand in Christian belief which emphasized the transcendent otherness of God in relation to his creatures. If the mystic were to merge with God, then God's transcendence with regard to the mystic would collapse. As we pointed out above, this strand of Christian belief derives from Judaism. In this respect Jewish mysticism is the exact opposite of the neo-Platonic ideal of merging: 'Throughout there remains an almost exaggerated conscious-ness of God's *otherness*, nor does the identity and individuality of the mystic become blurred even at the height of ecstatic passion.'[38] For this reason, as Singer points out, Jewish mystics generally characterize the love of God as the devotion of child to parent, and not as the union between lover and beloved.[39] But also in orthodox Christianity it is heretical to deny the transcendence of God in this way. Indeed in 1329 Pope John XXII condemned Eckhart for maintaining that: 'We are fully transformed and converted into God; in the same way as in the sacrament the bread is converted into the body of Christ, so I am converted into him, so that he converts me into his being as one, not as *like*. By the living God it is true that there is no

---

[36] St Bernard, *On Loving God*, chapter 10. [37] Ibid., chapter 10.
[38] Gershom G. Sholem, *Major Trends in Jewish Mysticism* (New York 1941), 55.
[39] Singer, *Nature of Love*, I, 219.

difference.'[40] Most Christian mystics are usually very aware of this threat of heresy and, even though they often use metaphors which are suggestive of merging, they take great pains to argue that this is not the case. Thus St Bernard goes to great lengths to show that the mystical union is in no way a *substantial* unification between Divine and human being or even between the Divine and the human will, but merely a perfect *accord* or coincidence between the will of the mystic and the Will of God. In this respect the mystical union between God and the mystic differs from the unity between the Persons of the Trinity.

There is in them … one essence and one will, and where there is only one, there can be no agreement or combining or incorporating or anything of that kind. For there must be at least two wills for there to be agreement, and two essences for there to be combining and uniting in agreement. There is none of these things in the Father and the Son since they have neither two essences nor two wills … If anyone would affirm that there is agreement between the Father and the Son, I do not contest it provided that it is understood that there is not a union of wills but a unity of will. But we think of God and man as dwelling in each other in a very different way, because their wills and their substances are distinct and different; that is, their substances are not intermingled, yet their wills are in agreement; and this union is for them a communion of wills and an agreement in charity. Happy is this union if you experience it, but compared with the other, it is no union at all.[41]

Clearly then, St Bernard avoids pantheism by sharply distinguishing between union and unity. But the dividing line between these two concepts is very fine indeed, and numerous Christian mystics have been suspected, cautioned or condemned for crossing it.[42]

---

[40] Eckhart, *Sermons and Treatises* I, xlviii.

[41] St Bernard, *Song of Songs*, Sermon 71. It is significant that Eckhart fails to maintain this distinction, but prays rather 'that Jesus may come into us … and make us one, as he is one with the Father and the Holy Ghost, one God, that we may become and remain eternally one with Him, so help us God' (*Sermons and Treatises* I, 61).

[42] A striking example of how fine this line is can be found in the history of Marguerite Porete who in 1310 was burned in Paris as a relapsed heretic. Marguerite was condemned on the basis of a book she had written which, according to the clerics who judged her, advocated pantheism. Marguerite's book was also burned, but copies survived. In later years, her authorship was forgotten, but the book itself became widely read, especially by monks and nuns. Before it was properly identified as the

A second difficulty with the ideal of merging, is that it denies the personhood of both God and the human mystic who tries to merge with him, and is thereby also inconsistent with the model of love understood in personal terms. As we shall argue at greater length in part IV, 'personhood' is a relational concept in the sense that one can only be a person in relation to other persons. In order to establish a personal relationship therefore necessarily involves two distinct persons. Since merging entails the abolition of the distinct personal identity of the partners, it also entails the abolition of the relationship as such. According to Friedrich Heiler 'the barriers between God and man disappear in the ecstatic experience; man vanishes in God, fuses with him in perfect unity. Every contrast, every difference, every dualism disappears in the mystic experience.'[43] If this is true, then the mystic ideal would not only abolish the personal identity of the mystic but also make the idea of a personal God superfluous. Merging presupposes an impersonal Absolute like the One of Plotinus rather than a personal God. Thus, according to Heiler, who holds this interpretation of mysticism,

the God whom the mystic adores is conceived as absolutely static. The spiritual Reality in which he by contemplation sinks himself, is a static ideal; the object of contemplation can only be an Ultimate, a Final... The God of mystical contemplation does not possess the strongly marked feature of personality which is peculiar to the idea of God in primitive prayer. It is significant that in mystical prayers God is so often addressed by such a neutral expression as *summum bonum*... Wherever aesthetic intuition and solemn adoration of the Highest Good takes the place of loving intercourse with God, there the features of the divine personality begin to fade.[44]

Clearly the ideal of merging is inconsistent with the model of 'loving intercourse' since the latter requires that the loving partners remain distinct individuals. In the words of St Bernard quoted above: 'There must be at least two wills for there to be agreement.'

work of a condemned heretic it was even published in modern English under the auspices of the Downside Benedictines with the nihil obstat and imprimatur. Marguerite's authorship was not re-established until 1946. See Sharon Brehm, 'Passionate love', in R. J. Sternberg and M. L. Barnes (eds.), *The Psychology of Love* (London 1988), 252.   [43] Heiler, *Prayer*, 169.   [44] Ibid., 197–8.

The third difficulty with the ideal of merging, is that it is well nigh impossible for us to form any coherent idea of what it could mean. As Singer puts it: 'To the extent that Christianity describes the mystical union as a kind of merging, it defies reason. It aligns itself to any number of primitive religions, wrapping its moral message within the orgiastic mystery of self-contradiction.'[45] There are two ways in which this difficulty might be removed. On the one hand it might be argued that our difficulty with imagining what it would mean for two persons to merge follows from the fact that in this life we think of persons as corporeal beings and as such unable to merge with one another. But this does not exclude the possibility of *non-corporeal beings* merging with each other. Does Gilson not suggest this with reference to St Bernard when he states that 'inter-communion of this kind is made possible by the immateriality of the soul on the one hand, and the absolute purity of the spirituality of God on the other'[46]? And is this not consistent with the view of many mystics, including St Bernard, that real mystical union can only be achieved in the next life when we are freed from our corporeal existence? It is doubtful, however, whether this solution is adequate. Apart from the difficulties involved in forming a coherent idea of non-corporeal existence, this way out fails to remove the two other major difficulties with the idea of merging which we discussed above. On the other hand, one might argue that the mystical union should not be interpreted as referring to a form of *real* ontological merging, but merely to an ectatic *experience* which is described as an experience of merging. Thus it might be more plausible to interpret the ultimate goal of mystic love as an ecstatic experience of union with God rather than as a form of ontological merging with the Divine. Let us examine this interpretation of mystic love more closely.

'Pure love, as conceived by St Bernard, is essentially a mystical experience. What we have to do with here is neither an idea, nor an habitual disposition, but the brief and perpetually in-

---

[45] Singer, *Nature of Love* I, 227.   [46] Gilson, *Mystical Theology*, 108.

terrupted *excessus* of the soul of the mystic, when God unites it
with himself by exceptional graces.'[47] As we explained above, St
Bernard distinguishes two aspects to this mystical state of
excessus: ecstasy and rapture. Ecstasy is a state of mystical
slumber or trance in which the bodily senses cease to function,
while rapture is the enjoyment of ineffable visions which cannot
be described or communicated to others. In her autobiography,
St Teresa of Avila describes this experience graphically as
follows:

While seeking God in this way, the soul becomes conscious that it is
fainting almost completely away, in a kind of swoon, with an
exceedingly great and sweet delight. It gradually ceases to breathe
and all its bodily strength begins to fail it; it cannot even move its hand
without great pain; its eyes involuntarily close, or, if they remain
open, they can hardly see.[48]

In the light of such statements, it is plausible to suppose that
mystics who would deny wanting to really merge with God, do
in fact aim at achieving ecstatic experiences which might be
described in terms of merging. Thus, according to Sharon
Brehm, it seems reasonable to suggest that although Teresa
firmly believed in the theology of essential difference and
distinctiveness, her own psychological experience may have
included the feeling that, at least for brief moments, her being
was annihilated and submerged in the Godhead.[49] But then it
would seem that the goal of the mystic's life is to achieve what
William James calls 'mystical states of consciousness'.[50]

This interpretation of the goal of mystic love has two
noteworthy implications. First of all, on this interpretation it
becomes meaningful to ask whether such states of mind could
not be induced in many other ways apart from following the
tortuous *via mystica*. Could we not as well achieve a state of
trance accompanied by visions of ineffable delight by means of
drugs? Thus Frits Staal distinguishes between 'the difficult

---

[47] Ibid., 143.
[48] Teresa of Avila, *The Book of Her Life*, chapter 18. (*Works*, 108).
[49] Brehm, 'Passionate love', 252.
[50] William James, *The Varieties of Religious Experience* (Glasgow 1982), 366.

ways of contemplation' and 'the easy way of drugs' by means of the following analogy:

Since a mystical experience is like entering a mental state or like gaining access to a domain of the brain, there are different methods which can bring this about, just as a house can be entered by various means: by climbing through a window, or breaking a wall, by digging a tunnel to reach the cellar, or by opening the front door with a key. Some methods are easier than others ... Someone who has just broken the wall of his home is irritated when he afterwards finds in his pocket a fitting key.[51]

Staal admits that this analogy is limited, since in the realm of mysticism we do not know whether it is really the same state which is reached by these different routes. However, according to him these differences may in fact result from the different religious and moral frames of reference or 'superstructures' in terms of which various mystics interpret their experiences, and have little to do with the mystical states themselves.[52] However, even if we were to maintain that the ecstatic experiences of mystics could also be different in themselves, apart from the various ways in which they are interpreted, it still does not necessarily follow that these differences run parallel with the different methods by which they are induced. The various mystical experiences achieved by means of 'the difficult ways of contemplation' are not necessarily the same, nor is it logically necessary that experiences induced through 'the easy way of drugs' should always be different. It is not logically impossible to achieve different experiences by the same technique nor to achieve the same experience by different techniques. This does not deny the distinction between genuine mystical ecstasy and pathological states of trance. However, the difference between these is not in the methods by which they are achieved, but, as we have seen Evelyn Underhill argue, in their fruits. There is no guarantee that meditative techniques could not lead to pathological states of trance. And why should we disagree with the

---

[51] Frits Staal, *Exploring Mysticism* (London 1975), 159–60.
[52] For an interesting defence of this kind of distinction between mystical experience and interpretation, see Ninian Smart, 'Interpretation and mystical experience', *Religious Studies* 1 (1965). For a critique of the distinction, see Katz.

claims of Staal, William James, Aldous Huxley, and others[53] that drugs could also induce genuine beneficial experiences of mystical ecstasy?

A second noteworthy implication of the view that the mystic's life is aimed at achieving 'mystical states of consciousness' is the following. States of consciousness do not necessarily require intentional objects. Thus if love were taken to be an ecstatic state of consciousness, achieving it does not necessarily require a real personal beloved. And if mystic love is taken to be an experience of mystical ecstasy, achieving it does not necessarily entail a relation to a real Divine Being. But in that case the pure love of the mystic is no more than a solipsistic state of narcissism. Then the mystic lover is as solipsistic as we have seen Stendhal's romantic lover to be: the latter is in love with his fantasies and the former with his ecstatic experiences, and neither of them necessarily requires a real personal beloved with whom to relate.

In the light of these implications, the view that the mystical union desired by the mystic is to be interpreted as a kind of ecstatic experience seems less than adequate. It might be that the difficulty lies in the concept of 'experience' which is being used here. In an illuminating essay, Grace Jantzen criticizes William James as the initiator of 'the subjective view of mysticism' according to which the definition of mysticism has shifted from the patristic emphasis on the objective content of experience to the modern emphasis on the subjective psychological states or feelings of the individual.[54] According to Jantzen, the basic difficulty with James' views on mysticism is that he confuses two senses of 'experience', a broader and a narrower one. In his chapter on mysticism, James presupposes the narrower concept of experience. The examples he gives are of particular states of consciousness: dream-like states, trances, an experience with chloroform, flashes of exaltation, experiences of ecstatic union. These, for James, are 'mystical experiences'.

[53] 'I know more than one person who is persuaded that in the nitrous oxide trance we have a genuine metaphysical revelation' (James, *Varieties of Religious Experience*, 373). See also Aldous Huxley, *The Doors of Perception* (London 1954) for a classic defence of this claim.

[54] Grace M. Jantzen, 'Mysticism and experience', *Religious Studies* 25 (1989), 295.

Subsequent philosophers have followed him in thinking of mysticism in terms of experiences in this narrower sense: voices, visions, ecstasies, and the like, to such an extent that in many people's minds phenomena of this sort are part of their conception of mysticism. Elsewhere, however, James also seems to presuppose a broader concept of religious experience which would also include a lifetime of 'being toward God', living in a conscious relationship with God. He describes those with a 'more habitual and so to speak chronic sense of God's presence', and says that this would be the self-description of 'thousands of unpretending Christians'. There are no trances here, no voices or visions or ecstasies; yet according to Jantzen it would be a great mistake to say that there is no experience of God. James cites the practice of the presence of God, recollection, and contemplation as disciplined ways of life into which one can increasingly enter. All this is experiential in the broad sense. According to Jantzen this continuous relationship with God is arguably the heart and centre of Christianity.[55] Jantzen does not deny that mystics like St Bernard, Julian of Norwich, and others do experience visions, ecstasies, etc. In fact such experiences 'in the narrower sense' play an important role in the life and works of a mystic like Julian. However, they are never a goal in themselves. They are only of value as a means for achieving mystical experience in the 'broader sense'. Thus visions, ecstasies, etc. could even be harmful if they fail to deepen the mystic's loving relationship with God. It is in this sense that the value of such experiences 'in the narrower sense' depends upon their fruits. Thus Jantzen concludes that union with God cannot be equated with intense experiences like voices and visions and subjective feelings of unity or ecstasy. Such phenomena can at best be no more than a help toward the ongoing project of increasing union with God. At worst, if one becomes fixated upon them, they are an impediment. They are never an end in themselves, and they are never essential even as a means to union with God.[56]

If we interpret mystical experience in this broad sense, we

---

[55] Ibid., 301–2.   [56] Ibid., 313.

also avoid the two consequences which we pointed out above. The experience of living your whole life in a loving relationship with God and the discipline of gradually transforming all your actions and attitudes to be in conformity with this relationship, can never be achieved by means of drugs. On the contrary, the kind of union sought for here, could hardly be achieved without going through something like the various stages of the *via mystica*. In the words of Grace Jantzen, 'it would be folly to suppose that union with God, the summit of Christian experience, could occur unless one were also serious about purification and illumination, and indeed were making progress in these areas' (307). Furthermore, this kind of mystical experience excludes all narcissistic solipsism, since it is by definition the experience of living in a loving *relationship* with God.

Interpreted in this way, the union of love sought by the mystic is neither a form of ontological merging, nor a mere ecstatic experience, but an intimate and life-transforming personal relationship with God. According to St Bernard, this consists of a perfect accord or coincidence between the will of the mystic and the Will of God. As we pointed out in the previous chapter, believers consider the Will of God to be the ultimate standard in the light of which all their value preferences are to be judged and their lives and characters are to be continuously remodelled. As we described it above, the *via mystica* is aimed at this process of remodelling in which the mystic's life is on the one hand purified from false ways of feeling, thinking, and acting which are contrary to the Will of God, and on the other hand regains the likeness of the Divine love which was lost through sin. In the words which we quoted from St Bernard, the mystic's soul is 'sprinkled with the hyssop of humility' and 'set alight by the fire of love'. We saw that both St Bernard and Henry Suso use the metaphor of a drop of water disappearing in a large amount of wine. The point of this metaphor is not to show how the mystic is merged into God, but rather to explain how the mystic's life is transformed into the likeness of God: the water takes on the taste and colour of the wine.

Does this also apply to the kind of union sought by romantic lovers? Does the intimate personal relationship which they seek also entail a union of wills? Does a human lover have to agree with the wishes and will of his or her beloved, or merely to identify with the beloved's interests or good even though they may differ in their views on what this could be? How does the union sought by romantic lovers differ from that between the mystic and God? We will have to return to this point in detail in part IV. For the present we can conclude, however, that the kind of loving union with God sought by the mystic, is an intimate personal relationship in which the whole life and character of the mystic is transformed in the likeness of the Divine love. For the mystic this life-transforming personal relationship is what constitutes ultimate bliss. In some respects, however, achieving it entails suffering. Let us now turn to an examination of the ways in which love is related to suffering.

CHAPTER 4

Passionate suffering

4.1 MYSTIC LOVE AND SUFFERING

Transforming our life and character in the likeness of God does not take place without self-sacrifice and suffering. This transformation cannot be achieved without discarding our old sinful self which loves itself rather than God and desires its own pleasure rather than God's Will. This can only be achieved through a rigorous process of mortification which, according to St Bernard, the monastic life of the Cistercians was designed to provide. Such purifying ascesis entails much bodily and mental suffering.

In his treatise *On Grace and Free Choice*, St Bernard distinguishes between three forms of freedom: first, the *liberum arbitrium* or radical indetermination of the will which is proper to our nature as human persons. This is freedom from necessity or compulsion, or the freedom to make choices. According to St Bernard this kind of freedom is in fact the *image* of God in us which cannot be taken away from us by sin. Sin does however destroy the Divine *likeness* in us which according to St Bernard consists of the other two forms of freedom, the *liberum consilium* and the *liberum a miseria*. The *liberum consilium* is the freedom from sin which enables the just to know God's Will and consistently choose to act in accordance with it. This kind of freedom can only be achieved by grace and not by nature. It does not guarantee, however, that the choice for good over evil will always be easy or pleasant for us. On the contrary, it will cost us bitter suffering to consistently do what we know to be God's Will for us, since doing so requires continual self-sacrifice and ascesis of body and mind. For this reason the *liberum consilium* is only half the Divine likeness. The other half is the *liberum a miseria* which is granted to those who not only do God's will but do so joyfully. Such people 'delight in goodness because they have a taste for it'.[1] They will find the highest joy in doing the Will of God, even if this involves mortification and the bearing of worldly tribulation. These are borne joyfully because they are experienced as participation in the suffering of Christ.[2] In its fullest sense, this freedom from suffering (or 'freedom of pleasure') is only granted to us in the next life, and on earth only in rare moments of mystic rapture.[3]

There is however a second sense in which the way to mystic union involves suffering. If in this life mystic union can only be achieved in rare moments of rapture, then, as we explained in the previous chapter, the mystic's life is characterized by vicissitude. Moments of mystic union are interrupted by long periods of languor in which the mystic suffers on account of the absence of God – the unhappiness of the lover longing for the return of the beloved.[4] Thus the mystic lover suffers in this life not only on account of the price to be paid for union with God,

---

[1] 'How many good actions are performed without the doers having any taste for them, because they are compelled to do them by their way of life or by some circumstance or necessity?... But those who... are wise... delight in goodness because they have a taste for it... Happy the mind which is protected by a taste for good and a hatred of evil, for this is what it means to be reformed in wisdom, and to know by experience and to rejoice in the victory of wisdom... It looks to virtue to sustain tribulation with fortitude, and to wisdom to rejoice in those tribulations.' *Song of Songs*, Sermon 85.

[2] 'It is none the less true that he will find henceforth a heartfelt joy in mortification. The pains he inflicts on his body he wills out of desire to associate himself with the suffering of Christ on the Cross. In his turn, he collaborates by means of his own affliction in the ransom of the sinner; his sufferings will have become, in the fullest sense of the term, a *compassion* with the Passion of Christ; He associates himself with the work of redemption, and thereby begins to re-establish a state in which the will shakes itself free from the misery into which it has fallen since the first sin... This accord of the will with the actual state in which man finds himself placed is precisely *libertas a miseria*.' Gilson, *Mystical Theology*, 83–4.

[3] 'On this earth, the contemplatives alone can in some way enjoy the freedom of pleasure, though only in part, in very small part, and on the rarest occasions.' *On Grace and Free Choice* v.15.

[4] 'And so, even in this body we can often enjoy the happiness of the Bridegroom's presence, but it is as happiness that is never complete because the joy of the visit is followed by the pain of his departure.' *Song of Songs*, Sermon 32.

but also on account of the imperfection of the union which can be achieved here.

In order to eliminate this latter misery during this life, the quietists tried to carry self-sacrifice to its logical conclusion by renouncing all desires – including the desire for God. If we have no desires at all, we cannot suffer through having our desires thwarted. Thus suffering is avoided by cultivating the kind of stoic apathy which the quietists called 'pure love'. This is described as follows by Madame Guyon:

The understanding is obscured, the will loses all elasticity, the slightest vital movement of the selfhood is dead. Wish, inclination, desire, aversion, antipathy – all are gone. The soul enters into the dark and awful state of mystical death since it has passed over into a state of complete absence of feeling. It has become utterly indifferent to the world, to itself, and to God. It neither loves nor hates any more; it neither suffers nor rejoices; it does nothing good and nothing evil, it does nothing at all. The soul has nothing, wills nothing, is nothing; it is in a state of nothingness.[5]

Obviously this is the exact opposite of that which St Bernard would call 'pure love'. For St Bernard pure love is the bliss of union with God; for the quietists it is the elimination of the desire for this bliss. For St Bernard it is the experience of momentary ecstasy during this life; for the quietists it is resignation to a permanent state of languor during this life. For St Bernard it is the elimination of desire by means of possession; for the quietists it is the elimination of desire by means of resignation. For St Bernard pure love of God eliminates suffering; for the quietists pure love of God is resignation to it.

A third form of pure love, quite distinct from that of the mystics and the quietists, is to be found in the medieval courtly tradition. Here love is related in a very different way to suffering. Unlike the mystics, who tried to overcome the distance to the beloved and so to eliminate the suffering which follows from it; and unlike the quietists who tried to eliminate the suffering by adopting an attitude of stoic resignation toward it, the courtly lover tried in a way to *cultivate* the distance and the

---

[5] Quoted by Heiler, *Prayer*, 197.

suffering which attends it. 'Pure courtly love is defined by exclusion of that precisely which constitutes the pure love of the mystics: the real union of lover and beloved ... The purity of courtly love keeps the lovers apart, while that of the mystics unites them.'[6] Let us now take a closer look at the medieval phenomenon of 'courtly love' and see how in that context love was related to suffering.

4.2 COURTLY LOVE AND THE SUFFERING OF TRISTAN

What do we mean by 'courtly love'? The term 'courtly love' or *amour courtois* was first introduced by the nineteenth century medievalist Gaston Paris to characterize a set of attitudes in relation to love which first manifested itself in the amorous social practices prevalent among twelfth-century knights and ladies at court and in the ways these were described and expressed in twelfth-century French literature. This does not mean, however, that 'courtly love' is a univocal term which refers to a single easily identifiable phenomenon. 'Strictly speaking, it is love as this was conceived in the courts, just as scholastic philosophy is the philosophy elaborated in the schools. This concept of love is by no means one: it varies from poet to poet and, according to his mood, in the same poet.'[7] Even more so than in the case of 'mysticism', the term 'courtly love' refers to a variety of phenomena which show no more than a family resemblance. Any attempt to specify defining characteristics for it can be opposed with counter-examples from the literature and the courtly practice of the period. This is further complicated by the distinction between representative and compensatory ideals introduced by Johan Huizinga when discussing the phenomenon: the former refer to symbols which actually exist in a culture, while the latter are compensations which do not actually occur but are considered desirable. According to Huizinga, courtly love was primarily an ideal of the second type.[8] Thus the concept of courtly love could also include

---

[6] Gilson, *Mystical Theology*, 192–3.   [7] Ibid., 171.

[8] Singer, *Nature of Love* II, 20. Huizinga makes this distinction in his book *The Waning of the Middle Ages* (New York 1954), particularly chapters 2–5, 8, and 9.

aspects which never occurred but were merely considered desirable in the period. The amorphous nature of the concept therefore gives rise to fruitless controversies about its origin[9] and its effects in later centuries.[10]

In what follows, we shall try to avoid these difficulties by concentrating our attention on three features which most authors agree to be fairly generally present in the courtly tradition: courtly love is based upon the dual morality maintained by the nobility of the period, it involves passionate suffering and it is generally expressed in a veiled or rhetorical fashion. We do not claim that these features exclude counter-examples or that they are the only features which characterize courtly love. But for our present purposes they will suffice. In his classic treatment of courtly love, Denis de Rougemont shows how these three features are all present in the myth of Tristan and Iseult. Like him we shall try to explain these features by referring to this myth.[11]

The myth of Tristan.[12] Tristan is born in misfortune – hence his name. His father has just died and his mother does not survive his birth. He is brought up by his uncle, King Mark of Cornwall. Upon reaching the age of knighthood, he slays the Morhout, an Irish giant who comes like a Minotaur to exact his tribute of Cornish maidens. Wounded by the Morhout's

---

[9] Thus, for example, C. S. Lewis holds it to be a novel invention of the twelfth century whereas Irving Singer tries to prove that it has many antecedents in classical and especially in Arabic literature and thought. See chapter 1 of C. S. Lewis, *The Allegory of Love* (Oxford 1936), and chapter 2 of Singer, *Nature of Love* II. Denis de Rougemont tries to prove that courtly love originated from and was in fact an expression of the Cathar heresy. See his *Love in the Western World* (New York 1956. 2nd edn.), chapter 2.

[10] Thus, for example, C. S. Lewis and Denis de Rougemont view it as the foundation for the ideas on love prevalent in romanticism since the eighteenth century, while Singer emphasizes the great differences between courtly love and romanticism.

[11] De Rougemont, *Western World*. De Rougemont's views on courtly love are now generally considered to be biased and unfounded. Singer refers to their 'propagandistic inaccuracy' (Singer, *Nature of Love* II, xi). Although we shall to some extent follow the line of de Rougemont's exposition, we shall not necessarily accept his interpretation.

[12] In broad outline we follow here the summary of the myth as given by De Rougemont in *Western World*, 26–30.

poisoned barb, Tristan begs to be set adrift with his sword and his harp in a boat without sail or oar. He lands in Ireland where the queen knows the secret of the poison. Since the Morhout was the queen's brother, Tristan is careful not to disclose how he came by his wound. Iseult, the queen's daughter, nurses him back to health. This is the Prologue.

A few years later King Mark sends Tristan to find for him as a bride the maiden whose golden hair has been brought to him by a bird. A storm brings the hero again to Ireland where he slays a dragon threatening the capital. Having been wounded by the dragon, he is again nursed by Iseult. When she learns that it was he who killed her uncle, she threatens to transfix him in his bath with his own sword. She spares him, however, when he tells her of his mission from King Mark, since she would like to become queen. (According to some versions, she also spares him because she finds him handsome). Tristan and Iseult set sail for Cornwall. At sea they are thirsty, and Iseult's maid Brangien unwittingly gives them the magic love-potion to drink which Iseult's mother had prepared for her and King Mark. This commits them to a fate from 'which they can never escape during the remainder of their lives, for they have drunk their destruction and death'. They confess their love and fall into each other's arms. Yet, since Tristan is still duty bound to fulfil his mission for King Mark, he delivers Iseult to the king despite his betrayal.

Four 'felon' barons now tell the king that Tristan and Iseult are lovers. Tristan is banished, but he tricks the king into believing his innocence and is allowed to return to the castle. Then the dwarf Froncin, who is in league with the barons, lays a trap for the lovers. He scatters flour in the spear-length between Tristan's bed and that of the queen. When in the night Tristan desires to embrace his mistress, he leaps across from his bed to hers, and in the effort reopens a wound in his leg inflicted the previous day by a boar. Froncin, the barons and the King enter the room and find the flour blood-stained. Mark accepts this evidence of adultery and Iseult is handed over to a company of lepers while Tristan is sentenced to the stake. Tristan escapes, rescues Iseult from the lepers, and together they hide for three years deep in the Forest of Morrois. One day King Mark comes upon them asleep in the forest. Between them Tristan has placed his drawn sword. Taking this as evidence of their innocence the King spares them. Without waking them, he replaces Tristan's sword with his own and leaves.

At the end of three years (when according to some versions of the myth the potency of the love-potion wears off), Tristan repents and Iseult wishes that she were queen again. Through the hermit Ogrin, Tristan offers peace to the king, saying that he will return Iseult. Mark promises forgiveness. As the royal party approaches, the lovers part. However, Iseult asks Tristan to stay in the vicinity till he has made sure that Mark will treat her well. She also declares that she will join him at the first sign he makes since 'neither tower, nor wall, nor stronghold' will stop her doing Tristan's bidding. They have several secret meetings in the hut of Orri the woodman, but the felon barons continue to watch over the queen's virtue. She then asks for a judgment of God to prove her innocence. Before grasping the red-hot iron which will not harm one who has spoken the truth, she swears that no man has ever held her in his arms save the King and the poor pilgrim who has just carried her ashore from a boat. The pilgrim is Tristan in disguise.

Fresh adventures carry Tristan far away from Iseult, and he supposes she no longer loves him. So he agrees to marry 'for her beauty and her name' another Iseult, 'Iseult of the White Hand'. After the marriage he preserves her virginity, and sighs for 'Iseult the Fair'. At last, wounded by a poisoned spear, Tristan is about to die and sends for the queen from Cornwall who alone can save him. As her ship draws near, it hoists a white sail as a sign of hope. Tormented by jealousy, Iseult of the White Hand tells Tristan that the sail is black, whereupon Tristan dies. Arriving at the castle, Iseult the Fair clasps the dead body of her lover and dies as well.

So much for the myth in broad outline. De Rougemont points out that if we examine it with the cool gaze of the present-day reader, we discover that it is riddled with puzzling contradictions. Firstly, the manners of the time sanctioned the right of the stronger. Why does Tristan not take advantage of this right and simply take Iseult away from the king? Secondly, why the sword of chastity between the two sleepers in the forest? At that moment they had no intention of turning from their adulterous ways, nor did they expect to be discovered by the king. Thirdly, why does Tristan return Iseult to the king after three years in the forest, even in the versions where the love-potion retains its power? And if they are truly repentant, why do they promise to meet each other again at the very moment they undertake to part? Why do the authors of the myth hold up Tristan as the model of chivalry when he shamelessly betrays the king, and Iseult as a virtuous lady when she is in fact an adulteress? And why are the barons called 'felons' when they are merely defending the honour of their lord the king? Fifthly, the authors of the myth ascribe various motives to Tristan and others in order to explain their behaviour. These are so unconvincing that one must suspect that the real motives are very different. Thus, after three years in the forest, Tristan returns Iseult to the king because the rule of suzerain fealty requires this of him. But after three years this compliance with the rule seems both very belated and hardly sincere, since he has scarcely given her up before trying to return to the castle to be with her again. Furthermore, the love-potion which was brewed for Mark and his queen is said in some versions to last for only three years. Since a guarantee of three years of married bliss does not amount to very much, one wonders why the potency was not made permanent. Finally, when Tristan marries another Iseult 'for her beauty and her name', one wonders why he fails to consummate the marriage, since nothing compelled him to marry her or to be guilty of this insulting chastity in relation to her.

4.3 CHARACTERISTIC FEATURES OF COURTLY LOVE

These puzzling features of the myth can all be explained if we take into account the three characteristic features of courtly love to which we referred above: dual morality, passionate suffering, and rhetorical expression. Let us now take a closer look at these three features.

Dual morality. The social life of medieval nobility was characterized by two mutually exclusive social and moral codes: the
feudal and the courtly. The official structure of feudal society
was strictly hierarchical. Each individual had a designated
place or function or role to fulfil within the system. This was not
a matter of individual choice but was fixed by considerations of
heredity or position within the aristocratic 'line' or 'house'.
The basic moral requirement was that each individual should
know his or her place within the system and should strive to
fulfil his or her designated role. Individual ambitions and
preferences should be made subservient to the demands of the
social system as a whole. The preferred values were obedience,
faithfulness, and responsibility. Looked at in these terms, the
barons in the myth of Tristan were faithfully fulfilling their duty
as vassals to guard the rights and the honour of their lord the
king. Not they, but Tristan was the unfaithful 'felon' who
dishonoured his lord the king, and failed to fulfil his feudal
duties.

In this context, marriage was considered 'a phase of feudal
business-management, since it consisted basically of the joining
of lands, the cementing of loyalties, and the production of heirs
and future defenders'.[13] The choice of marriage partners was
not a matter of individual choice or preference. It was
determined by the interests of the 'line' which required the
production of heirs or the 'house' which strove to be enriched
through dowries and needed to form alliances with other houses
in order to safeguard it against military aggression. All such
matches were matches of interest, and 'great families found it
advantageous to keep marriage fluid, a union which could be
dissolved when it was advantageous to one or both parties'.[14] In
spite of the efforts of the church to discourage divorce, feudal
families could always find ways to dissolve marriage bonds.
'When a "deal" turned out badly, the wife was repudiated.
The plea of incest was exploited in curious ways, and in the face

---

[13] Morton M. Hunt, *The Natural History of Love* (London 1960), 119.
[14] James A. Brundage, *Law, Sex and Christian Society in Medieval Europe* (Chicago 1987),
175.

of it the Church was powerless. To allege consanguinity of even the fourth degree, no matter on what slender evidence, was enough to secure an annulment.'[15] Wives were therefore little more than useful pieces of property to be managed and protected accordingly. Thus as Morton Hunt points out, canon law had long given husbands express permission to beat their wives, and civil law often followed suit. A notable thirteenth-century statute of the town of Villefranche in Gascony granted every man the right to beat his wife, 'provided death does not ensue'.[16] Marriage therefore had little to do with love, and sexual intercourse within marriage was only justified with a view to procreation, and not as an expression of love. C. S. Lewis points out that, according to the 'sexology' of the medieval church, passionate love itself was wicked and did not cease to be so if the object of it were your own wife.[17]

Courtly love developed as a form of idealized adultery among the nobility during the twelfth century. In many ways it functioned as a 'compensatory ideal' (Huizinga) in reaction to the 'official' feudal relations between the sexes. Gradually these new manners and morals were developed into a more or less formal code of conduct which was explicitly cultivated among the young knights and ladies at court. This was especially the case at the brilliant court which Eleanor of Aquitaine created at her castle in Poitiers and later at the court of her daughter Marie, the Countess of Champagne, at Troyes. One of the ways

---

[15] De Rougemont, *Western World*, 33–4. In 1215 the Fourth Lateran Council decreed that 'the prohibition against marriage shall not in future go beyond the fourth degree of consanguinity and of affinity, since the prohibition cannot now generally be observed to further degrees without grave harm'. See Norman P. Tanner, *Decrees of the Ecumenical Councils* (London 1990), I, 257. Before then, divorce was subject to the *Decretum* of Gratian which allowed the dissolution of marriage up to the *seventh* degree of consanguinity! Brundage points out that 'while Gratian accepted the rules that barred marriages between persons related within seven degrees of consanguinity, he was surely not unaware of the potential problems that those rules posed, since few marriages could have been entirely immune from attack under the seven-degree rule' (*Law, Sex and Christian Society*, 254).   [16] Hunt, *Natural History*, 126.

[17] Lewis, *Allegory*, 13–4. See 14–8 for an extended discussion on this point. Brundage points out that Gratian's *Decretum* 'outlined a scheme of sexual morality that was disciplined and austere, grounded on the premise that sex was licit only within marriage, and then primarily for procreation, never for sheer pleasure' (*Law, Sex and Christian Society*, 255). Brundage's book provides an exhaustive treatment of the subject.

in which Eleanor and Marie developed and propagated the ways of courtly love, was a formal piece of play-acting known as the *Court of Love*:[18] in mock-legal proceedings, an anonymous lover or his lady – speaking through representatives – could present a complaint and defence in a disputed question of love behaviour. Hearing the case and handing down the decision might be a single judge – a great lady such as Eleanor herself – or an entire panel of noble ladies acting as a jury. In the hands of Eleanor and Marie, such debates grew to be a semi-serious pedagogical device for perfecting the new relationships, codifying and clarifying them, and promulgating them among the nobility at Poitiers. Apart from a large number of fictional and poetic representations of these Courts of Love, there also survives an extensive description of these proceedings written by Andreas Capellanus (André the Chaplain)[19] who lived at the court of Eleanor in Poitiers and later became chaplain at the court of Marie in Troyes.

Briefly, the practice of courtly love was as follows. A knight would solemnly dedicate his life to the service of a lady of his choice and would seek to be rewarded by her love. Usually both of them would be married to others, and initially he may not even yet have actually seen her. In principle she should be his social superior, and for this reason could not be his own wife who was legally subjected to him.

The love that is to be the source of all that is beautiful in life and manners must be the reward freely given by the lady, and only our superiors can reward. But a wife is not a superior. As the wife of another, above all as the wife of a great lord, she may be queen of beauty and of love, the distributor of favours, the inspiration of all knightly virtues, and the bridle of 'villany'; but as your own wife, for whom you have bargained with her father, she sinks at once from lady into mere woman.[20]

---

[18] On this see Hunt, *Natural History*, 134–5. See also chapter 15 of Amy Kelly, *Eleonore of Aquitaine and the Four Kings* (New York 1957). This excellent biography of Eleonore provides a vivid picture of the historical and social context within which courtly love flourished.

[19] *Tractatus de Amore et de Amoris Remedio.* An edition in English was produced by John Jay Parry under the title *The Art of Courtly Love* (New York 1941)

[20] Lewis, *Allegory*, 36–7.

Apart from not being the knight's superior, there is a second reason why his wife cannot be the object of his courtly love. Such love can only be given and received freely. On the one hand, he has not chosen his wife freely out of love but has bargained for her for the sake of feudal interests.[21] On the other hand, she cannot return his love freely since she is duty bound to obey him. In this connection, Andreas quotes the following judgment by Countess Marie of Champagne:

We declare and we hold as firmly established that love cannot exert its powers between two people who are married to each other. For lovers give each other everything freely, under no compulsion of necessity, but married people are in duty bound to give in to each other's desires and deny themselves to each other in nothing.[22]

The knight would imagine himself to be seized by an overwhelming passion for his lady. At first he would worship her in secret. Then he would gradually and humbly reveal his love to her, while she would gradually and grudgingly grant him her recognition or favour. Such favour might in time advance to the stage of nude sex play in bed, but not to actual intercourse for

---

[21] From the start of the thirteenth century, the idea that love can only be freely given or it is not love at all began to be applied to marriage as well. This gradually led to the introduction of the concensual theory in Catholic marriage law. 'Central to the concensual theory was free choice of matrimonial partners, which thenceforth took ascendancy over family interests and parental wishes in Catholic marriage law. This legal doctrine produced basic changes in the definition of family relationships and had enormous consequences for the subsequent history of marriage and family throughout the West' (Brundage, *Law, Sex and Christian Society*, 414). Although the free consent of the partners became a necessary condition for a legitimate marriage, this did not exclude the use of various forms of 'persuasion' in order to bring about the consent. It was therefore not always clear how 'free' the consent was!

[22] Andreas, *Courtly Love*, 106–7. This opinion functions as the basis for decisions in a number of other cases described by Andreas. For example: 'A certain knight was in love with a woman who had given her love to another man, but he got from her this much hope of her love – that if it should ever happen that she lost the love of her beloved, then without a doubt her love would go to this man. A little while after this the woman married her lover. The other knight then demanded that she give him the fruit of the hope she had granted him, but this she absolutely refused to do, saying that she had not lost the love of her lover. In this affair the Queen [either Adèle of France or else Eleonore herself] gave her decision as follows: "We dare not oppose the opinion of the Countess of Champagne, who ruled that love can exert no power between husband and wife. Therefore we recommend that the lady should grant the love she has promised."' *Courtly Love*, 175.

that would be to go beyond the limits of 'pure love'[23] to become
vulgar and degrading to both the lover and the beloved. Thus

the many testimonials that remain as to the existence of the practice of
amor purus, or 'pure love', make it very clear that adult, healthy,
normally sexed lords and ladies frequently, and perhaps most of the
time, managed to limit themselves to this kind of dalliance in their
courtly love affairs – and considered it a finer form of love than the
completed act. 'He knows little or nothing of the service of women
who wishes to possess his lady entirely', wrote the troubadour Daude
de Pradas, and scores of rhapsodists of *l'amour courtois* scorned the
culmination of the sex act as 'false love' while extolling as 'true love'
the 'pure' kissing, touching, fondling, and naked contact of the
lovers.[24]

This ideal of 'pure love' explains the meaning of the 'sword of
chastity' between the sleeping Tristan and Iseult in the forest,
and also the strange fact that three years of making love in the
forest failed to result in Iseult becoming pregnant.[25]

The aim of a courtly love affair was not primarily sexual but
rather the spiritual ennoblement of both lover and beloved.[26]
This is what distinguished such relations from all others in
which the partners participated.

[23] 'One kind of love is pure, and one is called mixed. It is the pure love which binds
together the hearts of two lovers with every feeling of delight. This kind consists in the
contemplation of the mind and the affection of the heart; it goes as far as the kiss and
the embrace and the modest contact with the nude lover, omitting the final solace,
for that is not permitted to those who wish to love purely ... This love is distinguished
by being of such virtue that from it arises all excellence of character, and no injury
comes from it, and God sees very little offence in it. But that is called mixed love
which gets its effect from every delight of the flesh and culminates in the final act of
Venus ... This kind quickly fails and lasts but a short time, and one often regrets
having practised it; by it one's neighbour is injured, the Heavenly King is offended,
and from it come very grave dangers.' Andreas, *Courtly Love*, 122.

[24] Hunt, *Natural History*, 123.

[25] 'Although bastardy was quite common in the Middle Ages (nine per cent of the
villeins of a typical English manor in the time of Edward III were known bastards),
references to children born of courtly love affairs are practically nonexistent both in
romance and in historical writing.' Hunt, *Natural History*, 123–4.

[26] 'Now it is the effect of love that a true lover cannot be degraded with any avarice.
Love causes a rough and uncouth man to be distinguished for his handsomeness; it
can endow a man even of the humblest birth with nobility of character, it blesses the
proud with humility; and the man in love becomes accustomed to performing many
services gracefully for everyone. O what a wonderful thing is love, which makes a
man shine with so many virtues and teaches everyone, no matter who he is, so many
good traits of character!' Andreas, *Courtly Love*, 31.

A married woman might cheerfully submit to her husband's demands without thereby impugning her devotion to the man she loved in a way that she did not love her husband. In that event, her behaviour would simply parallel the virtue of a knight who served his lord and possibly the church as well as the lady he loves. Similarly, he might enjoy the sexuality of other women – his own wife, his mistresses, and even an occasional peasant girl – without confusing the pleasures experienced in such encounters with the special ecstasy to be found in the company of his beloved. His love for her was a spiritual dedication that could not exist in relations with other women; and correspondingly her fidelity to him would manifest that nothing outweighed the value of his service to her.[27]

Thus the courtly lady was not a sexual object for her lover, but rather the embodiment of an ideal and the focus of his chivalrous endeavours. In this way he was supposed to perform heroic feats in honour of his lady in order to prove the strength of his devotion to her. The greater and more dangerous the deed, the greater the devotion manifested by it. Often such deeds consisted in overcoming great hurdles which separated him from his beloved, such as geographical barriers or military opposition, and especially the hurdles resulting from the rules of feudal society. Thus, according to the order of courtly love, every contravention of the rules of feudal society could count as an heroic deed if it enabled the knight to come closer to his beloved. According to the rules of the courtly moral order, Tristan was therefore an heroic knight whereas the barons were felons who revealed the secrets of courtly love. It is clear that the authors of the myth chose the side of the courtly moral order against that of feudal society. In this way the love of Tristan and Iseult was caught up in the clash between the two moral orders of medieval society. In the end this clash seems to be the cause of their suffering and downfall.

Passionate suffering. According to Andreas,

love is a certain inborn suffering derived from the sight of and excessive meditation upon the beauty of the opposite sex, which causes each one to wish above all things the embraces of the other and by

---

[27] Singer, *Nature of Love* II, 26–7.

common desire to carry out all of love's precepts in the other's embrace. That love is suffering is easy to see ... since the lover is always in fear that his love may not gain its desire and that he is wasting his efforts ... Indeed he fears so many things that it would be difficult to tell them.[28]

Thus courtly love involves passionate suffering on account of all the many real and imagined obstacles which the lovers fear could prevent them from realizing their desire. In this way the myth of Tristan is a tale of an unhappy love, of passion which continually had to face insurmountable obstacles which arose between the lovers and created distance between them.

De Rougemont points out that there are two distinct kinds of obstacles involved here. On the one hand there are *external* obstacles of a physical or social nature which keep the lovers apart: the presence of the king, the suspiciousness of the barons, the Judgment of God, and more generally the rules of feudal society. When such obstacles threaten the lovers, Tristan invariably overcomes them with a feat of heroism. 'Tristan leaps over the obstruction (this is symbolized by his leap from his own bed to the queen's). He then does not mind the pain (his wound reopens) nor the danger to his life (he knows he is being spied upon). Passion is then so violent ... that ... he is oblivious to pain and peril alike.'[29] The knight's demeanour becomes strangely different, however, whenever there are no such external obstacles separating him from his beloved. Then suddenly he starts *creating* obstacles which keep him and his beloved apart: he lays his drawn sword between himself and Iseult in the forest, or he decides on unconvincing grounds to return Iseult to the king, or he leaves Iseult the Fair in order to marry Iseult of the White Hand. These obstacles are quite insurmountable for Tristan – because he has set them up himself. Whence this strange inclination for creating deliberate obstructions in order to keep his beloved at a distance?

According to De Rougemont, this behaviour results from the fact that Tristan and Iseult do not primarily love each other. The primary object of their love is love itself and the experience

[28] Andreas, *Courtly Love*, 28. [29] De Rougemont, *Western World*, 43.

of being in love. They only love each other to the extent that each is for the other the necessary focus for the passionate sensation of being in love. In a more guarded way, Irving Singer asserts the same:

There are two things idealized by fin' amors: first, the beloved, the lady supremely beautiful in all respects; second, love itself, as the longing and desire elicited by the goodness and beauty of this particular woman. Thus, on the one hand, Arnaut de Mareuil addresses his beloved: 'Good lady, perfect in all good qualities, so worthy are you above all the best women that I know' ... On the other hand, the troubadours idealized love itself, their own desire, their own condition as lovers. Bernard de Ventadour ... reveals the importance of yearning as an essential element in love: 'I crave so noble a love that my longing is already a gain.'[30]

Both these forms of idealization require that the beloved be kept at a distance. On the one hand, the yearning of love is only possible when the beloved is absent. On the other hand, the idealized perfection of the beloved can only be maintained when she is not seen as she really is, but when the imagination of the lover adorns her with imaginary perfections, in the way Stendhal describes in his theory of 'crystallization'.[31] Love dies when the crystallization is terminated and the beloved is looked upon as she really is – warts and all. But then, what Shirley Letwin writes about Stendhal applies also to the courtly lover: 'This means that a "beloved" is not strictly speaking an object of love. Instead, like the grit that irritates an oyster into producing a pearl, a "beloved" stimulates the imagination to conjure up desires and satisfactions; when the stimulus becomes associated with the resulting pleasures, it takes on the character of a "beloved".'[32] In this way Andreas' distinction between *pure love* which 'goes on increasing without end' because it stops short of its final consummation, and *mixed love* which does not do so and therefore 'quickly fails and lasts but a short time', applies not only to the sexuality of courtly love, but to the courtly

---

[30] Singer, *Nature of Love* II, 50. [31] See section 2.4 above.
[32] Shirley Robin Letwin, 'Romantic love and Christianity', *Philosophy* 52 (1977), 131.

relationship as such. The intense passion of courtly love as such as well as the idealization of the beloved who is its focus, can only be maintained and intensified when the beloved is kept at a distance and the final union with the beloved is not realized. For this reason the lovers need to continually create obstacles which keep them apart. According to De Rougemont, this explains the curious behaviour of Tristan and Iseult in relation to each other:

Tristan loves the awareness that he is loving far more than he loves Iseult the Fair. And Iseult does nothing to hold Tristan. All she needs is her passionate dream. Their need of one another is in order to be aflame, and they do not need one another as they are. What they need is not one another's presence, but one another's absence. Thus the partings of the lovers are dictated by their passion itself, and by the love they bestow on their passion rather than on its satisfaction or on its living object. That is why the Romance abounds in obstructions.[33]

They even seem to welcome the suffering which this brings upon them.

This suffering differs from all other kinds of suffering since it is undergone for the sake of love. Thus Chrétien de Troyes (a courtly poet and contemporary of Andreas at the court of Countess Marie of Champagne) could write:

From all other ills doth mine differ. It pleaseth me; I rejoice in it; my ill is what I want and my suffering is my health. So do I not see what I am complaining about; for my ill comes to me by my will; it is my willing that becomes my ill; but I am so pleased to want this that I suffer agreeably, and have so much joy in my pain that I am sick with delight.[34]

In this way the suffering of love becomes inherently desirable because it is experienced as a form of *martyrdom* in the service of love as this is idealized in the beloved. But then this idealized love is looked upon as an irresistible fate which has the lovers in its power and which they serve willingly even though they cannot help but do so. In the myth of Tristan, this is expressed in the symbol of the love-potion. Tristan and Iseult are not

---

[33] De Rougemont, *Western World*, 41–2.
[34] Quoted by De Rougemont, *Western World*, 38.

responsible for their love or for their actions, since these are the fate which has come over them on account of the love-potion. They are therefore relieved of all responsibility or guilt for the things they do. Their actions are performed in service to a fate which has them in its power, and their suffering is martyrdom which they gladly undergo in service of it. 'The love-potion is thus an *alibi* for passion. It enables each of the two unhappy lovers to say: "You see, I am not in the least to blame; you see, it is more than I can help."'[35]

Such an alibi is not the *real* reason for an action. It is an excuse which is put forward in order to avoid having to reveal the real reason. As we have argued above, courtly love is by definition *freely* given and received. It is freely chosen, or it cannot be love at all. For this reason Tristan and Iseult's love for one another cannot be an inevitable fate which they do not choose and for which they can bear no responsibility. But why then do they make such claims about their love when they and everybody else know these to be untrue? This brings us to the third feature of courtly love: its expression in the form of rhetoric.

Rhetorical expression. De Rougemont points out that there always exists a kind of tacit convention or secret 'conspiracy' between the author of a novel and the readers: they have a shared interest in the continuation of the story and therefore in the occurrence of ever new and unexpected developments which prevent the denouement from being reached. If we were to ignore this shared interest, many of the developments in the story would become improbable or lose their plausibility for us. Normally, however, this interest makes the reader overlook such improbabilities. If, on the other hand, this shared interest were to become the dominating motive of the author and the reader, the story becomes a fairy tale in which nothing is implausible any more. In this way the novel is based on rhetoric: we accept unlikely motives in the story since this enables us to keep the real motives hidden and thus avoid having to take note of them, since that would spoil our

---

[35] Ibid., 48.

enjoyment of the story. According to De Rougemont, the behaviour of Tristan and Iseult is governed by the same desire as that which governs the novel and is kept hidden in its rhetoric.

Objectively, not one of the barriers to the fulfilment of their love is insuperable, and yet each time they give up. It is not too much to say that they never miss a chance of getting parted. When there is no obstruction, they invent one, as in the case of the drawn sword and of Tristan's marriage. They invent obstructions as if on purpose, notwithstanding that such barriers are their bane... The demon of courtly love which prompts the lovers in their inmost selves to the devices which are the cause of their pain, is the very demon of *the novel* as we in the West like it to be.[36]

For this reason the lovers (and we as readers of the myth) tend to be satisfied with the implausible motives which are put forward as explanations for their behaviour.

Similarly, the fact that courtly love is based upon the idealization of the beloved, requires that it be expressed in rhetorical form. Through idealization the lover *bestows* perfection upon his beloved, and he can only love her because she in this way becomes perfect in his eyes. In other words, his love for her requires that he should *identify* her as she really is with the idealization which he bestows on her. This identification is only possible as long as he ignores the fact that it is an identification which he has brought about himself. Hence the rhetoric of perfection with which he addresses her and thinks about her. In brief, such love is based both on the idealization of the beloved and on the need to overlook the fact that it is so based. Hence the need for rhetoric.

Such rhetoric is also needed to mask the vulnerability of courtly love, which is one of the fundamental reasons for the suffering it brings about. Its continuation is dependent on idealizing and being idealized by the beloved. But this is a spell which could only be maintained by keeping the beloved at a distance, and could be broken by any number of factors which might arise at any moment. In their hearts the lovers know this

[36] Ibid., 37.

and fear that it might happen. In the words of Andreas quoted above: 'He fears so many things that it would be difficult to tell them.'

4.4 THE EFFECTS OF COURTLY LOVE

In spite of the influence of Christianity, the sexual mores and the treatment of women in medieval feudal society were unbelievably crude and barbaric. As we have noted, wives were treated as property. The *jus primae noctis* theoretically entitled the lord of a manor to deflower the bride of a vassal. Noblemen also considered it their right to rape any peasant women they met in a lonely spot. Thus even Andreas could advise his knightly readers with reference to peasant women, that 'you can hardly soften their inflexibility so far that they will grant you their embraces quietly or permit you to have the solaces you desire unless you first use a little compulsion as a convenient cure for their shyness'.[37] Prostitution was a generally accepted feature of society, and on the first crusade of the pious King Louis IX (who later became St Louis), the king's barons openly set up brothels around his royal tent.[38] Under these social circumstances, the advent of courtly love had a remarkably civilizing effect on feudal society. Although not all women were necessarily treated as ladies, at least the ladies at court were not to be treated as (mere) women any more. They had become the objects of courtly love and the forms of social life at court became civilized accordingly. Morton Hunt describes this development as follows:

Rather suddenly – in a mere handful of years – these fierce semi-primitive chieftains had begun to cultivate the arts of singing, dancing, and composing, in order to please the ladies of their courts. They put on finer clothing, started to use handkerchiefs, and began to bathe more often; they practised genteel discourse and sophisticated argumentation; and they took love vows in secret (though the secrets were discreetly told) and squandered both money and health on endless jousts and harrowing pilgrimages designed to gain merit in their ladies' eyes.[39]

[37] Andreas, *Courtly Love*, 150.   [38] Hunt, *Natural History*, 127.
[39] Ibid., 123.

It would not be too much to claim that the modern ideal of 'courteous' behaviour between the sexes was 'invented' in the twelfth century.

Although the practice of courtly love might at first sight seem strange to the modern beholder, many of its features have survived in the forms which romantic love assumes in our own day and age. Thus Dwight van de Vate points out that the 'American Credo of Romanticism'[40] consists of at least four beliefs. There is the belief in 'one person' or 'the only one in the world', the belief that for each individual there is a single predestined romantic partner. Second, one should 'fall in love': in the presence of that predestined partner, one is unexpectedly overcome by feelings too powerful to be resisted. Third, 'love is blind', for those smitten by it are oblivious to their partners' failings, even when those failings are obvious to everyone else. Finally, 'love conquers all': inspired by their feelings, lovers can overcome almost any social or physical obstacle. Van de Vate comments that, soberly set down, these beliefs do not invite the assent of the serious-minded. Since what we do with them is serious enough, the only conclusion possible is that they are the foundation of a coded rhetoric, an extravagant, disguised way of talking. We decode automatically, for we have been trained not to notice that this rhetoric is literally nonsensical. These observations of Van de Vate, which are probably recognizable for most of us, illustrate a number of features of contemporary romantic behaviour which were also characteristic of courtly love as we described it above. Apart from the use of rhetoric as such, as noted by Van de Vate, we find that the content of this rhetoric also includes the exclusive idealization of the one beloved, the overcoming of obstacles both physical and social and the idea that love is a kind of fate against which the lovers are as powerless as Tristan and Iseult were against the effects of the love-potion. C. S. Lewis points out that here too lovers tend to experience their love as a form of 'martyrdom' for the sake of love, and consequently as a justification for behaviour which is

[40] Dwight Van de Vate Jr., *Romantic Love. A Philosophical Inquiry* (University Park and London 1981), 52. For a more extended discussion of this 'Credo', see also Hunt, *Natural History*, 315–19.

contrary to the moral codes of society. In this sense the notion of a dual morality is found here as well:

When lovers say of some act which we might blame, 'Love made us do it,' notice the tone. A man saying, 'I did it because I was frightened,' or 'I did it because I was angry,' speaks quite differently. He is putting forward an excuse for what he feels to require excusing. But the lovers are seldom doing quite that. Notice how tremulously, almost how devoutly, they say the word *love*, not so much pleading an 'extenuating circumstance' as appealing to an authority. The confession can be almost a boast. There can be a shade of defiance in it. They 'feel like martyrs'.[41]

The one feature of courtly love which above all seems strange to us today, is the radical distinction between love and sex: sex being a means for the production of offspring within marriage and love being an attitude and form of behaviour between courtly lovers outside of marriage. The reason for marriage was therefore not love but posterity. This distinction was of course just as much the result of the views of the church on the purpose of sex and of the function which the institution of marriage had within the feudal system, as it was a feature of courtly love as such. In practice things were in fact not invariably as clear cut as this, even in the twelfth century. Thus Singer claims that in some of its versions, courtly love could very well occur between married people, as a supplement to matrimony and as a strengthening of it.[42] With the gradual erosion of the feudal system in the course of time, all this began to change. At the end of the eighteenth century Louis XVI of France had a secret passage built in the palace of Versailles between his state bedroom and that of his wife Marie Antoinette. According to the guide who took me through the palace a few years ago, this was due to the fact that Louis was so 'weird' as to love his wife. By the close of the middle ages, love had become not only possible within marriage but even a possible reason for marrying, whereas in our society it would be considered shameful to marry for any other reason.

[41] C. S. Lewis, *The Four Loves* (London 1977), 103.
[42] Singer, *Nature of Love* II, 29.

In section 2.5 we saw Ortega y Gasset hold that love cannot be equated with sex. Sex is quite possible without love, and love can also be expressed in other ways than through sex. Thus Sharon Brehm argues that it is a serious mistake to regard all forms of passionate love as essentially sexual in origin or purpose. Just as one can have a highly active sexual life without a trace of passionate love, so one can be passionately in love independent of one's sexual drives.[43] Nevertheless, sex could be a very important if not essential way of expressing love between persons. It is now clear that the function of sex in personal relations and the way sexuality is related to love, can vary in the course of time in accordance with changes in society and culture. In our time, it is usually considered an essential feature of sexuality that it should be an expression of love. Sex without love is frowned upon. However, this is not universally so even today, nor was it always so in the past. We shall return to this point again in section 7.4. For the present, we should note that these features of courtly love could help us to sort out an issue raised in section 2.1 above: if it is possible to distinguish in this way between romantic love and sexuality, then it should also be possible to apply romantic love as a conceptual model for our relationship with God without thereby having to think of this relationship in erotic terms. To what extent, then, could courtly love be used as a model for the love of God?

4.5 COURTLY LOVE AND GOD

Unlike mystic love, which we discussed in the previous chapter, courtly love was an exclusively secular phenomenon. It was in no way directed toward God but exclusively to a human courtly beloved. Since the practice of courtly love was in fact often frowned upon by the church, it would seem an unlikely candidate for use as a model for the love of God. However, if we note the fundamental reason why the church objected to courtly love, it would appear that the latter is more like the love of God than it would seem at first sight. In some respects courtly love

---

[43] Brehm, 'Passionate love', 257.

was a humanization of the kind of love which Christian mystics had generally reserved for human beings in relation to God.[44] This applies especially to the element of idealization. According to the Christian tradition, God alone is perfect and therefore our passionate devotion is due to God alone. Ultimate bliss can therefore only be found in the love of God. As we shall show in the next chapter, this point was crucial to Augustine's views on the love of God. In courtly love, however, a human beloved was idealized as the perfect object of passionate devotion and thus treated in a way which was only appropriate toward God. In fact, the idealization of courtly love came very close to idolization. Sometimes the courtly beloved is explicitly treated as though she were divine. Thus in his poem on the love of *Lancelot and Guinevere*, Chrétien de Troyes describes Lancelot as acting toward Guinevere in a way which deliberately apes religious devotion. When he comes before the bed where she lies, he kneels and adores her, and when he leaves her chamber after having made love to her, he genuflects before her bed as though he were before a shrine. If in this way the love which is appropriate toward God is being directed toward the courtly beloved, why cannot courtly love function in this respect as a conceptual model for the love of God? Yet, this rarely if ever occurs in Christian spirituality. An example of courtly devotion being used as a religious model is St Francis of Assisi. But then his courtly beloved is not God but Lady Poverty.

For the purposes of the present chapter, however, another aspect of courtly love is important: the passionate suffering which results from the distance which separates the lover from the beloved. To what extent does this feature of courtly love also apply to the love of God? In section 4.1 we pointed out that the mystic lover also suffers on account of the distance which separates him or her from God. However, the aim of the *via mystica* is to overcome this distance and become united with God, whereas courtly lovers seem to go to extreme lengths in order to maintain the distance in spite of the suffering which this involves. Here the distance between the lovers (and thus also the

---

[44] There are of course also differences, which are especially stressed by Gilson in Appendix VI of his *Mystical Theology*.

resultant suffering) is given a positive value. Could it be argued
that this is an essential feature of love as such and thus also of the
love of God?

An interesting example of someone who seems to defend this
position is Simone Weil. For her both distance and suffering
seem to be essential features of love in general and of the love of
God in particular. It seems to become a necessary truth that 'a
song of love is a sad song'. Moreover, for Simone Weil this does
not only apply to our love for God, but also to God's love for us.
Thus she argues that

religion teaches us that God creates finite beings of different degrees of
mediocrity. We human beings are aware that we are at the extreme
limit beyond which it is no longer possible to conceive or to love God.
Below us there are only the animals. We are as mediocre and as far
from God as it is possible for creatures endowed with reason to be. This
is a great privilege. It is for us, if he wants to come to us, that God has
to make the longest journey. When he has possessed and won and
transformed our hearts it is we in our turn who have to make the
longest journey in order to go to him. The love is in proportion to the
distance.[45]

Here the distance between the lovers is given a positive value,
since it becomes an index of the magnitude and the intensity of
the love which is required to bridge it: the greater the distance,
the greater the love. But is this not precisely what we found to
be the case in the attitude of courtly lovers toward each other?
The magnitude of the obstacles separating them is proof of the
magnitude of their love for each other.

This applies not only to the distance but also to the resultant
suffering. Thus Simone Weil argues that 'the evil which we see
everywhere in the world in the form of affliction and crime is a
sign of the distance between us and God. But this distance is love
and therefore it should be loved. This does not mean loving evil,
but loving God through evil.'[46] In accepting the evil and
suffering in the world, we show our love for God – we love God
through evil. Is this not similar to the attitude of courtly lovers?

Of course, Simone Weil is careful to distinguish between
'loving God through evil' and 'loving evil'. Presumably she

[45] Simone Weil, *Gateway to God* (London 1974), 80.   [46] Ibid., 81.

would not agree with the sentiments which we quoted Chrétien de Troyes expressing: she would not be *pleased by* suffering or *rejoice in* it. But then we need not interpret Chrétien in a masochistic way as someone who values suffering positively for its own sake. Suffering is only valued positively when it is undergone for the sake of love. The courtly lover may therefore very well agree with Simone Weil's rejection of a masochistic desire for suffering:

It is wrong to desire affliction; it is against nature, and it is a perversion; and moreover it is the essence of affliction that it is suffered unwillingly. So long as we are not submerged in affliction all that we can do is to desire that, if it should come, it may be a participation in the Cross of Christ. But what is in fact always present, and what it is therefore always permitted to love, is the possibility of affliction.[47]

Would the courtly lover also agree with the two remarks which Simone Weil adds here to her disavowal of the desire for suffering?

First of all, the desire that our own affliction may be experienced as 'participation in the Cross of Christ'. This is similar to the sentiments of the mystic who has 'a heartfelt joy in mortification' when his sufferings 'will have become, in the fullest sense of the term, a *compassion* with the passion of Christ'.[48] In a sense, the courtly lover would probably also value his own suffering positively to the extent that it is 'compassion with the passion of his beloved'. In this way, courtly love could therefore include the notion of *identification with the beloved* which, as we shall argue at length in part IV, is an essential feature of love as such. Is this also what Simone Weil means by 'participation in the cross of Christ'? We will return to this point in part IV.

---

[47] Ibid., 87–8.
[48] See the passage from Gilson, *Mystical Theology*, 83–4, to which we referred in section 4.1 above. Compare also the following contemporary expression of such sentiments by Anthony Bloom: 'But to share with Christ his passion, his crucifixion, his death, means to accept unreservedly all these events in the same spirit as he did, that is, to accept them in an act of free will, to suffer together with the man of sorrows, to be there in silence, the silence of real communion; not just the silence of pity, but of compassion, which allows us to grow into complete oneness with the other so that there is no longer one and the other, but only one life and one death.' Anthony Bloom, *Living Prayer* (London 1966), 16.

Secondly, there is Simone Weil's distinction between *affliction* (which it would be perverse to desire) and *the possibility of affliction* (which we are 'always permitted to love'). Would this distinction also apply in the case of the courtly lover? That depends on what is meant by this distinction. We shall also return to this point in detail in part IV.

PART III

Neighbourly love

CHAPTER 5

Need-love

5.1 INTRODUCTION: NEIGHBOURLY LOVE

In the foregoing chapters, we have analysed three views on the nature of love in which love is conceived primarily as romantic love, i.e. the sort of attitude which a lover adopts toward his or her beloved. Characteristic of romantic love in this general sense, is on the one hand its exclusiveness and on the other hand the fact that it is in some way or other associated with sexuality. The precise way in which romantic love is related to sexuality varies, as we have seen, in accordance with cultural changes and with changes in the institutional structures of society. It therefore becomes possible for us to attend to these attitudes as such, quite apart from their varying relations to sexuality. The question then becomes: what kind of attitude is this attitude called love? Is it exclusive attention to the beloved, as Ortega argues? Or is it an urge to become united with the beloved, as in mysticism? Or is it an experience of passionate suffering on account of the distance which separates the lover from the beloved, as in courtly love? Or should these rather be interpreted as complementary aspects of love as such? And could these also be complementary aspects of the love of God? We shall return to these questions again in part IV. Before doing that, however, we have first to attend to some other views which look on love as an attitude toward other persons in general and not merely to the one beloved person as in romantic love. Let us call these forms of *neighbourly love*.

Neighbourly love differs from romantic love in two important respects: on the one hand it has no direct connection with sexuality, and on the other it is not exclusive in the way that romantic love is, since it is an attitude toward other persons in general and not merely to the one exclusive beloved. This later feature of neighbourly love would seem to weaken the analogy to the kind of love which we owe to God, since God is unique and not like other people. If we want to use this as a model for loving God, we will therefore have to qualify it in such a way that God becomes a very special kind of 'neighbour'. Hence it will become crucial here to distinguish clearly between what Anders Nygren calls the *dimensions of love*: God's love for us, our love for God, our love of our neighbours and our love for ourselves.

The two most important views on neighbourly love in this general sense, are usually referred to as *eros* and *agape*. C. S. Lewis has coined two very useful terms to distinguish these: need-love and gift-love.[1] *Eros* (or need-love) is the desire to receive that from the other which I need in order to be happy or to flourish. *Agape* (or gift-love) is the attitude of giving myself in service to the other. Two of the most important classical examples of the view that love is to be understood in terms of *eros*, were Plato and Augustine, and one of the most severe critics of the ideal of *eros* was Anders Nygren. Nygren was one of the staunchest defenders of the ideal of *agape* against that of *eros*, while Friedrich Nietzsche was the great critic of *agape* as an alternative for *eros*. In this chapter we shall analyse the views of Plato and Augustine, and in the next those of Nygren and Nietzsche as well as the attempt by Max Scheler to reconcile these opposing views.

5.2 PLATO AND *EROS* FOR THE GOOD

Most of Plato's ideas on love are to be found in the *Symposium*. Here Socrates explains the nature of love to his fellow guests at a banquet. Love, says Socrates, is either the desire for something which I do not have, or, if I do have it, the desire never to lose it in the future. By definition love is therefore 'always poor'

---

[1] Lewis, *Four Loves*, chapter 1.

(*Symposium* 203C):[2] it entails that the lover lacks something now or in the future and desires to possess that which he lacks. For this reason a god cannot love, since the gods lack nothing (cf. *Symposium* 202D and 204A). They already possess everything which they could conceivably desire. But love is not the desire for just anything. Love desires beauty and not deformity, and since the good is also the beautiful, love is the desire for the good: that we may possess it and never lose it in all eternity. Hence, 'love may be described generally as the love of the everlasting possession of the good' (*Symposium* 206A). However, the everlasting possession of the good requires the immortality of the possessor. Hence 'all men will necessarily desire immortality together with good: whence it must follow that love is of immortality' (*Symposium* 207A). Furthermore, since the possession of the good is what makes someone happy, love of the everlasting possession of the good is at the same time the desire for eternal happiness. In this way Plato's views on love are directly connected with his eudaemonism in which the aim of all moral action is the perfection of the soul which is ultimate happiness. In this way Platonic love becomes man's[3] greatest effort toward self-perfection or *arete*. According to Singer, this term was used by the Greeks to signify that condition of a man's soul or character without which life was not worth living. The man without *arete* was better off dead; but the man who dies in the quest for this inner excellence had nothing to fear from death.[4]

---

[2] References to Plato are taken from the fourth edition of the Jowett translation of *The Dialogues of Plato* (Oxford 1953).

[3] In discussing Plato, I will not try to avoid 'masculinist' language, since Plato's views on love were developed in a purely 'masculinist' context. 'Regardless of how bodily desires are treated in Platonic love, it is clear that for Plato the bodies must always be male bodies. He never so much as intimates that true love can be experienced by women or really directed toward them. A man may desire a woman sexually; he may even devote his life to an overwhelming passion for the female sex. But none of this fits the Platonic ideal' (Singer, *Nature of Love* I, 74. See pages 72–82 for a discussion of Plato's views on sex and on women). It could be argued that Plato's misogynistic approach to women was a reflection of the general attitude toward women in Greek society at the time rather than a necessary implication of his philosophical views as such. For an interesting discussion of the position of women in Athenian society in Plato's time, see Hunt, *Natural History*, chapter 2.

[4] Singer, *Nature of Love* I, 70.

But how is this kind of love as 'the desire for the good' related to love for other persons? In the *Lysis* Socrates argues that the sick man loves his doctor for the sake of health (218E); the poor love the affluent and the weak the strong for the sake of aid (215D); and everyone who is ignorant has affection and love for the one who has knowledge (215D). In other words we love other persons for the sake of the good which we can achieve in or through them. Sometimes we love others for the sake of achieving through them the immortality which is required in order to attain eternal happiness. Thus Socrates argues in the *Symposium*: 'Marvel not then at the love which all men have of their offspring; for that universal love and interest is for the sake of immortality' (208B). This is also the reason why people love fame:

Think only of the ambition of men, and you will wonder at the senselessness of their ways, unless you consider how they are stirred by a love of an immortality of fame. They are ready to run all risks greater far than they would have run for their children, and to spend money and undergo any sort of toil, and even to die for the sake of leaving behind them a name which shall be eternal ... I am persuaded that all men do all things, and the better they are the more they do them, in the hope of the glorious fame of immortal virtue; for they desire the immortal. (*Symposium* 208c·D)

Hence we love persons not for their own sakes but for the sake of something else: as we love the doctor for the sake of our health, so we love health for the sake of something else – and so on until we reach a *proton philon*, i.e. a first or terminal object of love, for whose sake all other objects are loved (*Lysis* 219D). In this way there is an hierarchy of loves culminating in the *proton philon* which is the only object to be loved for its own sake. All other things should be loved for the sake of the *proton philon*. But what could count as the *proton philon* which alone must be loved for its own sake? According to Socrates, this can only be the eternal Goodness which is also the eternal Beauty. Thus Socrates reports the explanation of Diotima:

He who has been instructed thus far in the things of love, and who has learned to see the beautiful in due order and succession, when he comes toward the end will suddenly perceive a nature of wondrous beauty (and this, Socrates, is the final cause of all our former toils) – a nature which in the first place is everlasting, knowing not birth or death, growth or decay; secondly, not fair in one point and foul in another... but beauty absolute, separate, simple, and everlasting, which is imparted to the ever growing and perishing beauties of all other beautiful things, without itself suffering diminution, or increase or any change. (*Symposium* 210E–211B)

Only the possession of this eternal object is eternal happiness. Here the hierarchy culminates: there is no 'need to ask why a man desires happiness; the answer is already final' (*Symposium* 205A). Socrates warns against confusing the order of objects of love by loving something other than the real *proton philon* for its own sake. Clearly, he would have rejected the plea: 'I want to be loved for myself alone and not for my golden hair', since that would entail treating a perishable object as though it were the eternal *proton philon*. This would not only be contrary to the order of loves, but would also lead to disaster since eternal happiness can never be found in a perishable object.

In Plato's view, there are therefore two kinds of love: *eros* for the *proton philon* which is to be desired for its own sake since only the possession of the *proton philon* constitutes eternal happiness; and *eros* for everything else (including other people). These are not to be desired for their own sakes, but only for the sake of the *proton philon*, since they could enable us to achieve the *proton philon* and in this way eternal happiness.

This in brief is Plato's concept of love. There are two serious objections which are often raised against this concept: it is a love of ideals and not of persons and in the end it is a form of 'spiritualized egocentrism'.[5] Let us examine these objections more closely.

First of all, on Plato's view we cannot love persons for their own sakes but only to the extent that they instantiate or realize ideals or contribute to the realization of ideals. In the words of Vlastos:

---

[5] See for example Gregory Vlastos, 'The individual as an object of love in Plato', in *Platonic Studies* (Princeton 1973), and Singer, *Nature of Love* I, chapter 4. For an uncompromising presentation of especially the latter objection, see Anders Nygren, *Agape and Eros* (London 1982), chapter 2.

What it is really about is love for place-holders of the predicates 'useful' and 'beautiful' – of the former when it is only *philia*, of the latter, when it is *eros*. In this theory persons evoke *eros* if they have beautiful bodies, minds, or dispositions. But so do quite impersonal objects – social or political programmes, literary compositions, scientific theories, philosophical systems and, best of all, the Idea of Beauty itself. As objects of Platonic love all these are not only as good as persons, but distinctly better. Plato signifies their superiority by placing them in the higher reaches of that escalated figure that marks the lover's progress, relegating love of persons to its lower levels.[6]

The social effects of this view are well illustrated in Plato's description of the ideal society in the *Republic*.[7] This society is a political community held together by bonds of fraternal love (*philia*). Everyone loves the welfare of the city with the same love which they ordinarily feel for their own families. Although Plato does not give a formal definition of *philia* in the *Republic*, the definition which he provides in the *Lysis* fits very well. There Socrates tells Lysis: 'Therefore, my boy, if you become wise, all men will be your friends and kindred, for you will be useful and good; but if you are not wise, neither father nor mother nor kindred nor anyone else, will be your friends' (210D). In Plato's ideal state everyone is loved if and only if he contributes to the welfare of the city. In doing so he fulfils the norm of justice by discharging all his obligations and earning all his rights. This view has two highly questionable effects. First of all, persons are only valued as long as they are public assets. If they cease to be so, they lose their value as objects of love. In no way can I be 'loved for myself alone and not for my golden hair'. On the contrary, as soon as I lose my golden hair, I cease to be an object of love. Persons cannot be valued as indispensable individuals. Instead they become dispensable placeholders for ideals. Secondly, the freedom of the individual which was highly prized in Plato's Athens, is eliminated in the utopia which he describes in the *Republic*:

Participatory democracy vanishes without a trace. So does free speech and, what Plato realizes is at least as important, free song, free dance, free art. The rulers lose all right to personal privacy. Even their sex-life

[6] Vlastos, 'Love in Plato', 26.   [7] See ibid., 11–19.

belongs to the state. For the greater part of their adult years intercourse is permitted them only for purposes of eugenic breeding, with parties assigned them by state officials. The end in view is the communizing – one could almost say the homogenizing – of their value-preferences, their likes and dislikes.[8]

The second main objection which is often raised against Plato's view of love, is its 'spiritualized egocentricity'[9]. This follows from the fact, which we noted above, that Platonic love was in the final analysis an eudaemonistic effort toward achieving for yourself *arete* or that self-perfection which is identical with ultimate happiness. Of this Singer remarks: '*Arete* is 'egocentric' in the sense that salvation begins with individual effort and ends with individual achievement. It requires that each man search for his own personal excellence, putting his own honour and the purification of his soul before any other consideration.'[10] For Plato this does not mean that love is selfish. It does not seek personal advantage at the expense of other people. On the contrary, seeking my own good involves seeking the good of society as a whole and even of the universe as a whole, since all these goods are intimately connected. Hence seeking what is good for myself involves acting altruistically as well. However, all such altruistic action is in the end done for self-seeking reasons. 'For every outgoing act there will always be a motive originating in a desire for some egocentric good. The philosophic lover (and only he fulfils Plato's aretaic code) desires the principle of goodness itself. He seeks to possess it, thereby making himself infinitely good.'[11] In other words: I do not love you for yourself alone, but only in order to achieve ultimate happiness for myself. In this sense all love is self-love.

These seem to be quite serious objections. An interesting proposal for interpreting Plato in a way which avoids these difficulties is put forward by David L. Norton and Mary F. Kille.[12] According to them, these objections are the result of a

---

[8] Ibid., 17.
[9] Ibid., 30. Nygren drops all such qualifications and characterizes Platonic eros as 'acquisitive self-love'. See Nygren, *Agape and Eros*, chapter 2.
[10] Singer, *Nature of Love* I, 71.   [11] Ibid., 72.
[12] Norton and Kille, *Philosophies of Love* (Totowa, NJ 1983), 81–4.

confusion between the imperfect *actuality* of each individual
person (i.e. the imperfect way in which each individual
actualizes the Good or the Beautiful), and the perfect *potentiality*
of each individual person (i.e. the perfect potentiality which
each individual has for realizing the Good or the Beautiful in his
own person). What Plato lets Alcibiades say of Socrates could
be applied to every person: 'He is exactly like the busts of
Selinus, which are set up in the statuaries' shops, holding pipes
or flutes in their mouths; and they are made to open in the
middle and they have images of gods inside them' (*Symposium*
215A·B). The clay bust is his appearance to the world, and is
always to some degree flawed and misshapen. Thus Socrates,
like the semi-deity Selinus, was known for his lack of elegance
and physical beauty. But this is merely his imperfect actuality.
Inside the misshapen clay bust there is a golden figurine of a
god. This is his ideal potentiality to realize the Good. This
hidden potentiality is known as one's *daimon*. It is inborn and
constitutes an individual's true self. To know yourself is to know
your *daimon*. This *daimon* subsists in you not as an actuality, a
finished product, but as a possibility, as a task to be realized. To
know yourself, therefore, means to know your ideal possibility
which it is your task and responsibility to realize progressively in
your life. Finally, each person's *daimon* is unique, it is a form of
perfection which is different from that of every other person. To
the extent that someone fails to know his *daimon* and to live in
truth with it, and therefore becomes distracted from his destiny,
to that degree the unique value which he represents will be
lacking from the world.

If we were to interpret Plato's eudaemonism along these lines,
then it becomes possible to meet the criticisms which were raised
above against Plato's view on love. First of all, we can now see
how Platonic *eros* is not merely a love for ideals but also a love
for persons. But then loving another person is not loving his
imperfect actuality (i.e. the imperfect way in which he has
realized the ideal of Goodness and Beauty), but loving his
perfect potentiality. If our love were directed at someone's
actuality, it would tie him to his past and his present and
thereby deny him the freedom to realize his future potentialities.

In this way Platonic *eros*, as the knowledge and love of someone's individual *daimon*, is a liberating kind of love which frees him from his past and enables him to progress toward the realization of his personal destiny. In this way too, love offers someone consolation in distress by reminding him of the golden figurine within his bust of clay.

Secondly, although Platonic love is also self-love, it is not egoism. Egoism is love for your own actuality and therefore self-satisfaction. This is disastrous, since it ties you to your imperfect present and prevents you from realizing your true destiny in the future. True love for yourself is knowing and loving your own individual *daimon* and therefore striving to achieve virtue in your own life. *Eros* for yourself in this sense means knowing and having confidence in your own potentialities. Such self-confidence is by no means the same as self-satisfaction or egoism. Furthermore, self-love in this sense does not preclude love for others, but rather makes it possible. In the words of Norton and Kille:

> *Eros* is love for the ideal humanity *which all men share*. To love it in oneself is the *precondition* of loving it in others, by no means the preclusion. More concretely, through self-knowledge we discover our need for the special excellencies of others, for these cannot be realized by us but only by them. In Socrates' words, 'Everyone chooses his love from the ranks of beauty according to his own character.' (*Phaedrus*) In virtue of this 'division of labour,' to love human excellence is necessarily to love others no less than ourselves. It consists in the discernment and appreciation of excellences different from our own, and as such it is our need. But it is a need which is fulfilled by the other becoming *himself*, by his living in truth to his *daimon*.[13]

This interpretation of Platonic *eros* has a very 'modern' ring about it. Leaving aside the question of whether it is an accurate representation of Plato's own views, or instead a rational reconstruction which makes them more acceptable to the modern reader, it cannot be denied that in this way Plato's views on love become more plausible than his critics would allow. For our present purposes, the question is whether this

---

[13] Norton and Kille, *Philosophies of Love*, 83.

enables us to reconcile Platonic *eros* with the Christian faith? Here two answers might be given. We could either try to recast the views of Plato in Christian terms and in so doing turn it into a Christian ideal. This was the course adopted by Augustine. Or we could reject the *eros* ideal as un-Christian and contrary to the Christian ideal of *agape*. This was the response of Anders Nygren. Let us first examine Augustine's response.

5.3 AUGUSTINE AND *EROS* FOR GOD

Like Plato, Augustine approached the concept of love from an eudaemonistic point of view: love is essentially the desire for ultimate happiness. The key difference between them, from which all other differences follow, was in their view on what constitutes eternal happiness. For Plato ultimate happiness consists in knowing the Good; for Augustine it consists in enjoying God.[14]

In his *De Moribus Ecclesia Catholica*,[15] Augustine argues that 'no one can be happy who does not enjoy what is man's chief good, nor is there anyone who enjoys this who is not happy' (*De Mor. Eccl.* 3.4). But what is this chief good for human existence? It must be something 'than which there is nothing better' and at the same time something 'which cannot be lost against the will. For no one can feel confident regarding a good which he knows can be taken from him, although he wishes to keep and cherish it. But if a man feels no confidence regarding the good which he enjoys, how can he be happy while in such fear of losing it?' (*De Mor. Eccl.* 3.5). It is clear that God is the only Being who can fulfil these requirements: 'Our chief good which we must hasten to arrive at in preference to all other things is nothing else than God.' Since nothing can separate us from his love, this must be 'surer as well as better than any other good' (*De Mor. Eccl.* 11.18). From this Augustine concludes that 'God

[14] Augustine's eudaemonistic ideal is perfectly reflected in the answer to the first question in the *Westminster Shorter Catechism* of 1647: 'Man's chief end is to glorify God and enjoy him forever (*Deum glorificare eodemque frui in aeternum*)'.

[15] Quotations taken from 'On the morals of the Christian church', in Philip Schaff (ed.), *The Nicene and Post-Nicene Fathers* (Grand Rapids 1979), IV. Referred to as *De Mor. Eccl.*

then alone must be loved; and all this world, that is, all sensible things, are to be despised, – while they are to be used as this life requires' (*De Mor. Eccl.* 20.37).

Augustine is quick to add, however, that loving God in this way does not preclude loving yourself or loving your neighbour. As to the former, 'it is impossible for one who loves God not to love himself. For he alone has a proper love for himself who aims diligently to the attainment of the chief and true good; and if this is nothing else but God, as has been shown, what can prevent one who loves God from loving himself?' (*De Mor. Eccl.* 26.48). Thus, 'you love yourself suitably when you love God better than yourself' (*De Mor. Eccl.* 26.49). As for loving your neighbour, 'we can think of no surer step toward the love of God than the love of man to man' (*De Mor. Eccl.* 26.48). This love consists in bringing your neighbour to the same chief good which you desire for yourself. In doing this you love your neighbour, not 'better than yourself' as you should love God, but 'as yourself'. 'What, then, you aim at in yourself you must aim at in your neighbour, namely, that he may love God with a perfect affection. For you do not love him as yourself, unless you try to draw him to that good which you are yourself pursuing' (*De Mor. Eccl.* 26.49).

It is clear from this that Augustine, like Plato, held there to be an *hierarchical* order in the objects of our love. In his *De Doctrina Christiana*,[16] Augustine developed the notion of an *ordo amoris* in more detail:

Now he is a man of just and holy life who forms an unprejudiced estimate of things, and keeps his affections also under strict control, so that he neither loves what he ought not to love, nor fails to love what he ought to love, nor loves that more which ought to be loved less, nor loves that equally which ought to be loved less or more, nor loves that less or more which ought to be loved equally. No sinner is to be loved as a sinner; but every man is to be loved as a man for God's sake; but God is to be loved for his own sake. And if God is to be loved more than any man, each man ought to love God more than himself. Likewise we ought to love another man better than our own body, because all

---

[16] Quotations taken from 'On Christian doctrine', in Philip Schaff (ed.), *The Nicene and Post-Nicene Fathers* II. Referred to as *De Doctr. Chr.*

things are to be loved in reference to God, and another man can have
fellowship with us in the enjoyment of God, whereas our body cannot.
(*De Doctr. Chr.* 1.27.28)

As in Plato, the basic distinction underlying this *ordo amoris* is
that between the way in which we are to love God (or the *proton
philon*) and the way we are to love everything else: the latter is
subservient to the former, since 'all things are to be loved in
reference to God' (for Augustine) and in reference to the Good
(for Plato). Augustine marks this distinction with the terms *frui*
(enjoy) and *uti* (use): 'To enjoy a thing is to rest with satisfaction
in it for its own sake. To use, on the other hand, is to employ
whatever means are at one's disposal to obtain what one desires'
(*De Doctr. Chr.* 1.4.4).

Like Socrates, Augustine warns us against enjoying things (as
though they were the *proton philon*) which we should only use in
order to achieve that which alone is to be enjoyed. If we do that
we become diverted from our ultimate destiny. Augustine
explains this by means of the following image:

Suppose, then, we were wanderers in a strange country, and could not
live happily away from our fatherland, and that we felt wretched in
our wandering, and wishing to put an end to our misery, determined
to return home. We find, however, that we must make use of some
mode of conveyance, either by land or water, in order to reach that
fatherland where our enjoyment is to commence. But the beauty of the
country through which we pass, and the very pleasure of the motion,
charm our hearts, and turning these things which we ought to use into
objects of enjoyment, we become unwilling to hasten the end of our
journey; and becoming engrossed in a factitious delight, our thoughts
are diverted from that home whose delights would make us truly
happy. Such is a picture of our condition in this life of mortality. We
have wandered far from God; and if we wish to return to our Father's
home, this world must be used, not enjoyed. (*De Doctr. Chr.* 1.4.4)

From this Augustine concludes that, among all things, 'those
alone are the true objects of enjoyment which we have spoken of
as eternal and unchangeable. The rest are for use that we may
be able to arrive at the full enjoyment of the former' (*De Doctr.
Chr.* 1.22.20).

What does this entail for the way in which we should love our neighbours? For Augustine the answer is clear: 'We are commanded to love one another: but it is a question whether man is to be loved for his own sake, or for the sake of something else. If it is for his own sake, we enjoy him; if it is for the sake of something else, we use him. It seems to me, then, that he is to be loved for the sake of something else' (*De Doctr. Chr.* I.22.20). Augustine puts forward four arguments in support of this conclusion:

First of all, 'if a thing is to be loved for its own sake, then in the enjoyment of it consists a happy life, the hope of which at least, if not yet the reality, is our comfort in the present time. But a curse is pronounced on him who places his hope in man' (*De Doctr. Chr.* I.22.20). In his *Confessions* (IV.4–10), Augustine recounts how he had personally experienced this 'curse' in the form of his excessive sorrow at the death of his friend Nebridius:

The grief I felt for the loss of my friend had struck so easily into my inmost heart simply because I had poured out my soul upon him, like water upon sand, loving a man who was mortal as though he were never to die (8) ... Blessed are those who love you, O God, and love their friends in you and their enemies for your sake. They alone will never lose those who are dear to them, for they love them in one who is never lost, in God ... who made them. No one can lose you, my God, unless he forsakes you (9) ... For wherever the soul of man may turn, unless it turns to you, it clasps sorrow to itself. Even though it clings to things of beauty, if their beauty is outside God and outside the soul, it only clings to sorrow. Yet these things of beauty would not exist at all unless they came from you. Like the sun, they rise and set (10).

Secondly, 'no one ought to love even himself for his own sake, but for the sake of him who is the true object of enjoyment ... If, however, he loves himself for his own sake, he does not look at himself in relation to God, but turns his mind in upon himself, and so is not occupied with anything that is unchangeable ... Wherefore, if you ought not to love even yourself for your own sake, but for his in whom your love finds its most worthy object, no other man has the right to be angry if you love him too for God's sake' (*De Doctr. Chr.* I.22.21).

Thirdly, we can only *truly* love our neighbour (as we can only truly love ourselves) when we love them in God. Only then does our love truly serve their interests. 'Whoever, then, loves his neighbour aright, ought to urge upon him that he too should love God with his whole heart, and soul, and mind. For in this way, loving his neighbour as himself, a man turns the whole current of his love both for himself and for his neighbour into the channel of the love of God' (*De Doctr. Chr.* 1.22.21). What form is this 'urging' to take? In this connection it is significant to recall the words which we quoted above from the *De Moribus Ecclesia Catholica* (3.5) to the effect that God, as our chief good, must be 'something which cannot be lost against the will'. In other words, although he will never forsake us if we do not wish it, this does not exclude the possibility that, if we do so wish, we may forsake him. So too, in the words which we quoted from the *Confessions*: 'No one can lose you, O God, unless he forsakes you.' The implication is that God allows us to forsake him and does not *force* us to love him. Presumably we should therefore also shun the use of force when urging our neighbour 'that he too should love God with his whole heart, and soul, and mind'. However, Augustine himself did not always draw this con-clusion. Thus, as Burnaby points out, the Donatist controversy 'drove Augustine to betray his own most Christian principle of toleration, and to justify the use of force against the schismatic by that fatal interpretation of the *compelle intrare* of the parable which became a chief authority for the religious persecution of later ages'.[17]

Finally, in his second homily on the epistle of St John, Augustine argues that we should consider our fellow creatures as gifts given us by God, and that one should not love the gift more than the giver. He explains this point by means of the following image:

Suppose, brethren, a man should make a ring for his betrothed, and she should love the ring given her more than her betrothed who made it for her, would not her heart be convicted of infidelity in respect of the very gift of her betrothed, though what she loved were what he gave? Certainly let her love his gift; but if she should say, 'The ring is

---

[17] John Burnaby, *Amor Dei* (London 1947), 100–1. See also Augustine, Ep. 185, 'De Correctione Donatistarum'. For an extended discussion of Augustine's attitude to religious coercion, see Peter Brown, *Religion and Society in the Age of Saint Augustine* (London 1972), 260–78.

enough, I do not wish to see his face again,' what should we say of her?
... The pledge is given by the betrothed just that in his pledge he
himself may be loved. God, then, has given you all these things; love
him who made them. (Tract. in Ep. Joh. 2, 11)

For these reasons, then, our neighbours, like ourselves, should
be for us objects of *uti* rather than of *frui*. There is, however, a
special sense in which we might also be said to 'enjoy' our
neighbour: we can enjoy him 'in God'.[18] 'When you have joy
of a man in God, it is God rather than man that you enjoy ...
"Enjoy" is used [here] in the sense of to "use with delight". For
when the thing that we love is near us, it is a matter of course
that it should bring delight with it.' (*De Doctr. Chr.* 1.33.37). In
this way our love of other persons differs from our love of objects
– including our own bodies – which we can only 'use' and not
'enjoy in God' since, as we have seen above, 'another man can
have fellowship with us in the enjoyment of God, whereas our
bodies cannot' (*De Doctr. Chr.* 1.27.28). Here the words of Austin
Farrer are thoroughly Augustinian: 'Even in heaven, it is right
to think, we shall keep a fellow-feeling for our own kind, shall
love men more dearly than angels; shall not be able, even, to
delight in God himself, without calling in our friends to share
our delight, while we also delight in their delighting.'[19]
Although this way of 'enjoying our neighbour' is obviously
quite distinct from the way we can be said to 'enjoy God', it is
nevertheless intimately connected with the latter.

Finally, to whose advantage do we 'use our neighbour with
delight'? Of course, it is to our neighbour's advantage that we
should truly love him since in this way we bring him nearer to

---

[18] There appears to be something inappropriate in saying that we should 'use' our
neighbours, since this seems to treat them merely as a means for achieving our private
ends. Thus Singer criticizes Augustine for treating the neighbour as a 'mere
instrumentality' rather than as a person (*Nature of Love* I, 344–9). Oliver O'Donavan
points out that Augustine was probably sensitive to this difficulty with the term *uti*
introduced in his *De doctrina Christiana*, since 'there is no single instance in any later
writing of the verb *uti* being used for the love of men for other men. The pair "use"
and "enjoyment" continue to be a familiar mark on the landscape, but whenever
Augustine wishes to accommodate love-of-neighbour into this contrast, he does so by
means of the phrase "enjoy in the Lord".' *The Problem of Self-Love in St. Augustine*
(New Haven 1980), 29. See also O'Donovan, '*Usus* and *Fruitio* in Augustine, *De
doctrina Christiana I*', *Journal of Theological Studies* 33 (1982).

[19] Austin Farrer, *A Celebration of Faith* (London 1970), 116.

God and thus to eternal happiness. Plato would say that in this
way we help our neighbour realize his individual *daimon* and
thus achieve eternal happiness. Secondly, 'our own advantage
follows by a sort of natural consequence, for God does not leave
the mercy we show to him who needs it to go without reward.
Now this is our highest reward, that we should fully enjoy Him,
and that all who enjoy Him should enjoy one another in Him'
(*De Doctr. Chr.* 1.32.35). It is important to note that for Augustine
our own advantage is not the purpose but 'a sort of natural
consequence' of loving our neighbour.[20] In a similar sense,
Plato would say that in realizing the Good in someone else, we
also realize the Good in ourselves, and in this way progress
toward eternal happiness for ourselves. Furthermore, the
converse is also true: seeking the good for myself involves
seeking it for my neighbour, for as we have seen in the case of
Plato, *eros* is love for the ideal humanity which all men share.
This also holds for Augustine: 'If the *Summum Bonum* is by its
very nature the *bonum commune*, a good which can be possessed
only by being shared, then the desire and pursuit of it can never
be the desire and pursuit of a *bonum privatum*... Goodness is a
possession which is not only not diminished by being shared, but
is only possessed at all in so far as it *is* shared.'[21] Finally, it is not
to God's advantage (or disadvantage) that we love our
neighbour and bring him to love God. Like Plato, Augustine
held that, since divine perfection entails that God is self-
sufficient and lacks nothing, he can in no way be in need of my
love or that of my neighbour.

So much for the way in which we should love ourselves and
our neighbours and how these loves should be related to our
love for God. But how, according to Augustine, does God love
us? For Plato, as we have seen, the perfection and self-sufficiency
of the gods, entails that they are unable to love. As a Christian
theologian, Augustine could obviously not follow Plato in
drawing this conclusion. He therefore argues as follows:

---

[20] 'Certainly it is no part of the meaning or intention of neighbour-love to be good *for
me* but for me to prove good *for my neighbour*, though good may follow for me as a *quite
unintended* by-product.' Paul Ramsey, *Basic Christian Ethics* (Chicago 1950), 116.
[21] Burnaby, *Amor Dei*, 127. See also Augustine, *The City of God*, xv.5.

For God loves us, and Holy Scripture frequently sets before us the love he has toward us. In what way then does he love us? As objects of use or as objects of enjoyment? If he enjoys us, he must be in need of good from us, and no sane man will say that ... He does not enjoy us then, but makes use of us. For if he neither enjoys nor uses us, I am at a loss to discover in what way he can love us. (*De Doctr. Chr.* 1.31.34)

But how does God use us? He cannot do so in the sense in which we use things, 'for when we use objects, we do so with a view to the full enjoyment of the goodness of God ... That use, then, which God is said to make of us has no reference to his own advantage, but to ours only' (*De Doctr. Chr.* 1.32.35). In other words, because of God's self-sufficient perfection, his love for us can in no way be a form of need-love. It is purely gift-love, or *agape*. But did not Plato let Diotima say something similar to Socrates regarding the Good? Was not the eternal Goodness and Beauty described by her as the benevolent source of goodness and beauty in temporal things? The Good is self-sufficient and cannot have any need-love, but it can impart of its goodness and beauty to all else: 'beauty absolute, separate, simple, and everlasting, which without diminution and without increase, or any change, *is imparted* to the ever-growing and perishing beauties of all other things.' (*Symposium* 211B). Is this not gift-love – or *agape*? As we shall see in the next chapter, this was precisely the point of departure for Anders Nygren's view on the love of God.

Before turning to Nygren's views, let us in conclusion briefly summarize the way in which Augustine would distinguish between what Nygren calls the different 'dimensions of love':

(1) *God's love for us* is not *frui*, since God does not need us for his own fulfilment; Nor is it *uti* in our sense, since God does not use us to achieve his own *frui*; God's love for us is *uti* in order to achieve our advantage alone – but that seems to be the same as *agape*.

(2) *Our love for God* is to be *frui*, and God alone should be loved in this way, since in him alone can we achieve eternal happiness.

(3) *Our love for our neighbour* should not be *frui*, since that would divert us from finding eternal happiness in God rather than

helping us achieve it; Neighbour-love should therefore be *uti*, which involves urging my neighbour to seek with me his ultimate enjoyment in God alone. This is to my neighbour's advantage (since it brings him to eternal happiness) as well as to mine (since God will reward me by letting me enjoy him and enjoy my neighbour in him). It is not for the sake of God's advantage, however, since God is self-sufficient and not in need of my or my neighbour's love.

(4) *Self-love* cannot be *frui* in ourselves but *frui* in God, for in God alone can we find our eternal happiness. We therefore love ourselves rightly, when we love God more than ourselves and find our eternal happiness in him.

Why do we love God? Not for God's sake, since God is self-sufficient and does not need our love. But then we love God for our own sake, since in him we find eternal happiness. But does this not mean that in the end our love of God is really a form of acquisitive self-love? And if our love of all else is subservient to our love of God, does this not entail that *all* our loves are reduced to forms of egocentric self-love? But then the same doubts which arise with respect to Plato's eudaemonism, apply also to that of Augustine, in spite of all his attempts at qualifying it in a theocentric way. The question is whether his analysis of the concept of love in terms of *frui* and *uti*, 'does not emphasise the real weakness of all eudaemonist ethics, by fixing the self in apparently undisputed possession of the centre of things; whether the Ego as user and enjoyer does not face the world as a claimant, regarding it in all its aspects as so much matter for his use and enjoyment.'[22] It is these doubts which made Anders Nygren reject the *eros* ideal and the eudaemonism within which it is embedded, and argue instead that *agape* is the only valid form of love from a theocentric point of view. Let us now turn to an analysis of the views of Nygren.

[22] Burnaby, *Amor Dei*, 109.

CHAPTER 6

Gift-love

6.1 NYGREN: *AGAPE* CONTRA *EROS*

Until his death in 1977, Anders Nygren was bishop of Lund in the church of Sweden and a very influential Lutheran theologian. One of his most important books was *Agape and Eros*[1] which had a wide influence, especially in contemporary protestant theology. The main point of his book was to show how '*agape* and *eros* are contrasted with one another... as Christian and non-Christian fundamental motifs' (39), and how, in the course of the history of theology, 'an admixture of the *eros* motif has weakened the *agape* motif and rendered it more or less ineffective' (38–9). In discussing Nygren's views, we will in this section pay special attention to the way in which he contrasts *agape* and *eros*, and in the next section to the way in which he proposes to fill in the so-called 'dimensions of love' in the light of his concept of *agape*.

According to Nygren '*eros* and *agape* are the characteristic expressions of two different attitudes to life, two fundamentally opposed types of religion and ethics. They represent two streams that run through the whole history of religion, alternately clashing against one another and mingling with one another. They stand for what may be described as the egocentric and the theocentric attitude in religion' (205). The *eros*-motif defines the Greek-hellenistic attitude to life as this is expressed in the Platonic view on love which we described in the previous

---

[1] This book appeared in two parts during the 1930s in Swedish as well as in German and English translations. All page references to Nygren in this chapter are taken from the English translation by Philip S. Watson, which was re-issued in London in 1982.

chapter. The *agape*-motif, on the other hand, is the fundamental characteristic of the Christian attitude to life as this was described in all its purity by St Paul. These two motifs are in fact mirror images of each other, since at all points they are exact opposites: 'There seems in fact to be no possibility of discovering any idea common to them both which might serve as the starting-point for the comparison; for at every point the opposition between them makes itself felt' (209). The four most fundamental aspects of this opposition are the following.

First of all, *eros and agape move in diametrically opposite directions*: '*Eros* is an upward movement ... *agape* comes down' (210). *Eros* is the aspiration of the lower toward the higher, especially the aspiration of human beings toward achieving perfection through realizing their own *daimon*. In this sense *eros* is the attitude of eudaemonism. *Agape*, on the other hand, is the attitude of the higher in stooping down in service to the lower. Max Scheler explains this difference in terms of human attitudes as follows:

The Christian view boldly denies the Greek axiom that love is an aspiration of the lower toward the higher. On the contrary, now the criterion of love is that the nobler stoops to the vulgar, the healthy to the sick, the rich to the poor, the handsome to the ugly, the good and saintly to the bad and common, the Messiah to the sinners and publicans.[2]

For Nygren, *agape* is essentially the attitude of God who in his infinite Grace stoops down toward human persons in order to save them. 'There is thus no way for man to come to God, but only a way for God to come to man: the way of divine forgiveness, divine love. *Agape* is God's way to man' (80–1).

Secondly, *eros is born from want, agape from abundance*. '*Eros* is the will to get and possess which depends on want and need ... *agape* is freedom in giving, which depends on wealth and plenty' (210). *Eros* is need-love which is motivated by the desire for what it lacks. *Agape* is gift-love which flows spontaneously from its own abundance. Thus God's love for us is not *eros* but pure *agape*. '*Eros* is yearning desire; but with God there is no want or

---

[2] Scheler, *Ressentiment* (New York 1961), 86.

need and therefore no desire nor striving. God cannot ascend higher... Since *agape* is a love that descends, freely and generously giving of its superabundance, the main emphasis falls with inescapable necessity on the side of God' (212). God's love for us is therefore the spontaneous expression of the never-diminishing abundance of his own nature. 'God does not love in order to obtain any advantage thereby, but quite simply because it is his nature to love – with a love that seeks, not to get, but to give' (201). God's love for us has its origin in God himself, i.e. in the abundance of his own *agape*, and not in us, i.e. in some advantage which he desires to receive from us. But did not Plato argue in a similar way about the Good? It too was self-sufficiently perfect and could have no need-love; but it too could have gift-love which imparts of its own abundance 'to the ever-growing and perishing beauties of all other things'. And this form of divine *agape* became even more explicit in neo-Platonism since, according to Plotinus, God ('the One') created the world out of the *superabundance* of his own nature, by a process of overflow or *emanation*. From this it follows that the sole reason for God's creativity and love is his own nature, which spontaneously overflows itself without suffering the least depletion.[3]

Thirdly, *eros is conditional and agape unconditional. Eros* is the love I have for the other for the sake of the inherent possibility which the other has for either realizing the good or enabling me to achieve the good. But then it is conditional on the other having this inherent possibility. I can only desire goodness from you on condition that you have this possibility. *Agape*, on the other hand, is unconditional since it is not motivated by the qualities of the other, but only by the abundance of the giver himself. '*Eros* is determined by the quality, the beauty and worth, of its object; it is not spontaneous, but "evoked", "motivated"... *agape* is sovereign in relation to its object, and is directed to both "the evil and the good"; it is spontaneous, "overflowing", "unmotivated"'(210). This again applies especially to God's love for us:

---

[3] See Norton and Kille, *Philosophies of Love*, 154.

We look in vain for an explanation of God's love in the character of the man who is the object of his love. God's love is 'groundless' – though not, of course, in the sense that there is no ground for it at all, or that it is arbitrary or fortuitous. On the contrary, it is just to bring out the element of necessity in it that we describe it as 'groundless'; our purpose is to emphasise that there are no extrinsic grounds for it. The only ground for it is to be found in God himself. God's love is altogether *spontaneous*. (75)

This point has two important corollaries for Nygren. First, unlike *agape*, *eros* can be earned or merited. If you have those meritorious qualities which make *eros* appropriate toward you, you thereby merit my *eros* toward you. *Agape* can never be earned in this way but can only be spontaneously given, since *agape* is in no way grounded on any meritorious qualities which its object may or may not have. From this it follows, secondly, that unlike *eros*, *agape* is as Nygren says 'indifferent to value' (77). When God loves sinners, it is not because of an inversion of values whereby the sinners become more worthy of his love than the righteous. But neither are the righteous more worthy of the divine *agape* than are the sinners. God's love for the righteous is equally unmotivated and spontaneous and in no way based upon the qualities of the righteous: 'He causes the sun to rise on good and bad alike, and sends rain on the innocent and the wicked' (Matthew 5 : 45). This 'indifference to value' does raise a serious problem, since it seems to imply that God is indifferent to whether we are just or unjust, saints or sinners, believers or unbelievers. As Singer points out, 'God's love is not spontaneous and unmotivated if it may be guaranteed to "whosoever shall confess that Jesus is the Son of God". And neither can *agape* be indiscriminate if it is reserved only for one who thus accepts the Christian faith.'[4]

Finally, '*eros recognises value* in its object – and loves it ... *agape* loves – and *creates value* in its object' (210). Thus *eros* loves its object because of the value which it discovers in the latter, while *agape* is not based upon the value which is in some way present in its object, but rather bestows value on the object which the latter does not already have in itself. In this way

----

[4] Singer, *Nature of Love* I, 292.

agape is creative love. God does not love that which is already in itself worthy of love, but on the contrary, that which in itself has no worth acquires worth just by becoming the object of God's love. *Agape* has nothing to do with the kind of love that depends on the recognition of a valuable quality in its object; *agape* does not recognise value, but creates it. *Agape* loves, and imparts value by loving. The man who is loved by God has no value in himself; what gives him value is precisely the fact that God loves him. (78)

At this point, some further difficulties seem to surface in Nygren's views: is it not incoherent to claim both that *agape* bestows value on its object and that it is indifferent to the value in the object? Furthermore, the fact that I am loved by another does indeed bestow a value on me which I would not otherwise have had. It is however not quite clear whether *agape* in the sense in which Nygren conceives it, is the kind of love which can do this. We will have to return to these points in detail in part IV. For the present we can only note them down as items on our agenda. So much, then, for Nygren's concept of *agape* and the way in which he distinguishes it from *eros*. Let us now see how, in the light of this concept of love, he fills in the four 'dimensions of love': God's love for me, my love for God, my love for my neighbour, and my love for myself.

6.2 NYGREN: THE DIMENSIONS OF LOVE

First of all, what is the nature of *God's love for us*? For the same reason as Plato and Augustine, Nygren denies that God's love can be *eros*: 'With God there is no want or need, and therefore no desire or striving' (212). On the contrary, God's love is pure *agape*. This is so for two reasons. First of all, God's love is *agape* by definition: 'All love that has any right to be called *agape* is nothing else but an outflow from the divine love. It has its source in God. "God is *agape*". This, too, is a simple consequence of the meaning of the word *agape*' (212). Secondly, this is not merely a stipulation by Nygren, but a 'real definition': it is not a mere contingent fact about God that he is *agape*, but a necessary consequence of his essential nature as the superabundant source of all love. 'Since *agape* is a love that descends, freely and generously giving of its superabundance, the main emphasis falls with inescapable necessity on the side of God' (212).

This view on God's love raises a number of difficulties. First, if, as Nygren holds in common with Plato and Augustine, there is in God 'no need or want or desire', then presumably God cannot need nor want nor desire that we should return his love. In fact he would be unable to receive our love in any meaningful sense. Then God could be said to care *for* us but not *about* us. But then the doubt which Burnaby raises against Augustine, would also apply to Nygren: 'If perfect love is spiritual communion, a definition of charity which would restrict its proper activity to a "one-way" relationship, a giving without receiving, seems strangely inadequate.'[5] In this way Nygren's claim that '*agape* is the initiator of fellowship with God' (80), becomes quite vacuous. Is there any meaningful sense in which this kind of *agape* could still be said to initiate 'fellowship' or 'spiritual communion'? Secondly, in what sense could God's *agape* be said to be 'spontaneous' or 'freely given'? For Nygren this means that God's love is not motivated or necessitated by anything *outside* of God, and especially not by the qualities of its object. However, this does not mean that God's love is arbitrary. On the contrary, Nygren wants 'to bring out the element of necessity in it' (75) which is however intrinsic and not extrinsic to God himself. 'To the question, Why does God love? there can be only one right answer: Because it is his nature to love' (75). In this, too, Nygren's views are in accordance with those of Augustine (and Plato): 'On the one hand, the "need" or "necessity" which Augustine is concerned to exclude from the conception of God's activity is just that element in *eros* which makes it dependent on a good external to itself… On the other hand, creation is no arbitrary *fiat*. Augustine no more than Plotinus ascribes to God a freedom which is not the expression of his changeless nature.'[6] But then God does not love us by free choice, since his love is *necessitated* by his own unchanging nature, though not by the objects of his love. However, if God's

[5] Burnaby, *Amor Dei*, 307. According to Nygren, 'Love expresses a relationship between a subject who loves and an object who is loved' (211).
[6] Burnaby, *Amor Dei*, 165–6.

agape for us is neither freely chosen (since it is necessitated by his nature) nor accompanied by any 'want or need or desire' for reciprocation on our part, it could hardly be called love in any *personal* sense at all, nor could the 'fellowship' which it initiates be personal in any meaningful sense either. We will return to this point in more detail in part IV.

The second 'dimension of love' discussed by Nygren is *our love toward God*. According to Nygren, this can very well be *eros*. 'Human want and need seeks for satisfaction in the divine fullness. *Eros*-love is acquisitive desire, appetite, which as such strives to obtain advantages. Since God is the Highest Good, the sum of all conceivable good or desirable objects, it is natural that he should attract to himself all desire and love' (212). Strictly speaking, our love for God cannot be *agape*, since '*agape* is spontaneous, unmotivated love. But in relation to God, man's love can never be spontaneous and unmotivated. God's love always comes first and awakens man's love in response' (213). Our love for God is always motivated by an extrinsic cause in God. For this reason, Nygren doubts whether

agape can [any] longer fittingly be used to denote man's attitude to God. In relation to God, man is never spontaneous; he is not an independent centre of activity. His giving of himself to God is never more than a response. At its best and highest it is but a reflex of God's love, by which it is 'motivated'. Hence it is the very opposite of spontaneous and creative; it lacks all the essential marks of *agape*. Man's devotion to God must therefore be given another name: not *agape*, but *pistis*. (125–6)

Although this kind of love differs from *agape* in this way, there is a sense in which it is similar to *agape* and unlike *eros*: our love for God is a kind of gift-love in which we give ourselves to God, but then a kind of giving which is wholly caused by God. 'What we have here is a purely theocentric love, in which all choice on man's part is excluded. Man loves God, not because on comparing him with other things he finds him more satisfying than anything else, but because God's unmotivated love has overwhelmed him and taken control of him, so that he cannot do other than love God' (213–14).

Here too some problems arise regarding Nygren's views. First of all, if in relation to God, a human person 'is not an independent centre of activity' so that 'all choice on man's part is excluded', does he not by definition cease to be an agent and a person? Does this not turn us into mere objects of divine manipulation? Furthermore, can our relationship to God still count as a *personal* relationship if on the one hand God's *agape* for us is the inevitable result of his nature, and on the other hand our loving response is the inevitable effect of his *agape*? Is this not an extremely deterministic view on the divine–human relationship, and could we still refer to it with a highly personal concept like 'love'? Finally, Irving Singer points out the following implications of such divine determinism:

There seems to be no point in exhorting human beings to *anything*: either to love or to have faith in Jesus Christ. If *agape* so elects, they *will* have Christian faith ... If *agape* does not give them faith, the fault is not theirs ... [They] can only wait quietly for *agape* to descend. Such patience may be admirable, but it hardly counts as love ... Instead of being a *response* to *agape*, human love would merely illustrate it. The Great Commandments would not be injunctions so much as descriptions of God's loving immersion in the world. By this circuitous route, Christianity would have returned to a modified pantheism.[7]

The third 'dimension of love' is that of *love for one's neighbour*. Nygren argues that, both from the perspective of *eros* and from that of *agape*, neighbourly love can be said to be practised 'for God's sake'. But this phrase has a quite different meaning in the two cases. From the point of view of *eros*, loving my neighbour 'for God's sake', is loving my neighbour for the sake of the divine in my neighbour. It is *eros* for God by means of my neighbour. In the words of Augustine which we quoted in the previous chapter, it is love for my neighbour because there is 'no surer step toward the love of God than the love of man to man' (*De Mor. Eccl.* 26.48). According to Nygren, this means that 'a place is found ... for neighbourly love in the thought of man as fundamentally a divine being. To the extent that man participates in the divine, and only to that extent, is it right for me to love him' (215). Strictly speaking this is not love for my

---

[7] Singer, *Nature of Love* I, 293–4. Here again there appears to be an unintended similarity between Nygren and neo-Platonism.

neighbour as such, but only for the divine idea expressed or the divine potentiality realized in my neighbour. It is *eros* for God which passes by my neighbour. 'This means that it is no longer the concrete human being, but the divine idea of him, "God in him", that I really love. Moreover, from "God in my neighbour" my love must seek to pass on to God himself. For a love that actually seeks no other object beyond its neighbour there is no room whatsoever' (215). From this Nygren concludes that neighbourly love, when viewed from the perspective of *eros*, is nothing more than a means of reaching God and hence a means toward self-realization. 'The showing of love toward one's neighbour is regarded as a meritorious act, a step up on the way to God, and therein lies its justification' (215). '*Eros* does not seek the neighbour for himself; it seeks him in so far as it can utilise him as a means for its own ascent' (214).

From the point of view of *agape*, neighbourly love becomes something quite different. '*Agape*-love is directed to the neighbour himself, with no further thought in mind and no sidelong glances at anything else ... When my neighbour happens to be also my enemy, obviously no reason for my loving him can be found in his character or conduct' (215). But why should I love my neighbour? From the perspective of *eros* this is clear; from that of *agape* our neighbourly love becomes groundless.

So long as my love for my neighbour and my enemy is regarded as a meritorious achievement, whereby I make myself worthy of God's love, solid grounds can be given for loving my neighbour. But when this ulterior motive disappears – as it does when God's love for us is completely unmotivated, so that our love for our neighbour and our enemy cannot in any way help us to win God's love – does it not look as if neighbourly love were bereft of any actuating principle, and therefore itself reduced to unreality? (215)

From the point of view of *agape*, neighbourly love is indeed bereft of all grounds in ourselves or in our neighbours: its ground is in God alone. In this sense, it is love of the neighbour 'for God's sake'.

If it is asked what motive there is for Christian love toward one's neighbour, what inspires it and sets it in motion, there can only be one answer: God himself. Christian neighbourly love is a love 'for God's sake' – though this phrase, we must hasten to add, has now a quite different meaning from what it had before. God is not the end, the ultimate object, but the starting-point and permanent basis of neighbourly love. He is not its *causa finalis*, but its *causa efficiens* ... The phrase 'for God's sake' has no teleological but only a causal significance. Since God is *agape*, everyone who is loved by him and has been gripped and mastered by his love cannot but pass on this love to his neighbour. In this way God's love passes over directly into the Christian's love for his neighbour. (216)

Strictly speaking, *agape* cannot be the love of one human being for another. It can only apply to the love of God for human beings whereby he uses one human being as an instrument through which he funnels his *agape* to another. 'In relation to God and to his neighbour, the Christian can be likened to a tube, which by faith is open upwards, and by love downwards ... He has nothing of his own to give. He is merely the tube, the channel, through which God's love flows' (735).[8] It is therefore not we but God who does all the loving.

Not even here [can we] conceive of man as a centre of activity independent of God. In the life that is governed by *agape*, the acting subject is not man himself ... it is Christ who is the real subject of the Christian life ... The Christian has nothing of his own to give; the love which he shows to his neighbour is the love which God has infused into him ... The Christian's love for his neighbour is a manifestation of God's *agape*, which in this case uses the Christian, the 'spiritual' man, as its instrument. (129–30)

But if in this way *agape* is impossible between human beings, it would be better 'to reserve the name *agape* for God's love and Christ's love' (128).

Nygren denies, then, that human beings could be 'centres of activity', not only in relation to God, but also in relation to each other. Clearly, such a view on love depersonalizes us by viewing us not as personal agents but as impersonal objects of divine manipulation. But then, not only our relationship to God, but

---

[8] Nygren derives this 'hydraulic' metaphor from Luther, from whom he quotes the following passage: 'Faith and love, by which man is placed between God and his neighbour as a medium which receives from above and gives out again below, and is like a vessel or tube through which the stream of divine blessings must flow without intermission to other people.' (Weimar edition of Luther's works, 10,1,1, p.100, 9ff. (see also 45, p.591, 29ff.)

also our relationship to each other becomes impersonal: each of us becomes merely the impersonal 'tube' through whom God's *agape* flows like a 'pneumatic fluid' (129) to others. Could an impersonal relation like this still be referred to by means of a personal concept like 'love'?

The final dimension of love is that of *self-love*. According to Nygren, not only is self-love necessarily *eros*, but *eros* is necessarily self-love, since 'self-love is the basic form of all love that bears the stamp of *eros*. Love for God and love for one's neighbour (and for any other object than God) can alike be reduced to self-love. Neighbourly love... represents a stage in one's ascent to higher things. And love for God is firmly founded on the conviction that he is the satisfaction of all man's needs and desires' (216–17). Thus all forms of *eros* aim at self-realization and are therefore expressions of self-love. Unlike *eros*, however, *agape* 'excludes all self-love. Christianity does not recognize self-love as a legitimate form of love... It is self-love that alienates man from God, preventing him from sincerely giving himself up to God, and it is self-love that shuts up man's heart against his neighbour' (217).

In brief: according to Nygren, *eros* is in all cases equal to self-love; and *agape* is in all cases God's love toward or by means of human beings. The only kind of love which is possible for us is *eros* which 'Christianity does not recognize... as a legitimate form of love'. The most we can hope to be are the impersonal 'tubes' or 'canals' by means of which God can let his *agape* flow to the world. But then we are not the ones who love, since God does all the loving. It is clear that Nygren's claim that *agape*, in the sense put forward by him, is 'the centre of Christianity, the Christian fundamental motif *par excellence*' (48), could be said to present an image of the Christian faith as one which views human beings as objects of divine manipulation rather than as persons in relation to God and to each other. If the Christian faith entails a denial of the claim that human beings are 'independent centres of activity', then by implication it also denies that they are persons.

There are various ways in which one could respond to this representation of the Christian faith. One could accept Nygren's concept of *agape* and reject all eudaemonistic *eros* (including *eros* for God) as being, from the point of view of Christianity, an illegitimate form of self-love. But then one must also be willing to accept the conceptual price which this brings with it. This would amount to accepting a form of quietist 'pure love' which, as we pointed out in section 4.1 above, renounces all desire, including the desire for God. Irving Singer illustrates this attitude to life by referring to an episode in Dante's *Divine Comedy*. In paradise Dante encounters Piccarda, who as a young girl had taken religious vows and entered a convent. When her brother Corso decided to marry her off for political purposes, she yielded to his influence, broke her vows and left the convent. The result is that she now inhabits a low estate in heaven, the sphere of the inconstant moon. Piccarda accepts her lot and piously tells Dante that her heart joyously accepts whatever God has ordained for her. Surprised at such contentment, Dante wonders whether she does not yearn to move higher, to see God more nearly, and to be more dearly loved. She replies: 'Brother, the power of charity quiets our will and makes us will what we have and thirst for nothing else. Did we desire to be more exalted, our desire would be in discord with his will, who appoints us here.' Singer comments as follows on this example:

The blessed soul wants nothing on its own. Bathed in universal charity, it has no personal identity. It gives nothing, it takes nothing, it *is* nothing. In the medieval heaven there can be no reciprocity between persons. Piccarda and all the celestial host are just pawns within the game that God eternally plays in the process of loving himself. They do not love themselves, for they no longer have a separate self. They do not love others, for the others have no selves either. They do not love God, for it is he who does all the loving … God's love … is certainly not the love of persons.[9]

An alternative response would be to agree that a view on *agape* like that put forward by Nygren represents the 'centre of Christianity', but then to reject Christianity as a religion which is demeaning for human existence. An example of this line of

---

[9] Singer, *Nature of Love* I, 357–8. For this example from Dante, see 355–8. Even though Singer's interpretation of Dante fails to do justice to the latter's intentions, the example does illustrate the point we want to make here.

argument can be found in Friedrich Nietzsche's fervent defence of *eros* and equally fervent rejection of Christianity as the religion of *agape*. In section 6.3 we will briefly examine Nietzsche's views.

A third approach would be to claim that this view on *agape* does not do justice to the Christian faith, since the Christian concept of *agape* does not deny to human beings their identity as personal agents in relation to God and to each other. In this respect it is interesting to note that St Bernard would also have argued that Christian love is gift-love, but would not have believed that God has made us into mere 'channels' of his love. Like Nygren and Luther, he also uses this 'hydraulic' metaphor, but draws different conclusions from it:

> The man who is wise, therefore, will see his life as more like a reservoir than a canal. The canal simultaneously pours out what it receives; the reservoir retains the water till it is filled, then discharges the overflow without loss to itself... Today there are many in the Church who act like canals, the reservoirs are far too rare.[10]

This metaphor suggests that human beings have been created by God in such a way that they are able to bestow the contents of their own 'reservoir' of *agape* on God and on each other. In section 6.4 we will examine Max Scheler's attempt at defending the Christian faith against Nietzsche by putting forward a concept of Christian *agape* which in this way entails the autonomous identity of human beings as personal agents in relation to God and each other.

6.3 FRIEDRICH NIETZSCHE

Nietzsche would have agreed with Nygren that *eros* and *agape* represent two opposing forms of life, but then Nietzsche chose resolutely in favour of *eros* and rejected *agape* as decadent. He objected to the Judeo-Christian ideal of *agape* on two grounds, related to its origin and to its effects: on the one hand, he argued that the *agape* ideal originated in the resentment of the inferior to the superior; on the other hand, it resulted in a 'slave morality' which keeps humanity weak and inferior.

[10] St Bernard, *Song of Songs*, Sermon 18.

As to the origin of this ideal, Nietzsche argued that the Hebrews were an inferior nation of nomads, who were weaker and lower than the other nations who surrounded them. The only way in which they could maintain themselves among the other stronger nations was by idealizing their one distinguishing feature: their inferiority.

All the world's efforts against the 'aristocrats', the 'mighty', the 'masters', the 'holders of power', are negligible by comparison with what has been accomplished against those classes by *the Jews* – the Jews, that priestly nation which eventually realised that the one method of effecting satisfaction on its enemies and tyrants was by means of a radical transvaluation of values, which was at the same time an act of the *cleverest revenge* ... It was the Jews who, in opposition to the aristocratic equation (good = aristocratic = beautiful = happy = loved by the gods), dared with a terrifying logic to ... maintain with the teeth of the most profound hatred (the hatred of weakness) this contrary equation, namely, 'the wretched are alone the good; the poor, the weak, the lowly, are alone the good; the suffering, the needy, the sick, the loathsome, are the only ones who are pious, the only ones who are blessed, for them alone is salvation.[11]

They could sanction this inversion of values and look on themselves as a chosen people by inventing a God who loved the weak, the inferior and the deficient. 'The divinity of *décadence*, pruned of all its manliest drives and virtues, from now on necessarily becomes the God of the physiologically retarded, the weak.'[12] In this way they came to believe in a God of *agape*, whose love was indifferent to their inferiority and did not reject them on account of it, nor did he prefer their superior neighbours on account of their superiority. Thus their faith in a God of *agape* arose from their feelings of inferiority, and from their *resentment* against the other nations who were superior and more noble than they.

Regarding the effects of the *agape* ideal, Nietzsche argues that it keeps us inferior and prevents us from flourishing. *Agape*

[11] Nietzsche, *The Genealogy of Morals*, first essay, section 7. (Quoted from the translation of Horace B. Samuel, London 1923). See also Nietzsche, *Beyond Good and Evil*, aphorism 195.
[12] Nietzsche, *The Anti-Christ*, paragraph 17. (Quoted from the Penguin Classics edition of *Twilight of the Idols/ The Anti-Christ*, London 1990).

makes a virtue out of weakness, humility, poverty, abasement, and prevents people from developing and becoming strong and noble. By idealizing inferiority and denying the value of nobility, it keeps people inferior and dependent and makes them assume a slave-mentality. Through *agape* Christianity becomes a religion of pity for the weak, and therefore a decadent religion, since

pity on the whole thwarts the law of evolution, which is the law of *selection*. It preserves what is ripe for destruction; it defends life's disinherited and condemned; through the abundance of the ill-constituted of all kinds which it *retains* in life it gives life itself a gloomy and questionable aspect... This depressive and contagious instinct thwarts those instincts bent on preserving and enhancing the value of life: both as a *multiplier* of misery and as a *conservator* of everything miserable it is one of the chief instruments for the advancement of *décadence* – pity persuades to *nothingness*![13]

Nietzsche pleads instead for the classical ideal of *eros* which exhorts people to strive upward toward self-realization and strength, and which idealized the noble and not the weak. In this light the Christian conception of God as a God of *agape*, is corrupt:

The Christian conception of God – God as a God of the sick, God as spider, God as spirit – is one of the most corrupt conceptions of God arrived at on earth: perhaps it even represents the low-water mark in the descending development of the God type. God degenerates into the *contradiction of life*, instead of being its transfiguration and eternal *Yes*! In God a declaration of hostility toward life, nature, the will to life! With God war is declared on life, nature, and the will to life!... In God, nothingness is deified, the will to nothingness sanctified![14]

6.4 MAX SCHELER

Like Nygren and Nietzsche, Max Scheler held that the Christian ideal of *agape* was a reversal of the Greek ideal of *eros*. 'There takes place what might be called a *reversal in the movement of love*. The Christian view boldly denies the Greek axiom that love is an aspiration of the lower toward the higher. On the contrary,

---

[13] Nietzsche, *Anti-Christ*, paragraph 7.   [14] Nietzsche, *Anti-Christ*, paragraph 18.

now the criterion of love is that the nobler stoops to the vulgar.'[15] Furthermore, he also agrees with Nietzsche that *agape* becomes corrupt when it arises out of *self-hatred* or out of *resentment*. When that happens, *agape* is turned into mere altruism.

Thus, when I devote myself to another out of hatred or contempt for myself, the result is altruism rather than *agape*.

Turning to others is but the secondary consequence of that urge to flee from oneself. One cannot love anybody without turning away from oneself. However, the crucial question is whether this movement is prompted by the desire to turn toward a positive value, or whether the intention is a radical escape from oneself. 'Love' of the second variety is inspired by self-hatred, by hatred of one's own weakness and misery ... Modern philosophical jargon has found a revealing term for this phenomenon, one of the many modern substitutes for love: 'altruism'. (95)

Such altruism can also result from resentment (or *ressentiment* to use Scheler's German term). Because I despise my own weakness, I resent those who are strong since they have that which I miss in myself. As a result, I identify with the weak, since they are the very opposite of those whom I resent.

In *ressentiment* morality, love for the 'small', the 'poor', the 'weak', and the 'oppressed', is really disguised hatred, repressed envy, an impulse to detract, etc., directed against the opposite phenomena: 'wealth', 'strength', 'power', '*largesse*'. When hatred does not dare to come out into the open, it can be easily expressed in the form of ostensible love for something which has features that are the opposite of those of the hated object. (96)

Such resentment can also take on religious forms of expression. Thus for example,

when we are told ... that those people will be rewarded in 'heaven' for their distress, and that 'heaven' is the exact reverse of the earthly order ('the first shall be last'), we distinctly feel how the *ressentiment*-laden man transfers to God the vengeance he himself cannot wreak in the great. In this way he can satisfy his revenge at least in imagination, with the aid of an other-worldly mechanism of rewards and punishments. The core of the *ressentiment* Christian's idea of God is still the

---

[15] Scheler, *Ressentiment*, 86. All quotations from Scheler are taken from this text.

avenging Jehovah. The only difference is that vengeance is now masked as sham love for the 'small'. (97)

According to Scheler, Nietzsche is clearly correct in pointing out that Christian *agape* becomes corrupt when it is combined with a slave-mentality. However, he rejects Nietzsche's claim that such a slave-mentality is an essential characteristic of the Christian *agape*. The latter need not necessarily degenerate into altruism. It need not arise out of self-hatred or resentment, but could also be an expression of an inner strength and vitality. ' *This* kind of love and sacrifice for the weaker, the sick, and the small springs from inner security and vital plenitude. In addition to this vital security, there is that other feeling of bliss and security, that awareness of safety in the fortress of ultimate being itself (Jesus calls it "kingdom of God")' (90). Scheler illustrates this true Christian *agape* by means of the example of St Francis of Assisi.

When Francis of Assisi kisses festering wounds and does not even kill the bugs that bite him, but leaves his body to them as a hospitable home, these acts (if seen from the outside) could be signs of perverted instincts and of a perverted valuation. But this is not actually the case. It is not a lack of nausea or a delight in pus which makes St Francis act in this way. He has overcome his nausea through a deeper feeling of life and vigour! This attitude is completely different from that of recent modern realism in art and literature, the exposure of social misery, the description of little people, the wallowing in the morbid – a typical *ressentiment* phenomenon. Those people saw something buglike in everything that lives, whereas Francis sees the holiness of 'life' even in the bug. (91–2)

The acts of giving or helping others, are the adequate *expression* of love but not its *purpose*. The meaning of love lies in itself,

in the nobility of the loving soul in the act of love ... When the rich youth is told to divest himself of his riches and give them to the poor, it is really not in order to help the 'poor' and to effect a better distribution of property in the interests of general welfare. It is not because poverty as such is supposed to be better than wealth. The order is given because the *act* of giving away, and the spiritual freedom and abundance of love which manifest themselves in this act, ennoble the youth and make him even 'richer' than he is. (93)

It makes him richer, because it is the expression of the image of God in him. 'The Christian deity is a *personal* God who created the 'world' out of an infinite overflow of love – not because he wanted to help anyone or anything, for 'nothing' existed before, but only to express his superabundance of love. This new notion of the deity is the conceptual theological expression of the changed attitude toward life' (94–5). Because he believes that God is in this way a God of *agape*, the Christian 'acts in the peculiar pious conviction that through this "condescension", through this self-abasement and "self-renunciation", he gains the highest good and becomes equal to God' (86).

It is clear that *agape*, as conceived by Scheler, is not only the reversal of *eros*, but in a sense also its deepening and fulfilment: in *agape* we find the self-realization which *eros* desires.

Thus the picture has shifted immensely. This is no longer a band of men and things that surpass each other in striving up to the deity. It is a band in which every member looks back toward those who are further removed from God and comes to resemble the deity by helping and serving them – for this great urge to love, to serve, to bend down, is God's own essence. (88)

From the point of view of Nygren, there are two objections which might be raised against this alternative concept of *agape*. First of all, it might be objected that *agape* becomes here a means for realizing the objectives of *eros*. 'Scheler thus equates *eros* and *agape* as seeking higher value and then commends *agape* as the profounder in the common quest... It becomes hard not to conclude that Scheler has exchanged *agape* for a profounder *eros*.'[16] I do not think that Scheler need be interpreted in this way. He need not be taken to claim that the Christian should adopt an agapeistic attitude *in order to* 'gain the highest good and become equal to God'. Rather, this attitude is an expression of the fact that he has become so. If by adopting this attitude he also 'becomes even richer than he is', this is not the purpose but the unintended byproduct of his so doing. This is a similar point to that which we noted when discussing Augustine's views on neighbourly love in section 5.3: our own advantage is not the

---

[16] Norton and Kille, *Philosophies of Love*, 176.

purpose but 'a sort of natural consequence' of loving our neighbour. We could also state this point in terms of St Bernard's metaphor: loving our neighbour is not a way of filling our reservoir of *agape* (and thereby simulating God's superabundance of *agape*), but a natural consequence of the fact that it is so filled. However, this raises the second objection to Scheler's concept of *agape*: it seems to suppose that human persons are not only 'independent centres of activity' but also independent sources of *agape* apart from God and like God. Our agapeistic attitude is 'an expression of an inner strength and vitality' which we have apart from God. One could respond to this objection by granting on the one hand that human persons are free and independent centres of activity apart from God, who could act from an 'inner strength and vitality' as Scheler claims that we do. In other words, we are in fact independent reservoirs of *agape* who can actively overflow and not merely passive canals for conducting God's *agape* to the world. On the other hand, this does not mean that we have brought this about by ourselves. On the contrary, we are independent personal agents because God has made us so and we have the ability to love God and our neighbours because God enables and inspires us to do so. Our reservoirs are full because God has filled them.

Does this mean that in some sense human persons are *free* in their love for God and for one another? Is love something which we can freely do or is it something which overcomes us? In chapter 2 we saw Ortega argue that falling in love is not something which we can freely choose to do. It is something which happens to us when we fall under the spell of our beloved. And in section 6.2 we saw Nygren argue similarly with respect to our love for God (and our neighbour): 'Man loves God [and his neighbour] because God's unmotivated love has overwhelmed him and taken control of him, so that he cannot do other than love God [and his neighbour].' Are we free personal agents ('independent centres of action') in loving God and other people, or are we not? This is one of the questions which we shall have to discuss in the course of part IV below. Having now discussed a number of the most important views on both romantic love and neighbourly love, and having tried in a

preliminary way to see how these could be applied to the love of
God, we must now inquire whether all these views could be
integrated by means of a relational concept of love, whether this
will enable us to deal satisfactorily with all the conceptual
problems about love which were raised but not answered in the
previous chapters, and finally whether this will produce a
satisfactory conceptual model for the love of God.

PART IV

Love as a relationship

CHAPTER 7

Relationships

7.1 INTRODUCTION: FEELINGS, ATTITUDES, AND RELATIONSHIPS

It is sometimes argued that, since love is an emotion or feeling or sentiment and therefore inexpressible, the question as to its nature cannot be answered. Feelings must be experienced in order to be understood, and such understanding cannot be communicated to those who do not have the experience. 'Heightened discourse – poetry, music, fiction – may suggest what it is like, but suggestion is not expression, and ultimately love remains something each individual knows only within himself, if he knows it at all.'[1] This view fails to distinguish between 'existential understanding' and 'theoretical understanding'.[2] The former is the sort of understanding which we have of an experience if we know personally what it is like. It could be argued that this is only possible for those who have personally undergone the experience. 'A person who has been tortured with electric shocks can be said to know what that experience is like. I have never undergone this experience, so my understanding of what it is like is not very good, though of course I can imagine.'[3] But my imagination does not enable me to *have* your experiences, and therefore cannot strictly speaking provide me with existential understanding of them. In this sense it could be said that feelings of love are incommunicable: you can experience only your own feelings of love and not those of

---

[1] Van de Vate, *Romantic Love*, 8.
[2] See Ninian Smart, 'Understanding religious experience', in Katz, *Mysticism and Philosophical Analysis*, 10. [3] Ibid., 10.

149

other people. But then an experience or feeling is never an
isolated phenomenon, even for the person who has it. Our
experiences fit into our forms of life. Wittgenstein explains this
point with reference to sensations of pain: 'Pain has *this* position
in our life; has *these* connections; (That is to say: we only call
'pain' what has *this* position, *these* connections. Only surrounded
by certain normal manifestations of life, is there such a thing as
an expression of pain. Only surrounded by an even more far-
reaching particular manifestation of life, such a thing as the
expression of sorrow or affection. And so on.'[4] By referring to
and explaining these connections, I can talk about my feelings,
emotions, sentiments, experiences, etc., to you even though you
cannot *have* them yourself. In other words, I can communicate
a *theoretical* understanding of my feelings to you even though you
cannot experience them *existentially* yourself.

Unlike mere sensations (pains, itches, etc.), feelings, emotions, and sentiments are often intimately connected with the
attitudes we have toward ourselves and our surroundings. We
could also say that many (but not all) attitudes are 'feeling-
attitudes' in the sense that they involve feelings or emotions
toward their objects.[5] Such attitudes have three main characteristics: they are intentional, evaluative, and dispositional.[6]
Let us look at these three points in turn.

First of all, attitudes are *intentional* in the sense that they have
intentional objects. They are attitudes which we adopt toward
things, situations, events, persons, ideas, etc. Different attitudes
could be distinguished by the various kinds of intentional
objects which they presuppose. In this sense we might adapt a
term introduced by Van de Vate and classify love as a *social*

---

[4] Wittgenstein, *Zettel* (Oxford 1967), 533–4.
[5] 'But many attitudes have nothing to do with emotions since the latter are only one
variety of the former. There are attitudes of indifference, neutrality, detachment,
carelessness, scepticism, understanding, secretiveness, frankness, tolerance, con-
ciliation, decency, honesty, and a great host of other character traits that are not
themselves emotions and that need not incorporate any emotion.' Robert Brown,
Analyzing Love (Cambridge 1987), 98.
[6] For this view on the nature of attitudes, see section 7.18 of my *Theology and
Philosophical Inquiry.*

feeling-attitude, i.e. one which we have in relation to persons.[7]
Here it might be objected that this limitation is not reflected in
our ordinary use of the word 'love': 'English speakers, like
French and German speakers, quite commonly assert that they
love their dogs, their cars, their golf games, their swimming
pools, their jobs, the view from the front verandah, and their
native country.'[8] However, this verbal usage blurs the important conceptual difference between loving and cherishing.
'It is obvious that we can cherish particular situations, activities,
achievements, accomplishments, capacities, principles, and
beliefs in addition to animals and people. We can cherish all
these different things because we value them in themselves,
independently of their use as means to other ends.'[9] It is true
that loving someone involves cherishing that person, but as we
shall argue below, it is much more than cherishing alone.

Secondly, attitudes are *evaluative*, in the sense that they entail
a positive or a negative valuation of their intentional objects.
Thus love (like admiration, cherishing, appreciation, encour-
agement, etc.) entails a positive valuation, whereas contempt
(like indignation, ridicule, hate, disdain, etc.) entails a negative
valuation. However, there is an important difference between
the kinds of positive or negative valuation which different
attitudes entail. In this regard, Roger Scruton distinguishes
between those mental states which are directed toward things as
particulars, and those that are directed toward things as tokens
or instantiations of some type or property.[10] Thus I could have
admiration for James because he has some admirable characteristics. This implies on the one hand that I would admire
William as well if he should have the same characteristics, and
on the other that my admiration for James would stop if he
should lose his admirable characteristics or should prove not to

---

[7] 'Feelings whose objects are particular persons we may call "social feelings".' Van de
   Vate, *Romantic Love*, 14. This might be extended to include attitudes as well.
[8] Brown, *Analyzing Love*, 18.   [9] Ibid., 23.
[10] Roger Scruton, 'Attitudes, beliefs and reasons', in J. Casey (ed.), *Morality and Moral
   Reasoning* (London 1971), 41. We need not follow Scruton in his further claim that
   'those states which can be shown to be universal will normally be referred to as
   attitudes rather than emotions... Most of those states which are normally called
   emotions... are particular with respect to their objects' (42).

have had them in the first place. In other words, my admiration is directed primarily at James' characteristics and secondarily at James as the instantiation of these characteristics. In this respect love is different, since it is directed toward a person as a particular and not as an instantiation. Since I do not love you *because of* your characteristics, my love for you does not entail that I should similarly love everybody else who has the same characteristics, nor that I should stop loving you if you should no longer have these characteristics. My love for you is a love for *you* and not for your characteristics apart from you. I could also love you in spite of disapproving of your characteristics. The only thing which my love for you excludes is that I should be indifferent to your characteristics. The lover will feel an intimate concern about the continuance of good properties in the beloved and the diminishing of bad ones. But such concern would not be possible without an objective appraisal of the beloved.[11] In this sense love cannot be blind to the characteristics of the beloved. Thus both love and admiration require an objective appraisal of the characteristics of their intentional objects, but admiration is based on the outcome of this appraisal, whereas love is not.

Elsewhere Scruton makes this point as follows: 'It seems to me that we ought to be able to distinguish between emotions with a universal or abstract, and those with a particular or concrete, object ... Emotions like love and grief have particular objects. Others, such as contempt, admiration, and indignation, have universal objects.'[12] This distinction throws light on the two interpretations of Plato which we discussed in section 5.2. On the interpretation of Vlastos, Plato takes love to be an attitude primarily toward universal objects (ideas) and secondarily toward individual persons as instantiations of the ideas. On the interpretation of Norton and Kille, Plato takes love to be an attitude toward individual persons irrespective of their actual characteristics but with a concern that they should come to realize their potentiality for goodness. We shall return to this point in more detail below.

---

[11] See Singer, *Nature of Love* I, 9.
[12] Roger Scruton, 'Emotion, practical knowledge and common culture', in A. O. Rorty (ed.), *Explaining Emotions* (Berkeley 1980), 525.

The third characteristic feature of attitudes is that they are *dispositional*. Since they involve a valuation of their object, they entail a course of action in accordance with this valuation. Thus the Oxford English Dictionary defines 'attitudes' as 'forms of settled behaviour or manner of acting, as representative of feeling or opinion'. This does not deny the fact that feelings or emotions seem to overcome us rather than being deliberately adopted. 'We speak of feelings, sentiments and emotions as passivities, things that happen to us rather than things that we do. We are *struck* or *seized* by panic or remorse, *overcome* by fear, *driven* by lust – these metaphors picture us forced to feel.'[13] This also applies to becoming convinced of some truth and to falling in love with some person. However, since such feelings or emotions are imbedded in attitudes, they give rise to action in response to them. Thus fear prompts one to seek safety, resentment calls for revenge, and gratitude calls for expression in grateful behaviour. Similarly love gives rise to a complex form of behaviour in relation to the beloved.

Sometimes our feelings and emotions give rise to episodic responses, but not always. Often the response takes the form of a long-term disposition rather than a passing reaction to a specific occasion. Thus Gabriele Taylor points out that unlike many feelings and emotions, love is not 'occasional': while it is appropriate to speak of an occasion for being angry, afraid, grateful etc., we can hardly talk in this way of love. According to Taylor this is partly so because linking love with particular occasions would allow for the possibility of love being very short-lived indeed, and this we are not prepared to do.[14] In the case of social feeling-attitudes like love, the response is not merely an unintended long-term behavioural disposition caused by the emotion, but a purposive policy of action to which the lover commits him- or herself in relation to the beloved. Hence love is not merely a feeling or emotion but also a purposive commitment to adopt a complex pattern of actions and attitudes in relation to the beloved.

[13] Van de Vate, *Romantic Love*, 14.
[14] Gabriele Taylor, 'Love', in Ted Honderich and Myles Burnyeat (eds.), *Philosophy as It Is* (London 1979), 178.

Van de Vate points out that we tend to confuse feelings with the policies to which they give rise because they are often called by the same name.[15] However, if John says to Mary: 'I love you', this is not a report of a passing feeling or mental state in himself, but an expression of commitment to long-term action in relation to her. Feelings are passing states whereas policies are long-term commitments. Feelings are also private and can be kept secret, whereas policies necessarily issue in actions which are public. Furthermore, as we pointed out above, feelings are 'passivities' which overcome us and not activities which we decide to do. But the commitments to which they give rise are activities in the sense that we freely decide to make them. We may not have full control over our feelings, but we do have control over the policies to which we commit ourselves. In the case of love, our feelings might strongly *motivate* us to make the relevant commitments, but they do not *cause* these commitments in a way which makes them logically or physically unavoidable. We might willingly and gladly *consent* to feeling the way we do or, as Ortega puts it, fall in love because we want to; but we do not *decide* to feel that way. With our commitments, this is different: We may not only willingly consent to make them, we also have to freely decide to do so. In terms of the distinction which we made in section 2.3, we have the freedom of consent with respect to our feelings of love, but with respect to the policy-commitments to which these feelings give rise, we also have the freedom of choice. Hence, although we cannot be held responsible for our feelings, we can be held responsible for keeping our commitments. The sincerity of the commitments (and of expressions of the feelings which give rise to them) are therefore tested by the faithfulness of the lover. If he fails to keep his commitments we say that his love is not true. This prompts Wittgenstein to argue that, unlike pain, 'love is not a feeling. Love is put to the test, pain not. One does not say: "That was not true pain, or it would not have gone off so quickly."'[16]

Apart from these three characteristics which love shares with other attitudes, it also has a fourth characteristic which

---

[15] Van de Vate, *Romantic Love*, 15.   [16] Wittgenstein, *Zettel*, 504.

distinguishes it from most other attitudes: it entails a desire for reciprocation. When John says to Mary: 'I love you', this is not merely an expression of his feelings toward her and of the commitments to which they give rise, but also a plea that she should reciprocate these feelings and commitments. Love wants to be returned, requited, and in this way fulfilled in a relationship of mutual love. Of course this does not exclude the possibility of unrequited love. John's love for Mary is not *conditional* on her returning it, and his feelings and commitments toward her would not be any less real or sincere if she were not to reciprocate them. In this sense his love for her does not logically require her reciprocation, but it normally does entail that he should *wish* for her to reciprocate his love and so enter into a relationship with him. In this respect love is more than mere beneficence. Of course, love entails beneficence, but unlike beneficence it also seeks a relationship. I could act beneficently toward the starving people in the Third World without thereby seeking to establish a personal relationship with any of them. In fact my beneficence would most often be performed anonymously which effectively excludes the establishment of a relationship. Only under very abnormal circumstances might someone not want his or her love to be returned and fulfilled in this way. 'Because a person may be capable of giving love but be unable, for psychological reasons, to accept it in return, there is no logical absurdity in the case of a lover not caring about being well treated and valued by the beloved. It is a fact that some people can love others only if their affection is returned with ill-will, contempt, and punishment.'[17] Clearly such 'love' is defective, if not neurotic. Normally, therefore, the attitude of love entails the desire that its object should adopt a similar attitude in return.

John wants Mary to return his love, and if she should respond to his declaration of love by saying: 'I love you too, John', then, in the words of Van de Vate, 'she promises to adopt a policy that inter-meshes with the policy John promises, and we may say that a compact or contract or agreement is formed, a set of mutual obligations and expectations.'[18] When this happens, John's love is fulfilled in a relationship of mutual love between him and Mary. In this sense we could argue that love is primarily a relational concept rather than an attitudinal one, as was presupposed by all the views which we discussed in the previous chapters. Rather than looking on love as an attitude which might issue in a relationship, we could also look on love as a relationship which involves the partners adopting a complex set of attitudes toward each other.

This suggestion gives rise to two questions. First of all, what kind of relationship is this relationship of love? Is it adequate to refer to it as a 'compact or contract or agreement' as Van de Vate does? Secondly, how does this relationship involve the various attitudes identified with love in the views discussed in the previous chapters? And will sorting this out enable us to create some order in the 'Austro-Hungarian Empire' of love[19] to which we referred in section 2.1? The rest of this chapter and the next will be devoted to the first of these questions, and our final chapter to the second.

7.2 PERSONAL AND IMPERSONAL RELATIONS

In theory we could distinguish three basic types of relationship between people. Let us call them 'manipulative relations', 'agreements of rights and duties', and 'mutual fellowship'.[20] In this section and the next we will examine these three relation-types and try to decide to which of them a relation of love belongs. This inquiry will be complicated by the empirical fact that human relations are usually a mixture of all three. Although our concrete human relations could be characterized

---

[18] Van de Vate, *Romantic Love*, 15.

[19] 'Love is an Austro-Hungarian Empire, uniting all sorts of feelings, behaviours and attitudes, sometimes having little in common, under the rubric of "love".' Bernard Murstein, 'A taxonomy of love', 33.

[20] I have also developed these distinctions elsewhere. See my *What Are We Doing When We Pray?* and chapters 3 and 6 of my *Speaking of a Personal God*. For a similar distinction between three types of relationship, see John Macmurray, *Persons in Relation* (London 1961), chapters 5–7.

by any one of these, it is rare that human beings manage to sustain any one of them in its purity for any length of time. As human beings we are inconsistent in our dealings with each other, and our loves are therefore rarely pure. We could only avoid this inconsistency by becoming either divine or completely dehumanized. The distinctions we are to make are therefore not empirical but conceptual distinctions between relation-*types* which we approximate to a greater or lesser degree in our dealing with each other in the empirical world. Nevertheless these distinctions are essential for the description of human relations, since without them we would not be able to determine the extent in which our empirical relations approximate these types, nor describe the ways in which they are a mixture of all three of them. Similarly we would not be able to describe our impure human loves without first deciding to which relation-type love in all its purity should ideally belong.

The purpose of our inquiry is not merely to describe human relations but to find an adequate conceptual model for talking about our relationship with God. Here again, God is not like other people since God always remains faithful to his own character and therefore consistent in his dealings with us. As a conceptual model for God's relationship with us, we therefore need to choose one of these relation-types as such rather than the inconsistent mix of all three which is characteristic for our dealings with each other. God's love is pure and not inconsistent like ours. In the history of theology, all three of these relation-types have in fact from time to time been employed as conceptual models for the relationship between God and human beings. Let us briefly distinguish these three types of relationship and see which of them would be most adequate for talking about our relationship to a God of love.

We shall argue that in an important sense the first of these types (manipulative relations) is impersonal, while the other two (agreements of rights and duties and mutual fellowship) are personal. In this section we will try to distinguish between personal and impersonal relations and in the next between the two types of personal relations. Let us start then with manipulative relations. As human beings we often try to gain control over each other. In this sense Thomas Hobbes is correct in maintaining that every man is a wolf for his neighbour. To the extent that A manages to gain complete control over B, the relation between them becomes purely manipulative. Of course A need not necessarily exercise such manipulative control for selfish purposes. It could also be beneficent and exercised to B's advantage. However, no matter how beneficent A's control over B is, it nevertheless treats B as an object rather than as a person, since A adopts what Strawson calls an 'objective attitude' toward B: 'To adopt the objective attitude to another human being is to see him, perhaps, as an object of social policy; as a subject of what, in a wide range of sense, might be called treatment; as something certainly to be taken account, perhaps precautionary account, of; to be managed or handled or cured or trained.'[21]

In an important sense such relations are asymmetrical: only A is a personal agent, whereas B has become an object of A's manipulative power. The causal agency of A is both necessary and sufficient for establishing, maintaining, and amending the relation. In other words, A is able by him- or herself both to bring about, change, and terminate the relationship, whereas, to the extent that B has become an object of A's manipulative power, B loses the ability either to bring about or to prevent the relationship being established, changed, or terminated. The relationship therefore becomes impersonal in the sense that only one of the partners in the relationship is a personal agent. The other has become an object.

Personal relations, on the contrary, are symmetrical in this respect: both partners in the relation are free personal agents, and the free assent of both is necessary for the relation to be established or maintained. Either partner is able to terminate the relation by freely withdrawing from it, but neither is able by him- or herself to establish or to maintain the relation, since for this the assent of the other partner is also necessary. Of course, the fact that personal relations are symmetrical in *this* respect, does not exclude their being asymmetrical in many *other*

---

[21] P. F. Strawson, *Freedom and Resentment and Other Essays* (London 1974), 9.

respects. In fact there are no personal relations in which the partners do not differ from each other in an infinite number of ways.

In terms of this distinction, is love a personal or an impersonal relationship? If Hobbes is correct in his claim that all human relations necessarily tend to become manipulative, this should also apply to relations of love. And indeed, did we not in section 2.3 see Ortega argue that falling in love is a paralysis of attention 'which does not leave us any freedom of movement' and which can be brought about in the lover 'with irremissible mechanism'? And in section 2.2 we saw Ortega explain how manipulative the 'conquistadors of love' can make such relations become: 'Once a woman's attention is fixed upon a man, it is very easy for him to dominate her thought completely. A simple game of blowing hot and cold, of solicitousness and disdain, of presence and absence is all that is required. The rhythm of that technique acts upon a woman's attention like a pneumatic machine and ends by emptying her of all the rest of the world ... Most 'love affairs' are reduced to this mechanical play of the beloved upon the lover's attention.' However, in the previous section we argued that love is not merely a feeling or emotion but also a policy commitment in relation to the beloved. The feeling might be called up or caused by the beloved, but not the commitment to action. Although the feeling might strongly motivate the action, it does not cause it. To the extent, therefore, that love is a commitment to a course of action, the lover remains a personal agent in his or her loves, and love cannot be reduced to a purely manipulative relationship. But does this also apply to love in relation to God? In section 6.2 we saw Anders Nygren argue that human beings cannot freely decide to love either God or each other, since their love is the exclusive effect which the divine *agape* has on them. In loving God and other people, a human being 'is not an independent centre of activity' so that 'all choice on man's part is excluded'. God *causes* us to love him and each other. This seems to turn God into a kind of Heavenly Conquistador, except for the fact that human conquistadors presumably decide freely to embark on their conquistadorial activities, whereas God's *agape* is the inevitable effect of his essential nature as superabundant source of all *agape*. Clearly such views take love to be a highly impersonal concept and the relationship of love to be a very impersonal manipulative one.

On the other hand, we could also argue that love is a personal relationship in which the lovers freely commit themselves to one another. Their feelings toward each other might motivate them to make these commitments, but they do not cause the commitments. My feelings toward my beloved do provide me with a strong *reason* for committing myself to her in a loving relationship, but they do not make these commitments logically or physically inevitable. In loving her, I remain 'an independent centre of activity' who has chosen to enter into the relationship with her. As such, love is necessarily vulnerable, since each partner in a relationship of love is necessarily dependent on the freedom and responsibility of the other partner for establishing and for maintaining the relationship. It is logically impossible for either partner to establish or maintain the relationship by him or herself. For most people this fact causes an unbearable dilemma. Since love requires that we give up our autonomy and acknowledge our dependence on somebody else, love threatens our sense of security. For this reason most people are tempted to either force or oblige the other to return their love. The result is, however, that the relationship is perverted and love is lost, and the lover is left with an object rather than a beloved person.

In his perceptive analysis of the concept of love, Jean-Paul Sartre explains this as follows:

The man who wants to be loved does not desire the enslavement of the beloved. He is not bent on becoming the object of passion which flows forth mechanically. He does not want to possess an automaton, and if we want to humiliate him, we need only try to persuade him that the beloved's passion is the result of a psychological determinism. The lover will then feel that both his love and his being are cheapened ... If the beloved is transformed into an automaton, the lover finds himself alone.[22]

---

[22] Jean-Paul Sartre, *Being and Nothingness* (New York 1956), 367.

This is well illustrated in the popular song 'Paper Doll':

> I'm goin' to buy a paper doll that I can call my own,
> a doll that other fellows cannot steal.
> And then those flirty flirty guys
> with their flirty flirty eyes
> will have to flirt with dollies that are real.
> When I come home at night she will be waiting.
> She'll be the truest doll in all the world.
> I'd rather have a paper doll to call my own
> than have a fickle minded real live girl.

Far from being a song of love, this is a lament on account of the absence of love. In the words of Sartre quoted above: 'If the beloved is transformed into an automaton, the lover finds himself alone.'

It is clear that a relationship of love can only be maintained as long as the personal integrity and autonomy of *both* partners is upheld. The moment I let my partner become (or allow my partner to let me become) what Strawson calls 'an object to be managed or handled or cured or trained', the relationship between us becomes perverted to something other than love. Love must by its very nature be a relationship of free mutual give and take, otherwise it cannot be love at all.

If in my relation with you I insist on behaving generously toward you and refuse to accept your generosity in return, I make myself the giver and you the recipient. This is unjust to you. I put you in my debt and refuse to let you repay the debt. In that case I make the relation an unequal one. You are to have continual cause to be grateful to me, but I am not to be grateful to you. This is the worst kind of tyranny, and is shockingly unfair to you. It destroys the mutuality of the personal by destroying the equality which is its negative aspect. To maintain equality of persons in relation is justice; and without it generosity becomes purely sentimental and wholly egocentric. My care for you is only moral if it includes the intention to preserve your freedom as an agent, which is your independence of me. Even if you wish to be dependent on me, it is my business, for your sake, to prevent it.[23]

Here again it is clear that, even though love is impossible without beneficence, it is far more than that. In 1 Corinthians

---

[23] John Macmurray, *Persons in Relation*, 189–90.

13: 3 St Paul suggests that even when my beneficence should extend to giving away all I possess to the needy and giving up my body to be burned, it remains possible that in doing this I have no love.

If God is a God of love, as believers claim, then all this applies also to the sort of relationship which God wants to establish and maintain with human persons. For our present purposes two implications are especially important here. On the one hand this means that no human person is able autonomously to enter into or to maintain a relationship of love with God. For this human persons are dependent on the free assent of God. In the words of Anthony Bloom:

If we could mechanically draw him into an encounter, force him to meet us, simply because we have chosen this moment to meet him, there would be no relationship and no encounter. We can do that with an image, with the imagination, or with the various idols we can put in front of us instead of God; we can do nothing of the sort with the living God, any more than we can do it with a living person. A relationship must begin and develop in mutual freedom.[24]

Furthermore, if it is true, as we have seen Augustine argue, that the chief good and eternal happiness for human persons consists in being in the love of God, then no human person is able autonomously to achieve eternal happiness. Real human flourishing is only possible through the grace of God. Augustine does add, however, that the love of God differs from the love of other people because God can be counted upon to remain faithful in his love. God's love is 'something which cannot be lost against the will'. Because God is not like 'a fickle minded real live girl', Sartre's problem about the insecurity of love does not arise for the believer in the case of God's love. However, even though God's faithfulness can be *counted* upon, he should nevertheless not be *presumed* upon. It remains true that we depend on God's *free* grace in order to enter into and remain in a relation of love with God.

On the other hand, since love is a reciprocal relation, God is also dependent on the freedom and responsibility of human

---

[24] Anthony Bloom, *School for Prayer* (London 1970), 2.

persons in order to enter into a loving relation with them. Of course, this autonomy is *bestowed* on us by God as our creator. We do not owe our autonomy as persons to ourselves. Nevertheless, in creating human persons in order to love them, God necessarily assumes vulnerability in relation to them. In fact, in this relation he becomes even more vulnerable than we do, since he cannot count on the steadfastness of our love in the way we can count on his steadfastness. Simone Weil explains this point as follows:

God's creative love which maintains us in existence is not merely a superabundance of generosity, it is also renunciation and sacrifice. Not only the Passion but the Creation itself is a renunciation and sacrifice on the part of God. The Passion is simply its consummation. God already voids himself of his divinity by the Creation. He takes the form of a slave, submits to necessity, abases himself. His love maintains in existence, in a free and autonomous existence, beings other than himself, beings other than the good, mediocre beings. Through love he abandons them to affliction and sin. If he did not abandon them they would not exist.[25]

Even if we were to express this point in less extreme terms than Simone Weil, it remains true that if God did not grant us the ability to sin and cause affliction to him and to one another, we would not have the kind of free and autonomous existence necessary to enter into a relation of love with God and with one another. In the words of Sartre again: 'If the beloved is transformed into an automaton, the lover finds himself alone.'[26]

We can conclude from these considerations that love is a personal relationship in which the personal integrity of both partners is to be maintained. It follows that if God is a God of love, then our relationship with God must also be personal in this sense. But what kind of personal relationship is this relationship called 'love'?

---

[25] Simone Weil, *Gateway to God*, 80. For a Jewish view resembling that of Simone Weil, see Hans Jonas, 'The concept of God after Auschwitz', *The Journal of Religion* 67 (1987), 1–13.

[26] This clearly has far-reaching implications for the way in which we are to deal with the problem of evil and theodicy. For an extended treatment of these issues, see my *Speaking of a Personal God*, chapter 6.

7.3 AGREEMENTS AND FELLOWSHIP

At the beginning of the previous section, we referred to two
types of personal relation: 'agreements of rights and duties' and
'mutual fellowship'.[27] Agreements of rights and duties are the
sort of relations Rousseau had in mind in describing human
relations in terms of a social contract. In such relations two
persons accept certain rights and duties toward each other.
Thus in an agreement between an employer and an employee,
the employer accepts the duty to pay the employee a wage in
exchange for the right to the work which the employee has to do
for him, whereas the employee is given the right to receive wages
in exchange for the duty to do some work for the employer.
People enter into such agreements by recognizing the claims
which they make on each other with a view to the advantage
which each party can gain for himself. The goods or services
which each partner receives from the other in accordance with
the agreement constitute an interest which the recipient could
only realize for him or herself by means of such an agreement.
This is what typically distinguishes such relations from a relation
of mutual fellowship in which each of us chooses to serve the
interests of the other and not primarily our own. Or rather, I do
not merely *recognize* your interests and the claims you make on
me, but I *identify* myself with you by treating your interests and
your claims as my own. In serving these interests as my own, I
love you as myself.[28] 'If I love someone I care for him. I want his
good, not merely as much as I want my own, but as being my
own ... Aristotle's definition of a friend as a *heteros autos*, another
self, catches exactly the ambiguity ... I remain different from

---

[27] This distinction is similar to that which social scientists sometimes make between
primary and secondary relationships. See Van de Vate, *Romantic Love*, 19f. See also
C. H. Cooley, *Social Organization* (New York 1909). John Lucas refers to this
distinction as that between 'personal and business relations'. See his *Freedom and
Grace* (London 1976), 57–8. This is also parallel to the distinction between 'society
and community' made by John Macmurray. See his *Persons in Relation*, chapters 6–7.

[28] Compare the following words from Emil Brunner: 'Love is not the recognition of the
other person as an equal, but it is identification with the other person. Love not only
recognizes the claim of the other, but makes that claim her own; the truly loving
person loves her neighbour as herself.' *The Divine Imperative* (London 1937) 326.

you, but we are of one mind in wanting and hoping for those things that are good for you, and in fearing whatever is bad.'[29]

Furthermore, in agreements of rights and duties my partner, as well as the relationship, has an instrumental value for me as a means for furthering my own interests. As such they are replaceable by any other means which might be equally effective. As John Lucas explains,

> if I do business with you ... my good will toward you is conditional and limited. I will keep my side of the bargain provided you keep yours. Your value in my eyes is contingent on your doing certain things, whereby you are of use to me; and the good I am prepared to do you is proportional to your value to me. In the terminology of the Theory of Games, we form a coalition, because we each see that together we can achieve some of our respective interests better than we could separately. But our assessments of the outcome remains separate. Your good is not *eo ipso* my good, and your value in my eyes is simply as a person who can bring good things to me, as a furtherer of my own cause. Anybody else who could do the same would do equally well. I have no commitments to you as you, but only to you as a useful business partner.[30]

In relations of fellowship, however, where I identify with you and treat your interests as my own, your value and the value of our relationship become intrinsic for me. As such neither you nor our relationship can be replaced by another.

> If you are accepted because you are you, not only is your value in my eyes not conditional and not necessarily limited, but it is also unique. I can do business with anybody, but if I have a personal relationship [i.e. fellowship] with you, and value you because you are you, I cannot have *that* relationship with anybody else, just simply because anybody else is not you.[31]

Although relations of fellowship with other people could also be rewarding and satisfying, they could never be the same relationship, since you, as the person who is the reason for having the relationship, would be missing. It is clear that relations of fellowship play an essential role in human existence,

---

[29] Lucas, *Freedom and Grace*, 56.

[30] Ibid., 57. See also J. A. Brook, 'How to treat persons as persons', in A. Montefiore (ed.), *Philosophy and Personal Relations* (London 1973), 66, and Van de Vate, *Romantic Love*, 19f.   [31] Lucas, *Freedom and Grace*, 58.

since we owe our value and identity as persons to such relations. Personal value and identity are *bestowed* on me by the fact that others consider me irreplaceable to them.

To be esteemed by another secures one's own sense of self-esteem, and gives body to one's own sense of identity. To know that one is loved is to be able to anchor one's own existence in the affections of others. 'Who am I?' 'I am the person that Mother loves' or 'that Jill loves' or 'that God loves'. It means that my actions matter, not only to me but also to someone else in the outside world, and that therefore they have a significance which is not solely solipsistic.[32]

For religious believers this applies especially to fellowship with God. The ultimate value of my very existence is bestowed on it by the fact that God loves *me* and not merely my services apart from me.

Agreements between two persons can only come about if both partners freely decide to enter into them. The same applies to mutual fellowship: I can offer my fellowship to you but cannot cause you to return it. On the other hand, you cannot return my fellowship unless I have offered it to you first. As we pointed out in the previous section, both kinds of personal relations presuppose in this sense not only that both partners are personal agents, but that each acknowledges the freedom and responsibility of the other as well as his or her own dependence on the other for establishing and maintaining the relationship. From this it is clear that in seeking personal relations with other persons we become vulnerable in relation to them. Establishing such relationships entails taking a risk. In four respects, however, the risk I take in seeking your fellowship is infinitely greater than that involved in negotiating an agreement with you.

First of all, although agreements are not *coercive* in the sense in which manipulative relations are, they do create obligations. In fact it is their very purpose to do so. Through such an agreement I do not force you to serve my interests, but I do place you under an *obligation* to do so. In fact I earn your obligation to me by committing myself to the services which the agreement requires me to do for you in return. In this way I can limit the risk I take,

[32] Ibid., 60–1.

not by coercion but by obligation. With fellowship this is different since here you further my interests not because you are obliged to do so in order to merit my serving your interests in return, but because you freely identify with me and therefore treat my interests as your own. I can neither coerce nor oblige you to do this. In other words, I can buy or earn or merit your services but not your fellowship or your friendship or your love. If I try to do so, I merely succeed in perverting the fellowship I desire into an agreement of rights and duties. In the context of twelfth-century feudal society where marriage was in fact a business arrangement between feudal houses, Countess Marie of Champagne tried to make a very important conceptual point in her famous judgment which we quoted in section 4.3 above: 'We declare and we hold as firmly established that love cannot exert its powers between two people who are married to each other. For lovers give each other everything freely, under no compulsion of necessity, but married people are duty bound to give in to each other's desires and deny themselves to each other in nothing.'[33]

Secondly, fellowship is also much more risky than agreements, in the sense that much more is at stake in them. In an agreement it is the value of my services to you which is at stake, whereas in fellowship my value as a person is at stake. If you refuse to do business with me, you reject my services but not my person. If you refuse my fellowship, it is me that you reject. This difference is reflected in the ways in which we negotiate these two kinds of relationship. Van de Vate explains this as follows:

Business contracts, and in general secondary relationships, will be fitting matters for explicit formulation and open negotiation, for here the parties deal with duplicatable, dispensable goods, such as money. Such primary relationships as friendships and romances will not be fitting matters, however, for here the goods exchanged are held to be identical with the parties exchanging them. These latter negotiations are therefore especially risky. Should John offer to sell his car to Sidney for 500 dollars, he runs a risk in the offer, for Sidney or someone else might be willing to pay more. When John offers his friendship to

---

[33] Although a love relationship is not identical with a marriage bond, this of course does not necessarily exclude the possibility of love within marriage. We shall return to this point in section 7.4 below.

Sidney, however, he puts himself far more gravely at risk. 'John's friendship' is really another name for John himself. It is supposed to be desirable for its own sake, just as John himself is supposed to be desirable for his own sake. Sidney's spurning it threatens John's ability to conceive of himself as intrinsically worthy. That ability is John's very self. The more openly he offers himself to Sidney, the more difficult it will be for him to repair the damage done by a refusal. Therefore negotiations about primary relationships must be fundamentally tacit. Through this tacitness, negotiators minimize the risks to themselves.[34]

If I openly declare my love to you, I take responsibility for what I say. I therefore cannot easily disavow my declaration in order to save face if you should spurn it. If however I were to act toward you in a way which gives you the opportunity to infer that I love you, I can always hold you responsible for the inference and deny making any declarations at all. In section 4.3 we saw how De Rougemont argues that rhetoric is the essential form of expression for courtly love. It is now clear that this did not only hold for courtly love in the twelfth century, but is a necessary feature of the language of all forms of fellowship and therefore of love as such.

There is a third sense in which my fellowship with you puts me personally at risk in a way in which an agreement would not. In the latter I value you because of your services or your characteristics rather than for yourself. Your services or your characteristics are at stake here and not yourself. When valuing you for yourself, however, I also put *myself* personally at risk in a way which would not be the case if I were to value you for your services or your characteristics. Roger Scruton explains this point with the help of his distinction, referred to in section 7.1 above, between emotions like love or hate which have particular objects and those like contempt or admiration which have universal objects. Thus, if I despise you *because of* your cowardice, I really despise your cowardice as a universal characteristic and you merely as a contingent instantiation of it. My emotion (and the valuation on which it is based) applies equally to anyone who is a coward and only accidentally to you

---

[34] Van de Vate, *Romantic Love*, 26–7.

as an instantiation of cowardice. In this sense it is an objective evaluation which is abstracted from the particularity of its *object*. On the other hand, however, it is also abstracted from my particularity as its *subject*. While, as Scruton points out, it is *I* who feel contempt or indignation, I do so in obedience to an imperative which is applicable beyond my present situation, in accordance with a universal law. In this way such emotions seem not only to abstract from the particularity of their object but also from that of their subject: 'It is only accidentally *I* who am feeling this indignation – the call to indignation might have been addressed to and taken up by another. The emotion is as it were impersonal.'[35] Similarly, if I refuse to enter into an agreement with you because I do not value your services, or opt out of it because these services are not as good as they were promised to be, I do so on grounds that are valid for anyone else. Anyone else in my position should reject such a deal. In fact you might even admit that if you were in my position you would also have rejected it.

With fellowship or love this is radically different: 'I cannot regard the call to love someone as addressed only accidentally to me without losing all sense of myself as an agent in my situation. These emotions – love, hatred, grief, and the rest – are irremediably personal. The obligation to feel them cannot be shifted; if a man tries to shift it, then automatically he puts his personality at risk.'[36] In other words, my love for you involves me as a person and not merely as an impersonal evaluator of your services or your characteristics. As we argued in section 7.1, love *values* the beloved, but here this involves my personally *bestowing* value on my beloved and not merely making an impersonal evaluation of my partner in terms of universal criteria which could be applied with equal objectivity by all other evaluators. In this respect Nygren makes an important point in claiming, as we saw in section 6.1, that love *creates* value in its object, and does not merely *recognize* it.

In both cases my valuation of you commits me to actions and attitudes in relation to you in the future, but in the first the

---

[35] Scruton, 'Emotion, practical knowledge, etc.', 526.
[36] Ibid., 527. Scruton adds that 'it may seem strange to talk of "obligation" here'.

commitment is unconditional and in the second conditional. Recognizing your value commits me conditionally: if my evaluation should prove unfounded (since your services do not come up to expectations) or if you should change and lose the value which I now recognize in you, then my commitment is cancelled. Bestowing value on you commits me unconditionally: I have personally assumed responsibility for my actions toward you in future rather than having this responsibility thrust upon me by the value which I have discovered you to have. One could also say that in the one case I *predict* my future actions to be in accordance with the discovered value, and in the other case I *decide* on my future actions and take it upon myself to ensure that these actions will be performed. In the one case my future actions depend on external circumstances (i.e. your merits or demerits) and in the other on my own intentions. 'In order to form an intention...one must, to put it simply, 'identify' with one's future self. The attitude here contrasts with another – that of 'alienation' from one's future self – in which one sees oneself not as active and determining, but as the passive victim of external forces and of one's past, being driven along under the impulse of causes that are outside one's control.'[37] In brief: in an agreement of rights and duties, my future actions toward you depend upon you, while in fellowship they depend upon me. In becoming unfaithful to our fellowship, I become unfaithful to my very self. In an agreement, I can shift the obligation to you and avoid putting myself personally at risk. Love is risky because it constitutes the self of the lover whereas agreements of rights and duties do not.

In section 2.3 we found Ortega arguing that 'we can find in love the most decisive symptom of what a person is'. For Ortega this means that who we are determines whom we love. It is now clear that the relation between love and personal identity is rather the other way around: whom we choose to love determines the identity for which we assume responsibility. In loving you I identify with you and thereby assume responsibility for remaining faithful to this identification. Earlier in the

[37] Roger Scruton, *Sexual Desire* (London 1986), 51.

present section we argued that our identity as persons is bestowed on us in the love which others have for us. To this we must now add that our identity is equally determined by the love we have for others. In both senses we owe our identity as persons to the relationships of love and fellowship which we have with others.

This point suggests a fourth sense in which relationships of love or fellowship are risky. Such relationships depend on the partners remaining faithful to each other and to the identity which they adopt in identifying with each other. As human persons, however, we are not only able to become unfaithful to each other and thus to the identity which we adopt for ourselves, but the circumstances of our lives could give rise to changes in our identity which make it difficult for us to continue to identify with each other. Our identity as persons is not immutably stable. Thus you may change in the course of time in ways which make it increasingly difficult for me to identify with you with integrity. Or I myself may change in ways which prevent me from continuing to identify with you as before. Lovers and friends can grow apart in the course of time. According to Ortega y Gasset such changes in personal identity are normal and naturally give rise to changes in our amorous commitments:

This is the normal case. A personality experiences in the course of its life two or three great transformations, which are like different stages of the same moral trajectory. Without losing solidarity, or even the fundamental homogeneity of yesterday's feelings, we notice one day that we have entered upon a new phase or modulation of our characters ... Our innermost being seems, in each one of these two or three phases, to rotate a few degrees upon its axis, to shift toward another quadrant of the universe and to orient itself toward new constellations. Is it not a meaningful coincidence that the number of true loves which the normal man usually experiences is almost always the same in number: two or three? And, moreover, that each of these loves appears chronologically localized in each of these stages in character?[38]

Ortega is right that people can change in this way. However, he is wrong in thinking that such changes simply happen to us

---

[38] Ortega y Gasset, *On Love*, 82–3.

and are beyond our control. Changes in our personal identity do not follow with unavoidable necessity from changes in the circumstances of our lives, but they do result from the ways in which we decide to respond to such changes. If lovers respond to changing circumstances in ways which are incompatible, they will grow apart. If however they seek to respond in ways which are compatible, their personal identities will change and develop in concert and they will grow together in the course of time. In this sense a relationship of love or fellowship is a joint venture which in the long run can only be maintained to the extent that both partners commit themselves and manage to grow together with integrity in the ways in which they respond to changes in the circumstances of their lives. With this we are back with the first point which we raised above: such mutual commitments can only be fulfilled in mutual freedom. Neither partner can coerce or oblige the other to remain faithful without thereby implicitly perverting the relationship into a manipulative one or into a contractual agreement. Here too love or fellowship remains a risky venture which two persons enter into in relation to each other.

The partners in such a relationship can never have cast-iron guarantees that neither of them will ever change in ways which might lead them to grow apart. In this respect too, God is not like other people. Love of God is not risky like human love since God can not only be counted on to remain faithful to his character, but his character is also stable and unlike ours it does not change. Hence believers would claim that estrangement from God cannot result from God changing and growing apart from us, but only from our becoming unfaithful to God and forsaking him. In the words of Augustine which we quoted in section 5.3 above, God's love is something 'which cannot be lost against the will'. 'No one can lose you, my God, unless he forsakes you.'

It is now clear that, if we are to look on love as a personal relationship, it is a fellowship relation and not an agreement of rights and duties. In fact, we could say that love is the paradigmatic example of the sort of relation to which we have been referring as 'fellowship'. It is also now clear why we felt uneasy at the end of section 7.1 with Van de Vate's characterization of love as a 'compact or contract or agreement'.

By interpreting love as a paradigmatic form of fellowship and thus distinguishing it from manipulative relations and agreements of rights and duties, we are now able to deal more satisfactorily with three unresolved issues which were raised in chapter 2. First, what is the relation between love and sexuality? Second, in what sense is love free, and in what sense is it 'necessitated'? Third, in what sense does love provide the lover with 'knowledge' of the beloved? Especially the two latter questions have important implications for the nature of the love of God. The next section will be devoted to these issues.

In the next chapter we will inquire how the three types of relations distinguished in this chapter can be repaired when they become broken or damaged in some way, and especially how we can become reconciled to each other when we have marred our relationships of love. This question is especially important for our understanding of the doctrine of atonement which deals with the nature of reconciliation with God. What will be the conceptual price of applying the model of love in the doctrine of atonement? In our final chapter we will examine the way in which the attitudes discussed in previous chapters are involved in a relationship of love, and what this entails for the various 'dimensions of love', including the love of God.

7.4 LOVE, SEXUALITY, FREEDOM, AND KNOWLEDGE

In this section we will try to tie up some loose ends concerning the relation of love to sexuality, freedom, and knowledge. Let us start with the issue of sexuality.

How is human love related to human sexuality? In section 2.5 we found Ortega y Gasset argue that love cannot be equated with sex. A loving relationship, in the sense in which we described it above, is quite possible without any sexual involvement between the partners. Thus a relationship of love is possible between friends, between parents and children, and between human persons and God, as well as between sexual partners. Furthermore, sexual activity is possible without being connected with a loving relationship. Thus sexual involvement can also assume the form of a manipulative relationship or an agreement of rights and duties. In the former case sexual gratification becomes something which is forcibly extorted from someone else (as in rape), while in the latter case it becomes a commodity or a service which can be bought from someone else (as in prostitution) or exchanged in the sense that one partner provides the other with gratification in exchange for being gratified by the other. In all such cases sexuality turns to lust, i.e. the desire for sexual gratification irrespective of the partner who provides it. The partner becomes either a sexual object or a mere supplier of sexual gratification. In both cases the partner is replaceable by any other. It is the gratification that is desired and not the partner.

However, sexuality can also enter into a loving relationship. This can happen in two ways. First of all, as we have pointed out in section 7.1, feelings or emotions toward someone can provide a strong motive for entering into a relationship of love with that person. In the case of sexual love, it is sexual desire which fulfils this role. Although desire does not imply love, it does provide a motive for love. Hence 'falling in love' is not to be seen as a transition from the absence of love to the presence of love, but rather as the sudden acquisition of this motive.[39] However, sexual emotions are passing states whereas a loving relationship involves lasting commitments. Hence the emotions could motivate the relationship in the sense of initiating it, but cannot provide its lasting motive or purpose. In the long run, the relationship has to be valued for its own sake and thus provide its own motivation. Lovers come to value each other and their relationship for its own sake and not merely as a means for fulfilling their sexual desires. According to Scruton this explains why the course of desire is not the same as the course of love: love has a tendency to grow with time, while desire has a tendency to wither, and eventually desire is replaced by love based in trust and companionship.[40] In this way it is possible

---

[39] See Scruton, *Sexual Desire*, 238–9.   [40] Ibid., 244.

that the very passionate love that a husband and wife had for each other at the beginning of their marriage is weathered with age and deepened with the trials it survives. In such cases this love becomes more like a friendship without losing its sexual character.[41] But then, sexuality is no longer the *motivation* of love but rather its *expression*. This is the second way in which sexuality can enter into a loving relationship. 'Looking, caressing, and kissing are voluntary actions, but may be filled with love, because the agent himself can *mean* them in love. Such actions can be given all the structure of intentional communication; I may gaze at you with the intention that you recognize my love, by recognizing that such is my intention.'[42] But the sexual expression can only be meant in this way, when it can also be experienced thus by the beloved.

If the sexual experience can be received as an expression of love, it can also be used by the lover to express his love, since he can intend his love through it. This alone makes the experience into a vehicle of love ... Love can be felt *in* the experience of arousal, so that love becomes the arousal, as love becomes the caress, the kiss or the glance. This is what is meant by tenderness: the lover caresses and kisses his beloved, intending thereby to produce the perception of love. Such tenderness is an end in itself. The expressive gesture is a revelation of what I am and mean, and as such it is complete.[43]

Is love free or somehow 'necessitated'? In the previous sections we argued that love is by definition free. My feelings or emotions might motivate me to enter into and to maintain a loving relationship with you, but they neither coerce nor oblige me as a manipulative force might coerce or an agreement of rights and duties might oblige me to do so. Love can neither be extorted nor earned, it must be freely given. In the words of Countess Marie of Champagne: 'Lovers give each other everything freely, under no compulsion or necessity.' Thus, if I love you, I do so because I want to and not because I am forced to or obliged to.

---

[41] See Ilham Dilman, *Love and Human Separateness* (Oxford 1987), 90.
[42] Scruton, *Sexual Desire*, 245.   [43] Ibid., 248.

However, the fact that love is in this sense free does not mean that it is arbitrary. On the contrary, I have every reason for loving you. Thus my feelings or emotions (including my sexual feelings) might motivate me to love you, and in the long run my loving relationship with you might also provide its own motivation. As we have argued in the previous section, by identifying with you in love, our relationship becomes for me constitutive for my very self as a person. In becoming unfaithful to it, I would become unfaithful to myself and this would be the most unreasonable thing which I could do. As soon as I decide to let my identity as a self be constituted by my relationship with you, it follows that I can only renounce the relationship by renouncing myself and in fact assuming another self. Thus there is a sense in which we could say that love is 'necessitated': not because it is coercive or obligatory, but because I would have to become untrue to myself and in this sense unreasonable in order to renounce it. Becoming unfaithful to my love would be like acting against my conscience, since my conscience is my very self. I love you because I want to, and *I* could only cease to want this by becoming another 'I'. If we were to ask a lover why he does not become unfaithful to his beloved, this should strike *him* (being the person he is) as the most unreasonable thing to ask of him. For *him* his love is 'necessitated', not because he is coerced or obliged, but because, being the self he is, *he* cannot reasonably do otherwise any more than he can act against his conscience.

This 'necessity' is, however, not a lack of ability. Unfortunately in our moral weakness and on account of the instability of our characters, we human beings are all too often able to become untrue to ourselves and therefore to act against our conscience or become unfaithful to our loves. Because of our moral weakness of will and instability of character, society introduces legal sanctions in order to prevent the social chaos which could result from our lack of rationality. If we were always rational and remained true to ourselves, such legal sanctions would be unnecessary and society would naturally continue to function smoothly. Van de Vate explains this point as follows: the legal order functions as a backstop for the moral order, rightfully enforcing the civil peace which makes morality possible. Regarded in this way the contrast between morality and the law is a contrast between one part of the moral order and another – between the smooth, silent, automatic functioning of moral controls to which we are trained to aspire and the harsh justice which must now and then support it. According to van de Vate the relation of romantic love to marriage exemplifies this general conception of the relation of morals to the law: 'If everyone could always be trusted to do the right thing, then the tacit warmth of love would suffice to perpetuate the moral order. Persons in or out of love are sometimes untrustworthy, however, threatening not only one another but also such innocent third parties as the children they have produced. Therefore society employs explicit laws and forceful penalties to keep their behaviour within reasonable bounds.'[44] The legal institution of marriage is therefore not a logical consequence of the nature of a loving relationship between sexual lovers, but rather an admission of the moral weakness and instability which characterizes the partners in such a relationship as human beings. Thus the words of Jesus reported in Mark 12:25 could be seen to express an important conceptual point: 'When they rise from the dead, they neither marry nor are given in marriage, but are like angels in heaven.' If we were to love each other perfectly, like the angels in heaven, then marriage contracts would become superfluous. The Countess of Champagne was therefore correct in pointing out that a loving relationship is not the same as a marriage bond – and definitely not the same as a marriage bond in feudal society. She was wrong, however, in concluding that a marriage bond excludes a loving relationship. The fact that love is necessarily free does not entail that it is uncommitted. On the contrary, it entails a mutual commitment which the lovers freely enter and maintain in relation to each other. In a loving relationship between human sexual partners, it is therefore perfectly natural that they should admit their own human weakness and instability to each other and want to back up their own commitments to each other with the backstop of a contractual bond. But in that case

---

[44] Van de Vate, *Romantic Love*, 33.

they marry because they love each other; they do not love each other because they are contractually obliged to do so by their marriage bond.

In section 7.2 we argued that the consequence of interpreting the relationship between God and ourselves as a personal relationship is that both we and God are free persons in relation to each other. Thus God in his love freely identifies with us and makes our salvation his own concern. Unlike us, however, God does not suffer from moral weakness or instability of character. We can therefore *count* on him to remain true to his character, in a way in which he cannot count on us. Nevertheless, we should not *presume* on God since as a Person he remains free in his love for us. He does not love us because we somehow force or oblige him to do so, nor because he is somehow 'necessitated by his essential nature', as Nygren seems to hold. God loves us because he wants to and not because he lacks the ability to reject us.[45] Similarly, our love for God is also free. God does not want us to love him because we are forced or obliged to or because we lack the ability to turn our backs on him.[46] As we pointed out at the end of section 3.3, our love for God entails that we identify with him in the sense of making his will our own. However, we would not be able to do this if God did not himself in his trinitarian way *motivate* us: the Son makes God's will known to us, the Father enables us to do it, and the Spirit inspires us. But this does not exclude the need that we should freely choose to identify with God's will in love. This is well illustrated in St Bernard's views on human freedom to which we referred in section 4.1: without God in his grace providing us with the *liberum consilium* to know his will and to be able to do it, as well as with the *liberum a miseria* to be inspired and have a 'taste' for making his will our own, we will not be motivated to do so. However, although this is necessary, it is not a causally sufficient condition for our loving God: as persons we still have to exercise our *liberum arbitrium* and decide freely to turn to God. In the end God grants us the ability

---

[45] For a discussion of this claim in the light of the doctrine of divine *impeccabilitas*, see chapter 4 of my *Speaking of a Personal God*.

[46] For a discussion of this claim in the light of the doctrine of the irresistibility of Grace, see chapter 3 of my *Speaking of a Personal God*.

also to turn away from him. Doing so is of course 'rationally impossible' in the sense explained above. For a self who finds his eternal happiness in the love of God, it would be absurd to suggest that he might turn away from God. Since for him loving God is 'rationally necessary', he would dismiss the suggestion with the words attributed to Luther: 'Here I stand, I can do no other!' But this 'can do no other' is not an avowal of coercion or obligation but rather the expression of a motivated *liberum arbitrium*. The fact that God allows us as persons to retain the ability to turn away from him, excludes any form of universalism which holds that God's love *must* triumph in the end and cause all to love him. In the words of John Burnaby,

dogmatic universalism contradicts the very nature of love, by claiming for it the kind of omnipotence which it refuses. Love cannot, because it will not, compel the surrender of a single heart that holds out against it. Without the symbolism of warfare, of struggle and victory, our picture of the Christian life would be incomplete. But the comparison breaks down at the crucial point, for all the fighting of this world is with the weapon of force. Love never forces, and therefore there can be no certainty that it will overcome. But there may, and there must, be an unconquerable hope.[47]

Love and knowledge. Does love enable the lover to know the beloved, or does it clothe the beloved with illusions, as Stendhal claims? Does love make the lover blind or perspicacious about the beloved? Usually when we think of knowing something or someone, we think of knowing what characteristics that something or someone has. Of course love does require this kind of knowledge about the beloved, since, as we argued in section 7.1, the lover is intimately concerned about the continuance of the beloved's good characteristics and the diminishing of the bad ones. But then the lover cannot be blind to the beloved's characteristics. However, Ortega is correct in pointing out that, although love requires this kind of knowledge, it does not of itself provide it: we are more or less perspicacious or obtuse in love in the same way as we ordinarily are in judging our fellow beings.[48] In other words, love is not a privileged source of

---

[47] Burnaby, *Amor Dei*, 318.   [48] Ortega y Gasset, *On Love*, 35.

knowledge *about* the beloved, even though it does demand that
the lover should seek to acquire such knowledge. In the popular
song the lover states his dual aim in relation to his beloved with
the words: 'Getting to know you, getting to know all about
you.' The first half of this aim necessarily requires the second,
but it is not the same as the second. In what sense is 'getting to
know you' more than merely 'getting to know all about you'?

In section 2.4 we suggested that love enables the lover to
know the beloved *as a person*. What kind of 'knowledge' is this?
Ilham Dilman answers this question as follows:

We say we know someone with whom we have worked, someone by
whose side we have fought. In this sense we know a friend, a comrade,
a colleague, a neighbour; a husband knows his wife and wife her
husband. Here 'I know him' means more than 'I know what he is
like', though it includes that. In an important sense of 'know' if I
know him there are certain things I can ask of him, certain things I can
say to him, which I cannot ask of or say to a stranger. I can trust him
and vouch for him. At any rate I would feel let down if he lied to me.
Not simply because I was deceived *about* him, but because I was
deceived *by* him. In deceiving me what he does is to undo the
relationship of trust between us. We have to get back to it before I can
say I know him in the same way. Thus he may say he is sorry and I
may forgive him. That is the restoration of contact. Such contact has
to be sustained if I am to be able to continue to say that I know him.[49]

Love is not the *source* of this kind of knowledge, it *is* this kind of
knowledge. To know someone in this sense *is* to have fellowship
with or to love that person. The antithesis of this kind of
knowledge is not ignorance but estrangement. Thus the stranger
who says 'I don't know anyone around here' is not ignorant but
isolated.

Knowing someone in this sense means trusting or having faith
in that person. It therefore entails taking the risk of relying on
that person. This is not the risk of being mistaken but of being
let down. As we argued in section 7.2, this is precisely the sense
in which love is risky. Furthermore, such trust is expressed in the
unreserved candour in which the lover permits himself to say
things to or ask things of the beloved which he would not dream

---

[49] Dilman, *Human Separateness*, 121.

to say to or ask of a stranger. In this way it makes sense to say: 'I do not know him well enough to ask him that. You ask him, you know him better.' Of course, such candour also involves the risk of affronting the beloved by the things you say or ask. But then your love makes you trust that this will not be the case. Knowing someone therefore entails relying that the other will respond to you in fellowship or love. For this reason knowing someone requires a relationship of reciprocity. It takes two for there to be knowledge of another person in the same sense as it takes two for there to be a loving relationship. I could know many things about someone without that person knowing anything about me, but it would be a contradiction in terms to say: 'I know him but he does not know me.'

This also applies to knowing God. Here, too, knowing God means trusting God and consequently having unreserved candour in relation to God. This is precisely the sense in which in section 3.2 we saw St Bernard argue that the believer's love for God is *ardent*: it 'loses all thought of the greatness of its object' and overcomes all reticence in approaching God. The believer takes the risk of setting aside all such restraint, in the confident expectation of not being turned away by God. Of course the risk involved in thus knowing God is infinitely less than the risk involved in knowing other people. No matter how much we love and therefore know someone else, the chances are that our beloved will let us down from time to time, just as we will let our beloved down from time to time. When that happens, we have damaged our relationship and need to restore it if we are to continue to know each other as before. How are such loving relationships damaged or broken, and what is involved in restoring them? Let us in the next chapter consider these questions.

CHAPTER 8

Breaking and restoring relationships

8.1 RESTORING HUMAN RELATIONS

In section 1.3 we argued that Christians understand the meaning of their lives in the light of the way in which they are related to God. Life is significant because it is lived *coram Deo*, in the presence of God, and ultimate happiness consists in being in the right relation with God. Through sin, however, our relationship with God has been drastically disrupted. The fundamental religious issue which we all have to face, therefore, is how this relationship can be restored. How can we attain ultimate happiness by being reconciled with God? Basically, this is the issue with which the doctrine of atonement has to deal: 'The English word 'atonement' is derived from the words 'at-one-ment', to make two parties at one, to reconcile two parties one to another. It means essentially reconciliation ... In current usage, the phrase 'to atone for' means the undertaking of a course of action designed to undo the consequences of a wrong act with a view to the restoration of the relationship broken by the wrong act.'[1]

The nature of this reconciliation depends of course upon the nature of the relationship which has to be restored, and the variety of theories of atonement in Christian theology derive in the end from the variety of conceptual models in terms of which Christian theologians have tried to understand the divine–human relationship. In the previous chapter we distinguished

---

[1] James Atkinson, 'Atonement', in Alan Richardson (ed.), *A Dictionary of Christian Theology* (London 1969), 18. See also John Burnaby, *Christian Words and Christian Meanings* (London 1955), 95–6.

three basic types of relationship which could hold between human beings and argued that all three have from time to time been employed as conceptual models for the relationship between God and human beings. In this chapter[2] we will trace the implications which these models have for the theories of atonement which are based upon them, and see whether the model of love is adequate in this respect. Before we can do that, however, we must first examine how these three types of relationship can go wrong and what is required in order for them to be restored.

All three types of relationship discussed in the previous chapter can go wrong in various ways and then stand in need of repair. However, the sense in which the relationship can go wrong and the way in which it could be repaired, is different in each of these relation types. In a manipulative relation the passive partner becomes (in Strawson's phrase) an object 'to be managed or handled or cured or trained' by the active partner. If the condition of the passive partner should go wrong in some way or other, then it is up to the active partner to do something about it, since only the active partner is an agent in the relation. If the condition of the passive partner is remedied through the efforts of the active partner, the latter gets all the credit. If however no improvement is brought about, the active partner is the only one who can bear the blame. Since there is only one agent in this relationship, there is only one agent who can be responsible for bringing about what has to be done, and therefore only one candidate for both praise and blame.

In an agreement of rights and duties I commit myself to do certain things which you need to be done in return for the right to expect certain services from you. The relation breaks down, however, when one of us fails in his or her duty to provide the service to which the other is entitled, and thereby forfeits the right to whatever the other partner had a duty to do for him or her in return. Thus if you fail to fulfil your duties to me, my obligation to do something for you in return is suspended, and the agreement between us breaks down.

---

[2] In this chapter I make use of some material from my paper on 'Atonement and reconciliation', *Religious Studies* 28 (1992).

Basically there are three ways in which this sort of broken relation between us could be repaired and the balance of rights and duties between us restored. First, you could try after all to do for me that to which I am entitled, or, if this is no longer possible, you could perform some other equivalent service for me. In this way you would yet satisfy my rights and in so doing earn anew your right to the services which it was my duty to provide for you under the agreement. Thus the balance of rights and duties between us will be restored. However, you might for some reason or other be unwilling or unable to satisfy my rights. If you cannot or will not give me *satisfaction*, I could restore the balance by *punishing* you, i.e. I could withhold from you the services to which you would have been entitled if you had fulfilled your duties toward me. If you have borne your punishment and paid your penalty, your debt toward me is eliminated and the balance of rights and duties between us is restored. Providing satisfaction and being punished are therefore two ways in which the guilty party could *earn* reinstatement in the relation which he or she has broken. There is a third way in which a breach in a relation of rights and duties could also be restored: I could decide to *condone* what you have done by waiving my right to the duties which you have failed to fulfil. I decide that the service which you have failed to provide is not important to me and that it would not affect my interests if we were simply to amend the agreement in order to let you off the hook.

Relations of fellowship are those in which two persons identify with each other by each treating the other's interest as his or her own. In serving your interest as my own, I love you as myself. Owing to human weakness, we are all too often unable to sustain this sort of fellowship consistently. Through selfishness I put my own interests first, and intentionally or unintentionally act in ways which are contrary to your interests and thus cause you injury. Irrespective of whether the injury is serious or trivial, I have marred our relationship and given you grounds for resentment. In being resentful, you endorse the fact that our relationship has been damaged, if not broken.

Such a breach in our relationship can only be healed if you

refuse to be resentful, and instead adopt the opposite attitude, i.e. willingness to forgive. You have to consider the breach in our relationship a greater evil than the injury I have caused you, and therefore be willing to continue identifying with me and treating my interests as your own in spite of what I have done to you. 'The person who has been wronged can accept the wrong done to him: he can absorb as it were in his own suffering the consequences of the wrong that has caused it.'[3]

Such forgiveness can only be both real and effective on certain conditions. Thus it can only be *real* if there is something to forgive. It would make no sense to say that you forgive me unless I really caused you injury by failing to seek your interests as my own. In this respect forgiveness should not be confused with condonation. If you were to *condone* my action, you would thereby *deny* that it is an action which caused you injury, and thus also deny that there is anything to forgive. If, on the other hand, you *forgive* me for what I have done, you claim that my action did cause you injury, but that you would rather bear the injury than abandon the fellowship which I have marred by my action. 'The power to forgive is not to be obtained for nothing, it must be bought at a price, it must be paid for with the suffering of him who has been sinned against.'[4] One of the basic characteristics of forgiveness is therefore that the one who forgives is the one who suffers.[5] Thus forgiveness costs you something whereas condonation is a denial that there are any costs involved.[6]

Your forgiveness can only be *effective* in restoring our broken fellowship, on condition that I am sincerely penitent and express both contrition for damaging our fellowship and the desire that it should be restored. Forgiveness is your willingness

---

[3] Burnaby, *Christian Words and Christian Meanings*, 90.

[4] O. C. Quick, *Essays in Orthodoxy* (London 1916), 92–3.

[5] See J. Edwin Orr, *Full Surrender* (Edinburgh 1951), 22. See also Mark W. Thomsen, 'Jesus crucified and the mission of the church', *International Review of Missions* 77 (1988), 262.

[6] For a more detailed analysis of the differences between forgiveness and condonation, see R. S. Downie, 'Forgiveness', *Philosophical Quarterly* 15 (1965). See also Lucas, *Freedom and Grace*, 78f. An example of someone who interprets forgiveness in terms of condonation or pardon is A. Alhonsaari, *Prayer. An Analysis of Theological Terminology* (Helsinki 1973), 161f.

to identify with me in spite of what I did. But if I do not through penitence renounce the fact that I have broken our fellowship, your identification with me would not restore the relationship but rather entail your acquiescence in my breaking of it. It follows that my asking your forgiveness *entails* penitence and a change of heart on my part as well as the expression of these in penitential action.[7] The one would be incoherent without the other. 'To ask to be forgiven is in part to acknowledge that the attitude displayed in our actions was such as might properly be resented and in part to repudiate that attitude for the future (or at least for the immediate future); and to forgive is to accept the repudiation and to forswear the resentment.'[8]

Although my penitence is in this sense a *necessary* condition for your forgiveness, it is not a *sufficient* condition. My penitence can neither cause nor earn your forgiveness. Whether you are to identify with me again depends on your freely deciding to do so. It takes two to repair a personal fellowship just as it takes two to establish it in the first place. Forgiveness can only be freely given, and when it is forced or earned it ceases to be forgiveness. The same is true of penance and of my attempts to make good the injury I have caused. These cannot be more than an expression of my penitence or an attempt to put into practice my repudiation of what I have done. They can neither bring about nor earn your forgiveness since that remains up to you to decide. This is what distinguishes penitence and penance from punishment and satisfaction. Through bearing punishment or making satisfaction I can *earn* reinstatement in a relationship of rights and duties, and what I have earned you are obliged to give. Penitence and penance, however, can never *earn* reinstatement in a relation of fellowship, and therefore cannot in the same way create obligations. Furthermore, although penitence and penance are a necessary condition for forgiveness, punishment and satisfaction would make forgiveness unnecessary. If full satisfaction has been made or appropriate pun-

---

[7] 'Etymologically, of course, there is no difference between penance and penitence; both come from the same Latin source, *poenitentia*, but the existence of the two words in English makes it possible for us to distinguish between penitence, as an inner state, and penance, as a manifestation of it in action.' H. A. Hodges, *The Pattern of Atonement* (London 1955), 54.   [8] Strawson, *Freedom and Resentment*, 6.

ishment has been borne, there is nothing left to forgive. It follows that forgiveness after satisfaction has been fully made is no forgiveness at all.[9] Clearly then, I can never *demand* your forgiveness as a right which I have earned. I can only *ask* it as a favour. In asking your forgiveness (as in asking you anything else) I acknowledge my dependence on your free decision for granting my request. I may hope that you will forgive. I might even count on you to forgive me when I am penitent. But my penitence does not entitle me to your forgiveness and therefore I may not presume upon it.

If I repudiate the damage I have done to our fellowship by confessing myself in the wrong and by an act of penance try to demonstrate the sincerity of this repudiation, and if I express my desire for the restoration of our fellowship by asking your forgiveness; and if you, by forgiving me, show your willingness to identify with me again, then our fellowship will not only be restored, but might also be deepened and strengthened. In terms of the kind of 'knowledge' which we discussed in section 7.4, we have come to 'know' each other better than before.

We shall be to one another what we were before, save for one important difference. I know now that you are a person who can forgive, that you prefer to have suffered rather than to resent, and that to keep me as a friend, or to avoid becoming my enemy, is more important to you than to maintain your own rights. And you know that I am a person who is not too proud to acknowledge his fault, and that your goodwill is worth more to me than the maintenance of my own cause... Forgiveness does not only forestall or remove enmity: it strengthens love.[10]

In sum, whereas broken fellowship can only be restored by penitence and forgiveness, broken agreements of rights and duties are restored by satisfaction or by punishment or by condonation. If we do not clearly distinguish fellowship from an agreement of rights and duties, we will also tend to confuse penitence and penance with satisfaction or punishment, and forgiveness with condonation. We now have to see how these

---

[9] See G. W. H. Lampe, 'The atonement: Law and love', in A. R. Vidler, *Soundings* (Cambridge 1966), 185.

[10] Burnaby, *Christian Words and Christian Meanings*, 87.

distinctions apply to our understanding of the relation between God and human persons, and what this entails for our understanding of the doctrine of atonement.

8.2 ATONEMENT AND GRACE

A central axiom in the history of theology, and especially in Reformation theology, is that of *Sola gratia*: human salvation is by divine grace alone and therefore all the credit for our salvation should go to God and we have no grounds for claiming any of it for ourselves. The most radical way in which this primacy of grace could be maintained is by means of a manipulative model in which divine grace is the exclusive and sufficient cause of our salvation. In a theology which describes the divine–human relation in these terms, sin is usually not interpreted in relational terms, but viewed rather as a *condition* or state of corruption in which human beings find themselves, and which manifests itself in their sinful behaviour. Salvation does therefore not consist in reconciling a broken relationship but rather in being freed from a condition of corruption. This can exclusively be brought about by the action of an omnipotent God. God's agency is the necessary and sufficient condition for human salvation. The human partner in this relationship becomes a passive object ' to be managed or handled or cured or trained' by God, who is the only active partner in the relationship. The cause of this state of human corruption is the original sin of Adam which

carried permanent pollution with it, and a pollution which, because of the solidarity of the human race, would affect not only Adam but all his descendants as well. As a result of the fall the father of the human race could only pass on a depraved human nature to his offspring. From that unholy source sin flows on as an impure stream to all the generations of men, polluting everyone and everything with which it comes in contact.[11]

To the extent that the fall was the result of Adam's free decision to rebel against God, he is responsible for depriving

---

[11] Louis Berkhof, *Systematic Theology* (Grand Rapids 1982; 2nd. edn.), 221.

himself and all his descendants of the status of free agents before God and thus causing all human beings to be subject to a state of corruption. Sometimes, however, even the fall itself is said to result from the eternal decrees of God. In that case the human partner in the divine–human relation can at no time be other than a passive object of divine agency. From the very beginning God alone is an agent in his relationship to human beings. Thus John Calvin in his most uncompromisingly supralapsarian moments could argue that

before the first man was created, God in his eternal councel had determined what he willed to be done with the whole human race. In the hidden councel of God it was determined that Adam should fall from the unimpaired condition of his nature, and by his defection should involve all his posterity in sentence of eternal death. Upon the same decree depends the distinction between elect and reprobate: as he adopted some for himself for salvation, he destined others for eternal ruin.[12]

The theological advantage of this model is that it radically underpins the axiom of *Sola gratia* and excludes every trace of a 'theology of merit': 'For it is by his grace you are saved, through trusting him; it is not your own doing. It is God's gift, not a reward for work done. There is nothing for anyone to boast of' (Ephesians 2: 8–9). Since human beings cannot be agents in relation to God, they can in no way be the agents of meritorious acts before God. Thus human salvation is radically by grace alone, and can in no way be earned or merited by human actions. All credit belongs to God alone. *Soli Deo gloria*! However, the conceptual price to be paid for this advantage is rather high.

In the first place, if human beings are not agents in relation to God, they cannot perform meritorious acts, but neither can they perform acts which make them guilty before God. If we are merely objects of divine manipulation, we can in no way be held responsible for the way we behave or for the state in which we are. Human beings cannot claim any credit for being saved

---

[12] John Calvin, 'Articles concerning predestination', in J. K. S. Reid (ed.), *Calvin: Theological Treatises* (Philadelphia 1956), 179.

from their state of corruption. But neither can they be blamed for being in it in the first place.

Secondly, if God is the only agent in the relation, he is not only responsible for our salvation, but also for our state of corruption. Both the salvation (of some) and the eternal ruin (of others) result from God's 'eternal councel', which also 'determined that Adam should fall from the unimpaired condition of his nature, and by his defection should involve all his posterity in sentence of eternal death'. Then God is not only the origin of all good but also the author of all evil. It is logically incoherent to claim, as Calvin does in the *Articles concerning Predestination*, that 'while the will of God is the supreme and primary cause of all things, and God holds the devil and the godless subject to his will, nevertheless God cannot be called the cause of sin, nor the author of evil, nor subject to any guilt.'

Thirdly, on this model it becomes rather difficult to explain how the death of Christ on Calvary was *necessary* for our salvation. Our salvation results from God's 'eternal councel' rather than from the merit of Christ. The latter is at most a contingently chosen means for effecting the former, but in no way logically necessary. It would be quite conceivable for an omnipotent God to cancel our state of corruption by an exercise of his infinite power alone. Thus, in the articles quoted above, Calvin declares explicitly that 'while we are elected in Christ, nevertheless that God reckons us among his own is prior in order to his making us members of Christ'. But then the question arises as to what the merit of Christ adds to the *prior* fact that 'God reckons us among his own'. A similar question can be raised with reference to the following statement by Calvin:

When we treat of the merit of Christ, we do not place the beginning in him, but ascend to the ordination of God as the primary cause, because of his mere good pleasure he appointed a Mediator to purchase salvation for us... There is nothing to prevent the justification of man from being the gratuitous result of the mere mercy of God, and, at the same time, to prevent the merit of Christ from intervening in subordination to this mercy.[13]

[13] John Calvin, *Institutes of the Christian Religion* II.17.1., trans. Henry Beveridge (London 1953).

If the 'mere mercy of God' is sufficient, it is hard to see why the 'intervention of the merit of Christ' is necessary for the 'purchase of salvation for us'.[14]

8.3 ATONEMENT AND SATISFACTION

These difficulties can all be avoided by describing the divine–human relationship in terms of an agreement of rights and duties. In this model each partner is a personal agent who accepts certain obligations toward the other and can be held responsible for fulfilling these obligations. In the Christian tradition the covenant relationship between God and human persons has often been interpreted on the analogy of an agreement of rights and duties. Thus, according to F. W. Dillistone,

the archetypal model in this tradition is simply that of two individuals, each respecting the other's identity yet desiring some closer association with him. The essential pattern of action in such circumstances is that of give and take. Each commits himself to give: each, it follows, expresses his readiness to receive. Each deprives himself of some portion of his own strength or skill or possessions: each receives some valued addition to his own limited resources. While the process of interchange continues all is well. But what happens if one party clings tenaciously to that which he has promised to give? Or snatches more than he is entitled to receive? By such acts he becomes guilty ... That which he has withheld or snatched he must restore in full measure ... Any breaking of covenant obligations must therefore be summarily dealt with according to the uncomplicated law of direct retaliation.[15]

When this model is applied in this way to the divine–human relationship, then God is said to commit himself to providing us with eternal happiness while we in turn commit ourselves to honouring God by living our lives in obedience to his will. However, as sinners we fail to keep our side of the bargain. We

---

[14] Stephen Strehle shows how this feature in Calvinism implies that 'the work which Christ offered to the Father ... is made superfluous when it comes to applying the work in justification ... One wonders why the Father would deem it so necessary to send his innocent Son to death in the first place.' See Strehle, 'Calvinism, Augustinianism, and the will of God' in *Theologische Zeitschrift* 47 (1992), 231–2.

[15] F. W. Dillistone, *The Christian Understanding of Atonement* (London 1968), 212–13.

do not honour God with our obedience, we transgress the law of God and we live lives which are contrary to his will. In this way we do not give to God what is his right under the covenant agreement, and thereby forfeit our right to eternal happiness. Through our sinful behaviour we become guilty of radically disturbing the balance of rights and duties between God and ourselves. As we explained in section 8.1, there are three ways in which this balance can be restored: punishment or satisfaction or condonation. Thus, in the words of H. A. Hodges, 'our relation to God as sinners is this: We must pay a penalty appropriate and adequate to our wrong-doing, we must undergo punishment adequate to our guilt, we must make satisfaction adequate to the affront which we administer to God's honour, and by these means or by direct appeal to his mercy we must propitiate him.'[16]

God's justice prevents him from condoning our sins. He cannot take our rebellion lightly as though it does not really seriously damage his rights. Hence an appeal to God's mercy cannot take on the form of a request that he should condone our sins. From his side God could redress the balance between us by punishment adequate to our guilt. Thus he could withhold from us the eternal happiness to which we would otherwise have been entitled and bestow on us 'the pangs of eternal death' which are our just due. The only way in which we could avoid this fate, would be as yet 'to make satisfaction adequate to the affront which we administer to God's honour'. If this were possible, we could through good works *earn* reinstatement into the covenant agreement which we have broken and again merit the eternal happiness to which we were entitled under the agreement. This would seem to open the way again for a theology of merit in which we can claim the credit for our own salvation rather than saying *Soli Deo gloria*! and giving all the credit to God. As we argued above, the chief advantage of employing a manipulative model is precisely the radical exclusion of this kind of theology.

The way of satisfaction can only allow for a theology of merit on condition that sinners have the *capacity* to make adequate

---

[16] Hodges, *The Pattern of Atonement*, 45.

satisfaction. However, since God is infinite, it could be argued that our guilt before him is also infinite. The satisfaction required to restore the balance of rights and duties between God and ourselves is therefore far beyond our means. Since it is the achievement of Christ that he provided adequate satisfaction in our stead, all the credit for our salvation goes to him and not to us. Salvation still has to be earned, but by Christ rather than by us. *Soli Christo gloria*! This is the line of argument usually attributed to Anselm, whose theory of atonement is often interpreted as the classical example of a view based on this model. Thus Dillistone summarizes Anselm's position as follows:

Anselm's diagnosis of the human situation is fundamental to his argument. Man's failure to give due honour to God constitutes a weight, a debt, a doom. If he is to be saved from irretrievable disaster he must in some way make satisfaction. Yet it is obvious that this is quite outside his competence. How then can God's original purpose for man be fulfilled? Only if a new man can be found, a man who by perfect obedience can satisfy God's honour himself and by some work of complete supererogation can provide the means of paying the existing debt of his fellows. Such a one was the God-Man. By his unswerving obedience throughout his earthly life he perfectly fulfilled his own obligations as man: by his willing acceptance of death he established such a treasury of merit as would avail to pay the debts of all mankind if they would simply look to him, accept his grace and be saved.[17]

When developed along these lines, this model would seem to provide the basis for a theory of atonement which has all the advantages and none of the disadvantages of the manipulative model. It avoids a theology of merit without having to turn human beings into objects of divine manipulation. Thereby it can explain how we rather than God are the agents of our own downfall. God can in no way be held responsible for the fact that we have broken our agreement of rights and duties with him. Finally, this theory is able to explain how the work of Christ is essential for restoring the relation between God and ourselves and saving us from eternal punishment: only Christ is able to

---

[17] Dillistone, *The Christian Understanding of Atonement*, 193. I leave aside the question of whether this is the only legitimate interpretation of Anselm's position.

bring about the required satisfaction which is far beyond our means to provide. To him be all thanksgiving and glory. Nevertheless, these advantages are achieved at a price.

First of all, as we have pointed out in section 7.3, people participate in such agreements for the sake of the advantage which each party can gain for him or herself. Under such an agreement I do not value you for who you are but for the services which you are to provide for me, and you too value me merely as a provider of services under the agreement. As such you are not irreplaceable for me, nor am I for you. Anybody else who could provide the same services would do just as well. If this is the sort of relationship we have with God, it means that we do not love God for himself alone, but merely as a provider of eternal happiness. To put it crudely: we value heaven more than we value God. On the other hand, God does not love me for myself alone, but merely for the obedience with which I render him honour. To put it crudely: God values his own honour more than he values me. For this reason, too, I am replaceable for God by anybody else who is able to satisfy his honour adequately. It does not matter to him whether it is I or Christ in my stead who does so, provided his honour is satisfied. If, as we have argued, the ultimate value of my very existence is bestowed on it by the fact that God loves *me* and not merely my services apart from me, then it is clear that this model entails a concept of God which is radically defective from a religious point of view.

Secondly, the account which this theory of atonement provides of the work of Christ can hardly be said to do justice to the unity between the Persons of the Trinity. In this respect it is illuminating to recall the way in which in section 3.3 we saw St Bernard of Clairvaux distinguishing the *unity* between the Persons of the Trinity from the kind of *union* which a believer seeks with God:

There is in them [the Father and the Son] ... but one essence and one will, and where there is only one, there can be no agreement or combining or incorporation or anything of that kind. For there must be at least two wills for there to be agreement, and two essences for there to be combining and uniting in agreement. There is none of these things in the Father and the Son since they have neither two essences nor two wills... If anyone would affirm that there is agreement between the Father and the Son, I do not contest it provided that it is understood that there is not a union of wills but a unity of will. But we think of God and man as dwelling in each other in a very different way, because their wills and their substances are distinct and different; that is, their substances are not intermingled, yet their wills are in agreement; and this union is for them a communion of wills and an agreement in charity. Happy is this union if you experience it, but compared with the other, it is no union at all.[18]

Clearly, if the unity of the Father and the Son involves such a unity of will and essence, then their purpose and attitude toward us should be similarly identical: the purpose and attitude of the Son should be a direct expression of that of the Father. The substitution model of atonement entails a very different view of the relationship between the Father and the Son. In the words of David Smith:

The theory stands in direct and open contradiction to the fundamental article of the Christian faith, that Christ is one with God – one in character and purpose and disposition toward the children of men. It places a gulf between God and Christ, representing God as the stern Judge who insisted on the execution of justice, and Christ as the pitiful Saviour who interposes and satisfies his legal demand and appeases his righteous wrath. They are not one either in their attitudes toward sinners or in the part which they play. God is propitiated, Christ propitiates; God inflicts the punishment, Christ suffers it; God exacts the debt, Christ pays it. This is the fundamental postulate of the theory, God and Christ are not one in character or purpose or disposition toward sinners.[19]

Of course, this does not contradict the claim that the Father *agrees* with the Son adopting the 'character or purpose or disposition toward sinners' which he does. After all, it is the Father who 'gives' or 'sends' the Son to act as Mediator. However, 'agreeing' does not amount to 'sharing'. In terms of St Bernard's distinction, 'there must be at least two wills for

[18] St Bernard, *Song of Songs*, Sermon 71.
[19] David Smith, *The Atonement in the Light of History and the Modern Spirit* (London 1918), 106.

there to be agreement'. Agreement between the Father and the
Son would account for no more than a 'union of wills' and not
for the 'unity of will' which constitutes the unity between the
Father and the Son. Clearly, therefore, a theory of atonement
which is based on the conceptual model of an agreement of
rights and duties runs into both religious and theological
difficulties. Let us see whether these can be avoided by using the
model of fellowship or love.

8.4 ATONEMENT AND THE LOVE OF GOD

A relation of fellowship or love is one in which two personal
agents mutually identify with each other. Each partner in the
relationship freely identifies with the other by making the
interests of the other his or her own, and by pursuing these as his
or her own interests. Applied to our relationship with God, this
means that God identifies with us by making our salvation and
eternal happiness his own concern, and we identify with God by
making God's will our own or, in the words of St Bernard which
we quoted above, we seek to establish with God 'a communion
of wills and an agreement in charity'. Furthermore, this mutual
identification is necessarily free in the sense that one partner can
neither compel nor oblige the other to reciprocate the fellowship. In this sense we cannot *compel* God to love us. God
remains free in his love. Likewise, God cannot compel us to
reciprocate his love for us, since then our response would not be
love or fellowship. Neither can we *oblige* God to identify with us
by somehow earning his love through doing his will. This is
what distinguishes loving fellowship from an agreement of
rights and duties. God's love cannot be earned. Not because the
price is too high or our efforts too feeble, but because it is love,
and by definition love cannot be earned (nor given away
unearned). We simply cannot talk about love or fellowship in
terms of rewards which might or might not be merited. Thus we
cannot earn eternal salvation by doing God's will. Our salvation
remains a gracious favour freely bestowed on us by God. Every
trace of a theology of merit is therefore excluded by this model.
On the other hand, God does not try to 'earn' our love by his

offer of salvation. He wants us to love him because we identify with him, and not for the sake of that which we can receive from him in return. If we love heaven rather than God, then our efforts are directed toward our own interests and we fail to identify ourselves with the will of God.

This is in fact precisely what we do. We disrupt the fellowship with God by trying to pursue our own interests rather than identifying with his will. In terms of this model, therefore, sin is not primarily a state of corruption calling for a manipulative cure, nor guilt to be wiped out through punishment or satisfaction, but alienation from God requiring reconciliation. As we argued above, the necessary and sufficient conditions for this kind of reconciliation are not punishment or satisfaction or condonation, but penitence and forgiveness: if in penitence we repudiate the damage which through selfishness we have done to our fellowship with God, and through acts of penance try to demonstrate the sincerity of this repudiation, and if God should grant us our desire for restoration of our fellowship by forgiving us, then we shall be reconciled with him and our fellowship will be restored. Nothing more than this is required. In the words of D. M. Baillie: 'God will freely forgive even the greatest sins, if only the sinners will repent and turn from their evil ways. Nothing else is needed, no expiation, no offerings, for God has everything already. Sincere repentance is enough, and a real turning from sin to God; and then the sinner can count on God's mercy.'[20]

In these respects reconciliation with God is like reconciliation with other people. However, God is not like other people, and there are at least four important respects in which divine forgiveness differs from being forgiven by other people.[21] First of all, as we have pointed out above, your forgiveness depends on your free decision. Since it is in no way necessitated, there are limits to the extent to which I could count on it. Being human, you might find it difficult to forgive and suppress your resentment for the injury I caused you. With God this is

---

[20] D. M. Baillie, *God Was in Christ* (London 1961), 176.
[21] I have also developed these points elsewhere. See my *What Are We Doing When We Pray?*, 82–5.

different. Because he is *perfect* in love, there is never the slightest
likelihood that he will ever fail to forgive those who are truly
penitent. 'If we confess our sins, he is just and may be trusted to
forgive our sins and cleanse us from every kind of wrong'
(1 John 1 : 9). However, this does not contradict the claim that
his forgiveness is free and neither earned nor necessitated by our
penitence. As Peter Baelz explains,

the penitent is not only voicing his sincere grief and contrition when he
asks for forgiveness; he is also asking for something which he has no
moral right to expect. He is asking for a new, undeserved expression of
the divine love which will restore him to a right relationship. Although
in one sense he may be confident of the unchanging love of God, in
another sense that is just what he has no *right* to presume upon. To
presume upon love is to blaspheme against it: '*Dieu pardonnera, car c'est
son métier*'.[22]

Although I could be infinitely more confident of divine
forgiveness than of human forgiveness, both kinds of forgiveness
remain equally free and unmerited.

Secondly, when I express my penitence to someone whom I
have injured, I inform that person of the fact that I am penitent
and desire forgiveness. Without my expression of penitence, the
other cannot know that I am penitent and therefore cannot
forgive me either. With God this is different, for God knows the
secrets of my heart without my having to inform him. As
Kierkegaard explains, 'the person making the confession is not
... like one that confides in a friend to whom sooner or later he
reveals things that the friend did not previously know. The all-
knowing One does not get to know something about the maker
of the confession.'[23] Although our expressions of penitence do
not tell God something he does not already know, they do
acknowledge and welcome the fact that he knows it.

We confess in order to express our acceptance of this fact, our
willingness to be so known, and our desire to enter as far as we can into
this searching knowledge God has of us. We stop the life of
concealment, of pretending that no one knows or need know. We say

---

22 P. R. Baelz, *Prayer and Providence* (New York 1968), 107.
23 S. Kierkegaard, *Purity of Heart*, trans. D. V. Steere (New York 1956), 50.

we know we are living in the light, we are content to have it so, only more so, we want to be wholly in the light if possible.[24]

If divine forgiveness is to be effective in restoring the personal fellowship between God and the penitent, then this *acknowledgment* is a necessary condition for God to forgive. Without such acknowledgment the penitent remains an *object* of God's knowledge but does not become a *person* in relation to God. C. S. Lewis explains this point as follows:

To be known by God is to be... in the category of things. We are, like earthworms, cabbages and nebulae, objects of divine knowledge. But when we (a) become aware of the fact – the present fact, not the generalisation – and (b) assent with all our will to be so known, then we treat ourselves, in relation to God, not as things but as persons. We have unveiled. Not that any veil could have baffled his sight. The change is in us. The passive changes to the active. Instead of merely being known, we show, we tell, we offer ourselves to view... By unveiling, by confessing our sins and 'making known' our requests, we assume the high rank of persons before him. And he, descending, becomes a Person to us.[25]

It is therefore not sufficient to say with Kierkegaard that 'not God, but you, the maker of the confession, get to know something by your act of confession'.[26] As the maker of the confession, I do not merely get to *know* something about God and myself. I also assume the status of a person and therefore of the sort of being with whom God can restore a personal fellowship. In terms of the distinction we made in section 7.4, I come to *know God* and not merely to *know something about God*.

A third difference between divine and human forgiveness is the following. Since my asking *your* forgiveness is aimed at restoring the fellowship which I marred by injuring *you*, it only makes sense if I ask you to forgive what I did to you and not the injury I do to others or my moral transgressions in general. In fact, your forgiveness does not even cover the injury I do to you completely, for, as W. G. Maclagan points out, 'when... injury is considered not as injury but in its character of wickedness or

[24] J. N. Ward, *The Use of Praying* (London 1967), 43.
[25] C. S. Lewis, *Letters to Malcolm: Chiefly on Prayer* (London 1964), 33.
[26] Kierkegaard, *Purity of Heart*, 51. See also D. Z. Phillips, *The Concept of Prayer* (London 1968; 2nd edn.), chapter 4.

evil-doing we recognize that, so regarded, it is something that
no man, not even the person injured, can properly be said to
forgive. Men can forgive injuries; they cannot forgive sins.'[27]
Thus you can forgive my injuring *your good*, but not the fact that
in so doing I outrage *goodness* as such. At this point the parallel
between divine and human forgiveness breaks down: unlike us,
God can and does forgive sins. However, it does not break down
completely, for, as I have argued elsewhere,[28] a believer is
someone who accepts the will of God as *ultimate* standard of
goodness. It follows from this that all sin, as outrage against
goodness, is for the believer an outrage against the will of God
and as such an injury to God in which the loving fellowship with
God is marred. For this reason I can ask divine forgiveness for
all my sins, whereas I can only ask your forgiveness for injury I
do to you. 'What happens between man and man never
embraces the whole of our existence. A friend can only forgive
his friend the *particular* guilt through which he has become guilty
in relation to him personally. But the relationship to God does
embrace human existence as a whole, and his forgiving grace
bestows purity and newness without more ado.'[29]

This third difference between divine and human forgiveness
entails a fourth. If I am penitent and you forgive me, my
fellowship with you could be restored. But your forgiveness does
not restore my fellowship with God which was also marred by
the injury I did to you. For this reason, if I am a believer, I
would not be satisfied with your forgiveness alone. I would want
God's forgiveness as well. Only then would my sin be blotted out
completely. Of God alone can it be said that 'as far as the east
is from the west, so far does he remove our transgressions from
us' (Psalm 103: 12). Only if I know that God accepts me, can
I come to accept myself. Or stronger: if I know that God accepts
me, it would be meaningless for me *not* to accept myself. As
D. Z. Phillips explains: 'It makes sense to say, "My friend
forgives me, but I cannot forgive myself", but it makes no sense
to say, "God forgives me, but I cannot forgive myself"... Being

---

[27] W. G. Maclagan, *The Theological Frontier of Ethics* (London 1961), 161.
[28] See my *Speaking of a Personal God*, sections 4.3 and 4.4.
[29] Rudolf Bultmann, *Essays Philosophical and Theological* (London 1955), 179.

able to see that one is forgiven by God entails being able to live with oneself.'[30]

In brief: through sincere penitence and divine forgiveness I can be restored to loving fellowship with God. Such fellowship bestows ultimate meaning on my very existence and enables me to 'live with myself'. This in a nutshell is the view of atonement which follows if we interpret our relationship with God in terms of loving fellowship. Does this view succeed in overcoming the difficulties which we found in the views on atonement based on the other two relation models? It is indeed a fully *personal* view of atonement which emphasizes the personal nature of our relationship with God, as well as the fact that we and not God are responsible for the disruption of our fellowship with God. Furthermore, this model enables us to exclude every trace of a theology of merit: divine forgiveness can in no way be earned and remains a gracious favour freely bestowed on us. *Soli Deo gloria*!

Can this model be extended satisfactorily in order to take account of the Christological aspect of atonement? On the one hand, can this model, unlike the manipulative model, enable us to explain why the death of Christ on Calvary was necessary for our salvation? On the other hand, can it, unlike the substitution model, do so in a way which does justice to the trinitarian unity between the Father and the Son?

With respect to the latter point, we have argued above that on this model the person who forgives is the person who has to pay the price for reconciliation. Since, in restoring our fellowship with God, it is God who forgives, it is also God who has to pay the price and has to absorb into his own suffering the consequences of the wrong that we have done to him. On Calvary God reveals to us the cost of his forgiveness. Christ's suffering is the direct expression of God's suffering forgiveness. In this way the 'unity of will' between the Father and the Son, which we missed in the substitution model of atonement, is fully acknowledged here: Christ's attitude and purpose toward us sinners is a direct expression of God's attitude and purpose.

[30] Phillips, *The Concept of Prayer*, 63.

But this is not all. Christ's suffering is not merely the paradigmatic *revelation* of God's atoning forgiveness. Such a revelation is also a *necessary condition* for this forgiveness to achieve reconciliation. In this respect Christ's suffering on Calvary is also on this model necessary for our salvation. Let me explain. In section 7.4 we argued that loving fellowship entails knowing each other in the sense of adopting an attitude of mutual trust and open candour in relation to each other. If ultimate happiness consists of being in the love of God, it follows that we can only be ultimately happy to the extent that we know God. 'This is eternal life: to know you the only true God, and Jesus Christ whom you have sent' (John 17: 3).

Through sin, however, we have become estranged from God. Our lives are not characterized by loving trust and open candour in relation to God. But worse still, this estrangement has led to ignorance. Not only do we not know God; we do not even know who God is. For this reason we have lost the ability to seek reconciliation with God. We cannot seek a 'union of wills' with God, for we do not know what his will is. We cannot seek divine forgiveness, for we do not know whether God is long-suffering enough to forgive. In fact, we cannot repent, for we do not know whom we have offended. And since we are unable to repent, God's forgiveness cannot be effective. In the words of John Burnaby, 'there can be no effective forgiveness unless the wrong-doer repents of his wrong-doing, knows whom he has offended, and comes back to him with a changed mind ... The tragedy of the human situation lies in the fact that sinful man has lost the knowledge of the God against who he has sinned.'[31] In this way we could also understand St Bernard's claim that through sin we have lost the *liberum consilium* by which we are able to know God's will and consistently act in accordance with it. Even if we were to desire it through our *liberum arbitrium*, we are unable to achieve reconciliation and a 'union of wills' with God because we no longer know God and have become ignorant of his will. In spite of sin we remain free agents endowed with the *liberum arbitrium*. However, sin has deprived us of the *liberum*

---

[31] Burnaby, *Christian Words and Christian Meanings*, 94.

consilium which enables us freely to be reconciled with God. In this sense the will of the sinner is both free and at the same time held captive by sin. 'The sins of men have built their own prison, in which the windows are beyond the prisoners' reach: they have forgotten what the sunlit world of freedom is like. They *cannot* repent, because they do not know whom they have offended.'[32] It is therefore a necessary condition for our salvation that we should come to know God anew and to know what his will for us is.

However, we can only get to know God to the extent that he makes himself known to us, and we can only know what God wills for us to the extent that he reveals his will to us. As St Bernard points out, it is by God's grace alone that the *liberum consilium* can be restored to us and that we can be liberated from the captivity of sin. This God has brought about through the suffering of Christ. 'This is how he showed his love among us: he sent his only Son into the world that we might have life through him ... Thus we have come to know and believe in the love which God has for us' (1 John 4: 9, 16). Clearly then, the paradigmatic revelation of God's forgiving love through the suffering of Christ is a necessary condition for God's forgiveness to achieve reconciliation with us. 'By the death of his Son, God commends, proves, makes good his love toward us who were his enemies, and thereby reconciles us to himself.'[33] In Christ, God does not *cause* our repentance and thereby save us by turning us into objects 'to be managed or handled or cured or trained'. But by paradigmatically 'commending, proving and making good his love toward us' in Christ, he does *enable* us to repent and as persons to be readmitted to that fellowship with him which as believers we consider to be ultimate bliss. *Soli Deo gloria!*

So far so good. At this point, however, a further objection could be raised against this model of atonement, and one which does not necessarily apply to the substitution model.[34] In our day and age it is incumbent upon theology to provide an adequate view on the phenomenon of religious pluralism. Other religions have to be taken seriously and cannot be ignored or

---

[32] Ibid., 94–5.   [33] Ibid., 95.
[34] I am grateful to John Hick for pointing this out to me.

simply dismissed out of hand. Thus it is widely held by
contemporary theologians that an exclusivist theology, according to which there no salvation possible outside the
Christian church, is less than adequate. In the light of these
considerations, it could be argued that the substitution model of
atonement need not necessarily exclude a universalist interpretation. It is always possible to maintain that the merit of Christ
is sufficient for the salvation of all people irrespective of whether
they are members of the Christian church or even whether they
have ever heard of Christ Jesus.

In this respect the model of atonement defended in this
chapter would seem to be less satisfactory. If salvation depends
on knowing God as he has revealed himself in Jesus Christ, it
would seem to follow that salvation is impossible for those who
do not know Jesus Christ. Then, in the words of the commission
on faith of the United Church of Canada: 'Without the
particular knowledge of God in Jesus Christ, men do not really
know God at all.'[35] Wilfred Cantwell Smith responds to this
claim by making what he calls an 'empirical observation':

The evidence would seem overwhelming that in fact individual
Buddhists, Hindus, Muslims and others have known, and in fact do
know, God. I personally have friends from these communities whom it
seems to me preposterous to think about in any other way. (If we do
not have friends among these communities, we should probably
refrain from generalizations about them.)[36]

This observation would seem to confront us with a dilemma:
either we simply reject Smith's claim and agree with the
Canadian commission that without knowing Jesus Christ we
'do not really know God at all'. That would seem to entail an
unacceptably exclusivist theology. Or we agree with Smith that
people of other faiths can also be said to know God even though
they do not know or accept Jesus Christ. That would in turn
seem to prevent us from maintaining in the way we have done
here, that the incarnation and suffering of Christ is a necessary
condition for our salvation.

[35] Quoted by Wilfred Cantwell Smith in 'The Christian in a religiously plural world',
in John Hick and Brian Hebblethwaite, *Christianity and Other Religions* (Glasgow
1980), 98.   [36] Smith, 'Religiously plural world', 102.

Two remarks could be made in response to this challenge: first of all, we could agree with Smith that God in his almighty wisdom is able to make himself known in many ways, also to those who adhere to other faiths than Christianity. 'The God whom we have come to know...reaches out after all men everywhere, and speaks to all who will listen. Both within and without the Church men listen all too dimly. Yet both within and without the Church, so far as we can see, God does somehow enter into men's hearts.'[37] Secondly, however, Smith's claim about his friends in other religious communities knowing God, can hardly be called an 'empirical observation' in the way he does. It is far rather a claim which he makes in the light of his own Christian faith. In the sense in which we have been arguing in this and the previous chapter, we can only 'know God' to the extent that we have fellowship with God and achieve a 'union of wills' with God, and this will manifest itself in the Christlike character of our lives. Knowing God is leaving what St Bernard calls the land of unlikeness and returning to the land of likeness where our lives become like that of Christ. But then it is only possible in the light of our knowledge of God as revealed in Christ for us to discern that others (and ourselves) inside and outside the church can be said to 'know God'. In this sense the Christian will still have to claim, as we have done above, that the revelation of God's love in Christ is *paradigmatic* and therefore necessary, since it is only in the light of God's self-revelation in Jesus Christ that we can say what it means to 'know God' and be reconciled with him. Thus Smith has to admit that 'because God is what he is, because he is what Christ has shown him to be, *therefore* other men *do* live in his presence. Also, therefore, we (as Christians) know this to be so.'[38]

[37] Ibid., 107.   [38] Ibid., 106.

CHAPTER 9

The attitudes of love

Let us in this final chapter return to the five attitudes discussed in chapters 2–6 and see what role each of them has to fulfil within the relationship of love as described in chapters 7–8: in what sense is a relationship of love exclusive? (section 9.1); in what sense do the partners in such a relationship seek to be united with each other? (section 9.2); in what sense does such a relationship involve suffering for the partners? (section 9.3); in what sense do the partners in such a relationship have need of each other and of their relationship and therefore experience desire or *eros*? (section 9.4); in what sense is the attitude of the partners toward each other one of unconditional giving or *agape*? (section 9.5). In discussing these aspects of love, we will distinguish between the roles which they have within the following 'dimensions of love': romantic love, neighbourly love, our love for God, and God's love for us. In all this we must remember that God is not like other people. What then are the limits of using the model of love in talking about our relationship to God, and what is the conceptual price we have to pay for doing so?

9.1 EXCLUSIVE ATTENTION

In chapter 2 we saw Ortega y Gasset defending the view that exclusiveness is one of the most characteristic features of love: 'The world does not exist for the lover. His beloved has dislodged and replaced it.' The lover only has eyes for his or her beloved. All else is ignored. Similarly, the mystic is continually aware of the presence of God, and has great difficulty in paying attention to anything else: 'Every activity of the mystic's day brings him into contact with God, makes him revert to his idea.' Thus it would seem that if we love God, we cannot love anybody else. In this respect we referred to Abelard's injunction to Heloise that, since as a nun she has become the bride of Christ, Christ should now assume the exclusive place in her life which, as her lover, Abelard previously had. This is similar to the strategy of 'infinite resignation' in terms of which Kierkegaard felt obliged to break his engagement with Regina Olsen for the sake of an exclusive relationship with God. Walter Lowrie quotes Kierkegaard as saying of Regina: 'My engagement to her and the breaking of it is really my relation to God, my engagement to God, if I may dare to say so.'[1] Clearly, love which is exclusive in this sense is not only obsessive, but also in conflict with the Christian injunction that we should love *all* our neighbours. Even love for God cannot exclude love for others. Such exclusiveness would turn the love for God into a private obsession which not only removes the saint from human life but also prompts us to wonder whether in this way the true God does not turn out to be an idol after all.[2]

In chapter 5 we saw how Augustine tries to avoid this kind of obsessive exclusivism by means of the notion of an *ordo amoris*. We are not only to love God but also our neighbours, ourselves, and even our own bodies. Of course, this does not mean that we have to love them all in the same way. On the contrary, we have to love them all differently and to learn how to order our loves in the right way. If we love anything inordinately, our love leads to disaster. 'A man of just and holy life ... keeps his affections under strict control, so that he neither loves what he ought not to love, nor fails to love what he ought to love, nor loves that more that he ought to love less, nor loves that equally which ought to be loved less or more, nor loves that less or more which ought to be loved equally' (*De Doctr. Chr.* 1.27.28). However useful the notion of an *ordo amoris* may be, difficulties arise when it is interpreted hierarchically and our loves arranged in a

---

[1] Walter Lowrie, *A Short Life of Kierkegaard* (Princeton 1944), 147.
[2] See Helen Oppenheimer, *The Hope of Happiness* (London 1983), 160.

quantitative order of more and less as Augustine does here. In this way our loves are subordinated to each other and finally they are all made subservient to our love for God: God alone is to be enjoyed (*frui*), and all else is to be used (*uti*). In spite of all the perceptive things which Augustine has to say about love, we are left in the end with the lingering suspicion that his distinction between *frui* and *uti* treats all but God as means rather than ends and thus cannot account adequately for our love of anyone but God. Is Singer not correct in accusing Augustine of treating the neighbour as a 'mere instrumentality' rather than as a person?[3] In the end, Augustine concludes that 'God alone must be loved; and all this world, that is, all sensible things, are to be despised, – while they are to be used as this life requires' (*De Mor. Eccl.* 20.39). Is this mere hyperbole or the inevitable result of his hierarchical ordering of loves?

Similar difficulties arise with Kierkegaard's attempt at dealing with this in terms of the distinction between an absolute *telos* and relative ends:

> The task is to exercise the absolute relationship to the absolute *telos*, striving to reach the maximum of maintaining simultaneously a relationship to the absolute *telos* and to relative ends, not by mediating them, but by making the relationship to the absolute *telos* absolute, and the relation to the relative ends relative. The relative relationship belongs to the world, the absolute relationship to the individual himself; and it is not an easy thing to maintain an absolute relationship to the absolute *telos* and at the same time to participate like other men in this and that.[4]

Indeed, this task proved to be insurmountably difficult for Kierkegaard and, as Robert M. Adams points out, by the end of his life, Kierkegaard seems to have rejected the task, coming to the conclusion that, from a Christian point of view, it is a mistake to try to combine the enjoyment of finite goods with devotion to God. In fact, with reference to family relationships which for him provide the central cases of enjoyment of the finite, he implies in his last writings that marriage and the

[3] Singer, *Nature of Love* I, 344–9.
[4] S. Kierkegaard, *Concluding Unscientific Postscript* (Princeton 1941), 364–5.

begetting of children are displeasing to God.[5] In the end Kierkegaard failed to avoid his love for God as 'absolute *telos*' becoming obsessive and his love for 'relative ends' becoming impossible.

The solution to these difficulties could lie in reinterpreting Augustine's notion of an *ordo amoris* in a non-hierarchical way. Let me explain. In sections 7.1 and 7.3 we referred to Roger Scruton's claim that love is directed toward 'things as particulars' and not toward 'things as tokens or instantiations of some type or property'. This has two important implications. First of all, an object which is valued for instantiating a property is replaceable by any other object which instantiates the property equally well. As we argued in section 7.3, this applies in relationships of rights and duties where my partner as well as the relationship has an instrumental value for me as a means for furthering my own interests and as such are for me replaceable by any other means which might be equally effective. In love, however, the beloved is valued as an irreplaceable individual. As such the beloved can never be valued for his or her properties or usefulness as a means to an end. The beloved can never be looked on as a 'mere instrumentality' in the sense in which Singer accuses Augustine of treating the neighbour. But in that case love can be said to be exclusive in the sense that for the lover the beloved has intrinsic value as an irreplaceable individual. As such, no one else can fill the place which my beloved has in my life. Secondly, objects which are valued for their properties or uses can be graded in terms of the extent to which they instantiate the property or usefulness. If we were to love things as instantiations of properties (or usefulness or goodness), then our love for them would be in proportion to the extent in which they instantiate the property (or usefulness or goodness). The result would be an hierarchical *ordo amoris* as in Plato and Augustine: God or the Good is to be loved absolutely, and all other things (and persons) are to be loved relatively in proportion to the extent to which they 'approximate' God or the Good in some way either actually or potentially. If however,

[5] Robert. M. Adams, 'The knight of faith', *Faith and Philosophy* 7 (1990), 390.

as we argued in section 7.3, love treats the beloved as a unique and irreplaceable individual, it becomes impossible to grade our loves in an hierarchical order. Like their objects, each of our loves is irreplaceable by and incomparable to any other. For this reason the *ordo amoris* is qualitative rather than quantitative: we do not love different things more or less on an hierarchical scale, but we love them all differently, because they are all incomparably different.

This is well illustrated in the way parents should love their children. We all agree that it is wrong for parents to have favourites among their children, loving some *more* than others. However, the alternative to making favourites among our children is not to love them 'all alike': it is to love them all differently, so differently that comparisons of 'amounts' of love are not just odious but impossible. Since persons are not units of value, no one can adequately stand in for another. If one is lost, the loss is irreparable.[6] In this way the various 'dimensions of love' are incommensurable with each other: my love for my wife is incommensurable with my love for God, which in turn is incommensurable with my love for my child or my love for my next-door neighbour or my colleague or my friend or the stranger at the gate. Each of these is different and irreplaceable by any of the others.

In the case of romantic love, this incommensurability is clear. For the lover and the beloved their relationship is not one relationship among others. It is thought of as having and is given a special and even unique position in their lives. 'It becomes their centre, the single centre of two lives. For one party to share its fruits and privileges with someone else is for the relation to be wrenched from such a position and would be seen by the other as a debasing or downgrading of it.'[7] In the marriage service according to the *Book of Common Prayer*, the bride and bridegroom are charged: 'forsaking all others, keep thee only unto her/him, as long as ye both shall live'. However, this 'forsaking all others' is not intended to insulate the lover

[6] See Oppenheimer, *Hope of Happiness*, 81.
[7] Ilham Dilman, *Love and Human Separateness*, 84.

and the beloved from what lies outside their love. It does not prevent them from having relations of fellowship or love with other people or with God. It only excludes them sharing the 'fruits and privileges' of their unique relationship with anybody else. No one else can fill the position in my life which belongs to my (romantic) beloved – not even God. To argue like Abelard and Kierkegaard that we need to choose between loving God and loving our romantic beloved, is to misconstrue not only the unique nature of romantic love but also that of loving God. Martin Buber's comment on Kierkegaard's break with Regina Olsen, brings this point out very well indeed: 'God one object beside other objects, the chosen one beside the rejected ones? God as Regina's successful rival? Is that still God?'[8]

Similarly the believer's love for God is incommensurable with any other love. Augustine is right in his warnings about loving anything or anybody else in the way which is appropriate only in relation to God. To do so would be idolatry. Loving God also requires the believer to 'forsake all others'. As in the case of romantic love, however, this does not insulate believers from all else outside their relationship to God, nor does it prevent them from having relationships of fellowship or love with persons other than God. It only excludes others from the position in their lives which God alone can fill.

Mutatis mutandis this also applies to the way God loves each of us. God's love is not an equalizing love. It does not treat us as though we were all equal in his sight and therefore able to replace each other in his affection. The whole point about persons is precisely that they are not equal. One is not as good as another. No human being is worth less than another in God's sight. However, this is not because they are all worth the same, but because each one is irreplaceable.[9] In this way God's love

---

[8] Martin Buber, *Between Man and Man* (London 1947), 57. In a perceptive essay, Janet Soskice shows how spirituality becomes very inadequate if attention to other people (and paradigmatically of mothers for their children) is regarded as a rival to and an impediment for attention to God. See her essay on 'Love and attention' in Michael McGhee, *Philosophy, Religion and the Spiritual Life* (Cambridge 1992), 59–72. In this connection, compare also St. Bernard's considerations, referred to in section 3.2 above, regarding the value of vicissitude in the mystic's experience of God.

[9] See Oppenheimer, *Hope of Happiness*, 81.

for us is not impartial but partial in the sense in which 'partiality is a matter of looking to see what the special individuality of the other person really is and attending positively to it. God can have this kind of special love for each of his creatures.'[10] Elsewhere Helen Oppenheimer expands this point as follows:

> God loves each creature: but even 'each' is still too abstract here, and to bring out the full sense one must risk the subjective, 'God loves *me*': not externally but with a 'partial' love which enters completely and as of right into my unique point of view ... God abides in me in this sense, that he associates himself to the point of identification with the pettiness as well as the glory of every creature he has made ... To form the idea that God is the 'ground of one's being' in the sense that he is more concerned for one, more 'partial' to one, more on one's side, than one is oneself; that one's humanly private point of view is so to say anchored onto the divine: is assuredly to feel that one has 'got more than one bargained for'.[11]

The way in which God loves us is the perfect example on which we should try to pattern our love for each other. Thus as Shirley Letwin points out, God's love of human beings can be understood as a supreme appreciation of the individuality of each person. Similarly, when we love our neighbours, we will imitate, in a necessarily incomplete fashion, God's appreciation of the individuality of each neighbour as a person.[12] In other words, we do not love our neighbour as an instantiation of the property of being a neighbour. That would be an equalizing love which makes every neighbour as good as and therefore replaceable by any other in our sight. Does this mean that we should be 'partial' in loving our neighbours in the way in which God is 'partial' in loving us? At this point our finitude sets limits to what we can do.

What is wrong with 'taking sides' is not the good we do one side but the hurt we may do the other. For this reason, human beings dare not be as partial as God. 'Impartiality' is not a divine virtue, but a human expedient to make up for the limits of our concern on the one hand and

---

[10] Ibid., 135.
[11] Oppenheimer, *Incarnation and Immanence* (London 1973), 191–2.
[12] See Shirley R. Letwin, 'Romantic love and Christianity', 138.

the corruptibility of our affections on the other. If we find ourselves neglecting, or spoiling, or abusing, we need to be more even-handed and partiality becomes a vice; but the august partiality of God is a taking hold of the special character of each creature as uniquely significant.[13]

It is now clear that learning to order our loves, means learning to differentiate between them qualitatively and not learning to grade them in a quantitative hierarchical order. Learning this entails being able to do two things. First of all, we should acquire the ability to look on others as irreplaceable individuals rather than as instantiations of universal properties or values. Helen Oppenheimer argues that our self-awareness could be the necessary clue in this regard.

Each of us knows as a matter of plain fact what it is to be 'special'... I know at first hand that if I were snuffed out something irreplaceable would have gone. My difficulty is not to apprehend my own value but to put it in its proper place, maybe an entirely insignificant one behind a pillar, so to say, in God's temple. Even if I am a lost sheep, there is not much difficulty in imagining the Shepherd leaving all the others to come and look for me. One's own failings are lovable, one's own peculiarities are interesting, one's own talents are important, one's own embarrassments are ghastly, one's own virtues are solid. We avert our eyes from all this because we have been taught that it is wicked to be self-centred, forgetting that repressed self-centredness is likely to be at least as dangerous as repressed sex. It makes more sense to start with ourselves as we are and use our consciousness of ourselves to illuminate what a self is. By being me, I know what it is to be irreplaceable. I acknowledge my own claim, because I am the claimant... What we have to do is ascribe this same irreplaceability to other people. If we do this we know, really know, what the intrinsic value of a person is.[14]

If we really know that every single person, both human and divine, is irreplaceable, we also know that they are all different and that our love for them should be differentiated accordingly. We should not love them all alike since they are not all alike. This is the second ability which we need to acquire: to differentiate our loves in the appropriate way. The ideal of universal love does not require us to bestow equal quantities of

---

[13] Oppenheimer, *Hope of Happiness*, 131.   [14] Ibid., 82.

identical love on all persons. However, as Singer points out, it does require us to love indiscriminately, 'in whatever way is relevant to the other's reality and our own'. Although such love will vary from object to object, it will exclude no human being *a priori*. It is equal not in strength or configuration, but in availability.[15]

This is more easily said than done. In order to differentiate our loves correctly, we must know what it means to love every person 'in whatever way is relevant to the other's reality and to our own'. How do we decide on that? This may have to do with the various ways in which we seek to achieve union with each other. Let us now turn to an examination of this feature of the relationship called love.

9.2 THE UNION OF LOVE

We can now return to the question which we raised at the beginning of chapter 3: what is nature of the union which lovers seek to achieve with each other? In what sense do they desire to be 'melted and fused together' by Hephaestus? In chapter 7 we argued that love is the paradigmatic form of personal fellowship and that for this reason the union between lovers cannot be such that the personal autonomy of the lovers in relation to each other is in any way denied. Fellowship presupposes that both partners are persons, i.e. free and autonomous centres of agency in relation to each other. If I were to relinquish my personal autonomy and integrity in relation to you or fail to recognize yours in relation to me, then one of us is turned into an object of the other's agency and the relationship between us is perverted into something other than love. The union of love cannot therefore be anything like the sort of self-annihilating absorption into God which the so-called unitive mystics seem to seek. As we argued in chapter 3, mystic merging with God would eliminate God's transcendence as a person in relation to the mystic. Similarly, to be merged or fused with a human beloved would eliminate the transcendence which the lovers have toward each

[15] Singer, *Nature of Love* I, 305.

other as persons. Lovers necessarily remain distinct individuals who in loving each other should acknowledge and respect each other's separate identity.

The wonder of friendship and the magic of love depend on the separateness of friends and lovers; it is this which makes their response to one another a gift, something they can treasure. Without it, where the other person becomes a mere shadow or extension of one, one only loves oneself in her; and in the opposite case, where one has become no more than an extension of her, one merely participates in her love of herself.[16]

Singer argues that it is in this respect that the Aristotelian ideal of *philia* or the sort of friendship in which like loves like, is inadequate. Aristotle neglects the joy of loving those who are not like ourselves, persons who are not mere extensions of our own personality. According to Singer, loving others as persons entails bestowing value whether or not they are so like us that we can love ourselves in them, and despite those imperfections that prevent them from embodying our own ideal for ourselves. Hence, to love others as persons, we must accept their independence.[17] In no way should the union of love therefore become a form of *identity* between the lovers. In the poetic words of Kahlil Gibran: 'Let there be spaces in your togetherness. And let the winds of heaven dance between you.'[18]

Although the union of love is not a form of identity, it could nevertheless, as we explained in section 7.3, be characterized as a form of mutual *identification*: I identify with you by treating your interests as my own. In serving these interests as my own, I love you as myself. As Ortega y Gasset explains, 'this is partly what we mean when, at a difficult time, we say to someone: "Count on me, for I am at your side"; that is to say, your cause is mine, and I will stick by you'.[19] But what do we mean by *interests* in this connection? When do I look on some cause as *your cause* which I am to consider to be my own when loving you as myself?

One possible answer would be to say that by 'your interests' we mean 'your good'. If I love you I care for you in the sense

[16] Dilman, *Love and Human Separateness*, 106.
[17] Singer, *Nature of Love* I, 102.
[18] *The Prophet* (London 1980), 16.
[19] Ortega, *On Love*, 17.

that I want your good, not merely as I want my own, but as being my own. Although I remain different from you, we are of one mind in wanting and hoping for those things that are good for you, and in fearing whatever is bad.[20] This comes very close to the view we discussed in chapter 5 which Norton and Kille ascribe to Plato: loving you means identifying with your individual *daimon*, your own potentiality for realizing the good in your life, and not with your imperfect actuality. Augustine would say that loving you means making your eternal happiness my own concern and therefore 'turning the whole current of my love both for myself and for you into the channel of the love of God'. However, identifying with your good in this sense is not the same as identifying with your will or your wishes or desires, since doing so might very well be contrary to your good. Loving you does not necessarily imply that 'your every wish is my command'. The accord which exists between human lovers need therefore not go as far as to become a perfect coincidence of wills. Love between humans does not necessarily entail agreement on all issues and could also include the agreement to disagree on many issues. Human lovers are and remain distinct individuals with distinct points of view which need not necessarily coincide on all points.

Although loving you does not require me always to identify with your wishes and will, it does exclude my being indifferent to these. If I love you, I will mind about the things you mind about and be concerned about your concerns. I cannot ignore your wishes, and even when I do not share them, they will always concern me as do my own in the sense that I will always take them into account in my practical reasoning in the same way as I take my own wishes into account.

Your desires are then reasons for me, in exactly the same way, and to the same extent, that my desires are reasons for me. If I oppose your desires, it is in the way that I oppose my own, out of a sense of what is good or right in the long run. The mere fact that you want something enters the forum of my practical reasoning with all the imperative character of a desire that is already mine. If I cannot dissuade you, I must accept your desire, and decree in my heart 'let it be done'.[21]

---

[20] See Lucas, *Freedom and Grace*, 56.   [21] Scruton, *Sexual Desire*, 230.

My attitude toward your wishes and will involves both appraisal and bestowal. In loving you I will feel an intimate concern about the continuance of your good characteristics and the diminishing of bad ones. This requires my objective appraisal of your characteristics, actions, opinions, wishes, desires, etc. If I did not attempt to appraise these objectively, I would not be taking you seriously. But then, this also applies to my attitude toward myself. If I take myself seriously, I have to be equally honest with myself with regard to my own characteristics and desires since my desires are also not necessarily identical with my good. Here too an objective appraisal is required of me. However, my appraisal of your characteristics and desires, as of my own, will always be accompanied by a bestowal of significance or importance. Your wishes are not merely neutral objects of appraisal but are important to me because they are *yours*, in the same way as my wishes are important for me because they are mine.

Appraisal without bestowal may lead us to change people regardless of what they want. As moralists or legislators, or as dutiful parents, we may even think that this is how we *ought* to behave... On this moral attitude great institutions are often built. But it is not a loving attitude. We are not responding affirmatively toward others. We are only doing what is (we hope) in their best interests, or else society's.[22]

In brief, the union of love between two people can never be an identity of personalities which excludes the acknowledgment of each other's distinct individuality and the mutual acceptance of each other's right to a distinct point of view and distinct personal character preferences. However it does entail mutual identification with each other's good and the bestowal of significance or importance on each other's wishes and will. My love for you does not make me blind to your faults, but in an important sense it does make those faults dear to me.

Our human finitude sets limits to the range and to the intensity with which we can in this way identify with others. Thus real friendship takes time and energy which human beings

[22] Singer, *Nature of Love* I, 10.

have in limited amounts. 'We cannot have too many friends for
the same reason as we cannot do too much work. We cannot
spread ourselves too thin.'[23] Apart from such restrictions of time
and energy, it is especially the limits of our knowledge of one
another which determine the range and intensity of our
fellowship with others. As we argued in section 7.4, fellowship is
only possible to the extent that we not only know each other but
also gain knowledge about each other. I can only identify with
your good to the extent that I know what your good is, and I
can only take your feelings, desires, intentions, dispositions,
values, preferences, characteristics, etc. into account in my own
practical reasoning to the extent that these are known to me.
For this reason love cannot do without information. Lovers
remain relentlessly curious as to each other's sorrows, joys, and
desires, since these concern them as their own.[24] Clearly then,
since the number of people whom we can come to know and the
amount of knowledge we can acquire about them is limited,
there is also a limit to the number of people with whom we can
achieve real fellowship and great differences in the intensity of
the fellowship which we are able to establish and maintain with
different people.

Finally, even with regard to those who are closest to me, my
ability to identify with them is limited by the extent to which I
can do so with integrity. As Roger Scruton explains,

love is intelligible only on the assumption that it too has a state of
'rest': an unchallenging 'being with', in which I know that you know
that I know that you know that neither of us seeks from the other any
more than he can willingly give ... I must be able to regard [your
faults], not as great moral failings, but as weaknesses, and as qualities
which endear you to me. For I must be able to accept your weaknesses
as part of my practical reasoning. I can make allowances for your
laziness, your selfishness, your lack of essential refinements. For these
do not place you outside the reasoning whereby I conduct my life. But
can I make allowances for your cowardice, your viciousness, your
character, say, as a murderer or a rapist? ... If I cannot condone your

<hr>

[23] Oppenheimer, *Hope of Happiness*, 136. Cf. Emil Brunner's statement that 'a person
who claims friendship with everyone has not begun to understand the meaning of
friendship' (*The Divine Imperative*, 518).   [24] Scruton, *Sexual Desire*, 231.

vice, it must inevitably erode my love for you, since it introduces calculations that cannot enter my reasoning as they enter yours. (He who freely and happily loves a criminal is always capable of being himself an accomplice in crime.)[25]

Even when out of loyalty or for some other reason I refuse to break with you in such circumstances, the quality of our fellowship will be strained and severely limited, and will most likely become reduced to little more than a tacit agreement of rights and duties.

These factors do not only limit the range and intensity of the fellowship which we can establish and maintain with others. They also determine the way in which we differentiate our loves according to the qualitative *ordo amoris* referred to above in section 9.1, and decide how to love in whatever way is relevant to the other's reality and our own. Obviously, my identification with my neighbour whom I know will be different from that with the stranger whom I do not. 'An ethic of undifferentiated love which allows of no application to proximate relations could have little relevance for embodied human beings who can be at only one place at a time and must needs be closer to some people than to others.'[26] For this reason too, 'loving a stranger does not mean treating him as a member of one's family; for that he is not. We love the stranger by responding to him as one who *is* a stranger, and therefore different from us. We bestow value by accepting his separateness, not by giving him intimate rights to which he has no claim.'[27] Thus we could have feelings of benevolence toward the stranger, but our mutual fellowship will be limited because of the limited extent to which we know each other. Similarly, our fellowship with many people will be limited to those areas in life which we share and where we therefore have mutual interests in which we can identify with each other. We will respect their separateness in other areas and tend to be reticent in intruding in their lives beyond the limits

---

[25] Ibid., 240. Similarly, 'my demand for your virtue is the demand that, in identifying with you, I do not enter into conflict with myself. You must be what I endorse.' *Sexual Desire*, 230.

[26] Oliver O'Donovan, *Resurrection and the Moral Order* (Leicester 1986), 240.

[27] Singer, *Nature of Love* I, 304.

which they tacitly set us, and beyond which we do not know whether we could identify with them with integrity. As we argued in section 7.3, establishing and extending relationships of fellowship is a risky affair and normally negotiated tacitly and with caution. Thus we can differentiate our fellowships with others in terms of the extent to which our lives overlap and give rise to mutual concerns in which we can identify with each other. Probably the most intensive form of fellowship, in which the range of mutual identification is the widest, is that aimed at in romantic love. Here two people aim to share their lives with each other in the most central and intimate respects where others are not allowed to intrude. Romantic lovers usually seek to know each other more intimately and therefore have greater mutual trust and unreserved candour toward each other than will be characteristic of their relations with other people.

In section 7.2 we pointed out that as human beings we are inconsistent in our dealings with each other. Our loves are therefore rarely pure. To a greater or lesser extent, our relations of fellowship are always accompanied by attempts to gain control over each other or to create mutual obligations through tacit agreements of rights and duties. Often our relationships with others do not even reach the stage of fellowship or mutual identification, and when they do, the range and intensity of the fellowship can vary considerably. Even when I manage to identify with others in the same way as I identify with myself, the range and intensity of this identification differs from person to person. In these ways our loves are differentiated from person to person. In this respect God's love for us is different. Not only is God consistent in his dealings with us, but his identification with each of us is not subject to the strictures of finitude which apply to ours. God's love for each of us is infinite because he knows each of us infinitely. To him 'all hearts are open, all desires known', and from him 'no secrets are hid'. God knows each of us perfectly and is therefore able to identify with each of us in perfect love as we in our finitude and mutual ignorance are unable to identify with each other. If we fail to achieve such perfect fellowship with God, this is not because God has become unfaithful and has forsaken us, but because we fail to put our trust in the One who alone can be trusted never to forsake us but always to remain true in his love for each and every one of us. In the words of Augustine quoted in section 5.3: 'No one can lose you, my God, unless he forsakes you' (*Confessions* IV.9).

We have argued above that, in loving you, I identify with your good and not with your will for the simple reason that your will, like mine, is fallible and therefore not necessarily in accordance with your good. I will therefore always have to appraise your wishes and your will in the light of a higher standard of goodness in order to determine whether granting your wishes would further your good. In the case of our love for God, this is different. As we argued in chapter 3, the union of love which the believer seeks with God consists precisely in a perfect accord of the believer's will with the Will of God. Within the Christian faith, the Will of God is affirmed to be the ultimate standard of goodness. For the Christian, God is the *proton philon*, to use Plato's term. God's Will is absolutely good, and not good relative to some more ultimate standard of goodness.[28] Hence the judgment 'what God wants is good' is not the outcome of an appraisal of God's Will in the light of some higher standard of goodness, but an affirmation that his Will *is* the ultimate standard. For the believer there can be no more ultimate standard of goodness in the light of which the Will of God could be judged. On the contrary, believers consider the Will of God to be the ultimate standard in the light of which all their own wishes and value preferences are to be judged and their lives and characters are to be continuously remodelled. As we described in chapter 3, the *via mystica* is aimed at this process of remodelling in which the believer's life is on the one hand purified from false ways of feeling, thinking, and acting which are contrary to the Will of God, and on the other hand regains the likeness of the Divine love which was lost through sin. In the words which we quoted from St Bernard, the believer's soul is 'sprinkled with the hyssop of humility' and 'set alight by the fire of love'.

---

[28] On the distinction between absolute and relative standards of goodness in this connection, see my *Speaking of a Personal God*, 96–101, D. Z. Phillips, *Faith and Philosophical Enquiry* (London 1970), 79f, and Patterson Brown, 'God and the good', *Religious Studies* 2 (1967), 269–76.

In this way love for God turns into *worship* or unconditional obedience, and for the believer God alone is worthy of worship. In this respect the believer's love for God is essentially different from love for other persons. From one human being to another, there can never be an absolute duty of obedience. Our obedience to each other always requires justification, and we should never obey a human being for no other reason than that he is what he is. Unconditional obedience is due to God alone.[29] This seems to raise a problem, as James Rachels explains:

The idea that any being could be *worthy* of worship is much more problematical than we might have at first imagined. For in admitting that a being is worthy of worship we would be recognising him as having an unqualified claim on our obedience. The question, then, is whether there could be such an unqualified claim... Such a recognition could never be made by a moral agent... To be a moral agent is to be an autonomous or self-directing agent... [Hence] to deliver oneself over to a moral authority for directions about what to do is simply incompatible with being a moral agent. To say 'I will follow so-and-so's directions no matter what they are and no matter what my own conscience would otherwise direct me to do' is to opt out of moral thinking altogether; it is to abandon one's role as a moral agent.[30]

In other words, it seems that subjecting oneself unconditionally to the Will of God in this way, entails the abandonment of one's own moral autonomy as a person which, as we have argued above, is a necessary condition for one's relationship with God to be a relation of loving fellowship. In this way we would seem to allow our relationship with God to be perverted into a manipulative one.

This objection is flawed in two respects. First of all, a moral agent must be able to decide whether a course of action is right in the light of some standard of value, which in turn will have to be justified in terms of higher standards of value and ultimately in terms of an ultimate standard which is itself not relative to any higher standard. Thus, being a moral agent entails recognizing some standard of value as ultimate. This rec-

---

[29] See John Burnaby, *Amor Dei*, 311.
[30] James Rachels, 'God and human attitudes', in Paul Helm (ed.), *Divine Commands and Morality* (Oxford 1981), 44.

ognition must necessarily be unconditional in the sense that a standard logically cannot be recognized as ultimate *on condition that* it fulfils some still higher standard: being ultimate logically excludes the existence of any such higher standard. Far from excluding the unconditional recognition of some standard as ultimate, being a moral agent therefore logically requires such recognition. Thus every moral agent necessarily has to submit unconditionally to some ultimate standard of value, some *proton philon*, whether it be the Guru or the Great Dictator, the good of Humanity or some platonic ideal of the Ultimate Good – or the Will of God. As a moral agent, the believer ascribes this role to the Will of God. Secondly, the moral agency of the believer does not exclude the unconditional recognition of God's Will as ultimate standard of value, since such recognition is neither arbitrary nor necessitated. As we argued in section 7.4, such recognition is not arbitrary since God motivates us in his trinitarian way to turn to him. On the other hand, since motivation is not coercion, it still requires us as persons and as moral agents to exercise our *liberum arbitrium* and decide freely to turn to God. Neither is such motivation the imposition of an external moral obligation to which the believer is subjected. Believers do not worship God out of obligation, but because they want to. 'God's claim for obedience is always for an obedience that springs from love and therefore is wholly free.'[31] Believers enjoy what St Bernard calls the *liberum a miseria*. In fact, believers worship God joyfully since for them ultimate bliss consists in 'glorifying God and enjoying him for ever'.

9.3 THE SUFFERING OF LOVE

For us, loving God and loving each other can both be the source of bliss. As we argued in chapter 4, it can also involve suffering. In the words of Ortega which we quoted in section 2.6: 'Who doubts that the lover can find happiness in his beloved? But it is no less certain that love is sometimes sad, as sad as death – a supreme and mortal torment.' The suffering of love results from the distance which separates the lover from the beloved, and

[31] Burnaby, *Amor Dei*, 312.

this distance follows in turn from the fact that the partners in a relation of fellowship are necessarily free and autonomous agents in relation to each other. As we argued in section 7.3, this makes lovers vulnerable and dependent on each other's freedom and faithfulness in order to establish and to maintain their fellowship. Such vulnerability breeds uncertainty and suffering. In the words of Andreas Capellanus, quoted in section 4.3, 'that love is suffering is easy to see ... since the lover is always in fear that his love may not gain its desire and that he is wasting his efforts ... Indeed he fears so many things that it would be difficult to tell them.'

As we have shown in previous chapters, there are various ways in which lovers could respond to this distance and to the suffering to which it gives rise. One such response would be to accept the vulnerability and suffering of love, turn it into a chosen way of life and revel in it. In chapter 4 we noted this tendency within the courtly tradition, and quoted the words of Chrétien de Troyes: 'From all other ills doth mine differ. It pleaseth me; I rejoice in it; my ill is what I want and my suffering is my health.' This is perverse. In the words of Simone Weil quoted in section 4.5, 'it is wrong to desire affliction; it is against nature, and it is a perversion; and moreover it is the essence of affliction that it is suffered unwillingly.' Furthermore, as De Rougemont points out, this is no longer love for the beloved but enjoyment of the passionate sensation of being in love. As such the courtly lover, like Stendhal's lover and William James' mystic, becomes a solipsist who loves his or her own sensations or fantasies or ecstatic experiences.

A second response would be like that of the quietist who renounces all desire for the love of the beloved. The lover could still serve the good of the beloved, but has given up the desire for his or her love to be reciprocated. In this way the lover becomes invulnerable to the response of the beloved, and to the suffering which results when the beloved fails to return his or her love. This is beneficence but not love for it treats the beloved as an object of care rather than a personal partner in fellowship.

A third (and the most common) response to the vulnerability of love, is that in which we seek invulnerability by trying to gain control over the response of the beloved, either by coercion or obligation. As we argued at length in sections 7.2 and 7.3, this merely perverts love into a form of manipulation or into an agreement of rights and duties.

These three responses to the vulnerability of love all end in perverting love into something else. The only response which does not pervert the love which it seeks is to accept the vulnerability, not for its own sake, but for the sake of love itself. I long for your love, but I will restrain this longing when it tries to control your love and prevents you from bestowing it on me freely. I long for your love as a gift which only you can freely bestow on me, and I wait on you to bestow it rather than trying to earn or extort it from you. I put my trust in you to bestow your love on me and not in my own capacity to earn or extort your love from you. I know that such efforts on my part will only pervert the fellowship which they seek to establish. In other words, I value our mutual fellowship more than the invulnerability which I can attain by denying your freedom as a person to let me down from time to time. I am willing to bear the affliction of being let down rather than to pervert the fellowship with you. In this sense we can agree with Simone Weil's claim that, although love does not desire affliction, it is always permitted to love 'the possibility of affliction', which is another name for the vulnerability of love. For the sake of love I am willing to forgive you when you should let me down, and I trust that for the sake of love you will also be willing to forgive me when I should let you down. And, as we explained in section 8.1 above, the one who forgives is the one who suffers.

This response entails a tension between longing and restraint which Ilham Dilman describes as follows:

The lover has to learn to contain the longing which his very love inspires for the sake of the loved one, and he can only do so because he loves her, because his love is more than this longing. Yet the aspect of his love from which the longing comes and the aspect which enables him to learn to contain it are different and conflicting aspects of the same love. Everything in the passion from which the longing comes fights against the containing of it.[32]

[32] Dilman, *Love and Human Separateness*, 89.

As we argued in the previous section, our human finitude limits the extent to which our loves can bear this tension without our having to sacrifice our integrity as persons, which in turn would also entail a perversion of our love. Thus in the end, as Dilham explains, the degree to which this longing has to be contained depends on the compatibility between the lover and the beloved – compatibility in temperament, in sensibility, in intelligence, in imagination, etc. The limits of such compatibility stretch in many directions and admit of great flexibility. Nevertheless, when they are stretched too far in a particular case, this puts a strain on the maintenance of reciprocity.[33]

Longing and restraint are characteristic too for the way in which God loves us. In his love, God identifies with us and longs for us to come and be reconciled with him and so to receive salvation and eternal happiness. In the words of Julian of Norwich, God

> wants us to see our wretchedness and meekly to acknowledge it; but he does not want us to remain there, or to be much occupied in self-accusation, nor does he want us to be too full of our own misery. But he wants us quickly to attend to him, for he stands all alone, and he waits for us continually, moaning and mourning until we come. And he hastens to bring us to him, for we are his joy and delight, and he is the remedy of our life.[34]

This divine longing is accompanied by infinite restraint. As we have argued at length in previous chapters, God does not coerce or oblige us to return his love, but has infinite patience in waiting on us to do so. He never gives up his willingness to forgive those who turn to him. The Greek word used in the Bible for this divine patience, *makrothymia*, is rendered very well in English as 'long-suffering'.

Unlike ours, the longing and restraint of God's love are both infinite. In these respects too, God's love is not subject to the strictures of finitude like ours. As we explained above, there are limits to the extent in which our love for each other can withstand the strain of being unrequited. Sooner or later we

---

[33] Ibid., 89.
[34] *Showings* (Classics of Western Spirituality, London 1978), chapter 79.

either lose our patience (or long-suffering) and give up loving each other or we try to coerce or oblige each other to respond. God's desire for our love, however, is infinite and is never diminished by the fact that we continually turn against him. Nor does he ever abandon the patient or long-suffering restraint with which he waits for us, and try instead to coerce or oblige us to return his love. Unlike ours, his willingness to forgive those who turn to him is infinite. As a God of love, he chooses to remain infinitely vulnerable in relation to us. In this respect the cross of Christ is for Christians the paradigmatic revelation of God's loving readiness to suffer on account of the evil that we do to him and to each other.[35] This provides a basis for believers to find consolation by experiencing their own affliction as participation in the long-suffering love of God. In this light we can now understand the view of Simone Weil to which we referred in section 4.5: 'So long as we are not submerged in affliction, all we can do is to desire that, if it should come, it may be a participation in the Cross of Christ.'[36]

It is clear that this view of the love of God conflicts with the traditional doctrine of divine impassibility, according to which God's perfection entails that he lacks nothing and therefore can have no desires which could be thwarted, causing him to suffer. As we have shown in chapters 5 and 6, this is the view of divine perfection which was put forward by Plato and was self-evident for a vast number of theologians in the Christian tradition, including Augustine and Nygren. In terms of our argument above, this view turns God into a quietist who avoids vulnerability and suffering by renouncing all desires. Such a God could be infinitely beneficent toward us, but as we have argued at length, he cannot be the God of love. Part of the conceptual price of looking on God as a God of love is therefore that we should give up the doctrine of divine impassibility. In contemporary theology, however, most theologians seem to have

---

[35] On the cross of Christ as the paradigmatic revelation of God's suffering, see for example John R. Stott, *The Cross of Christ* (Leicester 1987), 331-2, and H. J. M. Nouwen, D. P. McNeill and D. A. Morrison, *Compassion* (London 1989), 15-16, 23-4, 39.

[36] *Gateway to God*, 88. On consolation in this sense, see also section 6.6 of my *Speaking of a Personal God*.

very little difficulty in doing so. As Ronald Goetz points out, 'the rejection of the ancient doctrine of divine impassibility has become a theological commonplace'.[37]

Does our love for God also involve vulnerability and suffering, and is it also characterized by longing and restraint? If, as believers claim, our eternal happiness consists in being in the love of God, it is obvious that believers should desire and long for the love of God. Thus, as we saw in section 6.2, even Anders Nygren admits that 'since God is the Highest Good, the sum of all conceivable good and desirable objects, it is natural that he should attract to himself all desire and love'. Furthermore, since what we long for is the *gift* of God's love which he must bestow on us freely, we have to wait on him to bestow it and restrain our urge to coerce or oblige him. We must put our trust in him to be merciful rather than in our own capacity to earn or cause his love for us.

Among finite persons, such self-restraint is especially difficult since it requires us to surrender ourselves to other finite beings whom we know from experience to be as undependable and prone to become unfaithful as we are ourselves. We have great difficulty in risking such surrender without demanding some sort of guarantee that we will not be let down. In section 7.3 we pointed out how we try to limit such risks by means of the fundamentally tacit or indirect way in which we establish and maintain our fellowship with each other. We must first get to know one another well before we can bring ourselves to assume an attitude of unreserved trust and open candour toward each other. Such unreserved surrender is risky and many are never able to take the risk. As Rudolf Bultmann explains:

From human intercourse we know as it is – whether from ourselves or by observation of others – how difficult *sheer surrender* is. Many human beings long for friendship and love, and in this they basically long for surrender of themselves, in which their being is to be fulfilled. Yet they are incapable of taking the decision of unreserved surrender in the

---

[37] Ronald Goetz, 'The suffering God', *The Christian Century* 103 (1986), 385. For an exhaustive discussion and a detailed critical assessment of the conceptual price of either accepting or rejecting this traditional doctrine, see Marcel Sarot, *God, Passibility and Corporeality* (Kampen 1992).

encounters of life, or of trusting simply, without being able to hold on to a support, without a guarantee. Many a friendship and many a marriage is wrecked by man's inability to win this victory over himself.[38]

In brief, love is risky, and many are reluctant to take the risk.

Is loving God also risky in this way? Does such unreserved surrender to God also involve taking the risk of being let down by him? In the Christian tradition it has invariably been held that in this respect God's love differs essentially from that of finite human persons. With finite persons we always risk being let down while there is not the slightest likelihood that God will ever forsake us. An important strand throughout the Christian tradition has tended to interpret this claim in an essentialistic way: As in neo-Platonism, God is viewed as an eternal fountain from which goodness flows forth with eternal necessity. Since it belongs to God's essential nature to be good and faithful, it is 'logically' impossible for him ever to let us down. Thus for example, as we saw in chapter 6, Anders Nygren seems to hold that God is somehow necessitated by his essential nature to love us. And, more recently, Richard Swinburne argues that God 'always does what is good for that is how he is made'![39] In previous chapters we have argued that this view denies God's freedom as a personal agent. On this view God does not love us or remain faithful to us because he freely decides to do so, but because his essential nature deprives him of the ability to do otherwise. We need not *trust* God not to let us down, since we can rest assured that he lacks the ability to do so. Personal terms like 'trust' and 'love' would no longer apply. Love that is not freely given is not love at all. In section 7.2 we quoted Jean-Paul Sartre's remark that 'the man who wants to be loved ... is not bent on becoming the object of passion which flows forth mechanically. He does not want to possess an automaton ... [whose] passion is the result of a psychological determinism.' The essentialistic view of God's love is similarly flawed, since it takes God's love for us to be the result of an 'ontological' determinism. This excludes the possibility of having a loving

[38] Rudolf Bultmann, *Essays Philosophical and Theological* (London 1955), 174–5.
[39] Richard Swinburne, *The Coherence of Theism* (Oxford 1977), 182.

relationship with God. In the words of Sartre, 'if the beloved is transformed into an automaton, the lover finds himself alone'. In brief, it is incoherent to try to avoid the risk involved in loving God by denying God the ability to reject us or become unfaithful to us. We cannot thus avoid the conclusion that faith involves a leap.

On the other hand, the claim that God's love does not flow forth mechanically and that he loves us because he freely decides to do so, does not imply that God is fickle-minded like a finite person. On the contrary, unlike us, God does not suffer from weakness of will, and therefore always remains consistent and faithful to his own character.[40] In this sense God is not like other people. The risk we take in loving God is incomparably less than that involved in loving finite persons. We can never be quite certain that other people will not let us down, while there is never the slightest likelihood that God will ever act out of character by forsaking us. We cannot always count on other people forgiving us when we are penitent about letting them down, while with God we can be sure that 'if we confess our sins, he is just and may be trusted to forgive our sins and cleanse us from every kind of wrong' (1 John 1: 9).

In spite of the fact that, unlike human persons, God is infinitely trustworthy, we humans remain reluctant to take the leap of faith and surrender ourselves unconditionally to the love of God. Instead of taking the risk of putting our trust in God's grace, we seek prior guarantees by imagining that our own goodness and merit make us worthy of God's love and therefore somehow *oblige* him to love us. 'No sooner do we believe that God loves us than there is an impulse to believe that he does so, not because he is Love, but because we are intrinsically lovable.'[41] It is precisely the illusion that we could be deserving in the eyes of God which logically stands in the way of our receiving the love of God as a gift. We confuse the gift of love with reward for work done, and have therefore continually to be reminded that 'it is by grace you are saved through faith; it is

---

[40] For a defence of this claim and an extended criticism of the essentialistic interpretation of God's impeccability, see chapter 4 of my *Speaking of a Personal God*.
[41] Lewis, *Four Loves*, 119.

not your own doing. It is God's gift, not a reward for work done' (Ephesians 2: 8–9). Thus, as Bultmann explains,

faith is obedience, because in it man's pride is broken. What is actually a foregone conclusion becomes for man in pride what is most difficult …He thinks that he will be lost if he surrenders himself – if he surrenders himself as the man he has made of himself, but he is *supposed* to lose himself in order to find himself for the first time. He is supposed to bow, to humble himself, to let his pride go, in order to come to himself in this way.[42]

In this light it is now clear why the first step in the *via mystica* as we described this in section 3.2, is that in which we learn repentance, self-denial and humility. In order to be able to receive the gift of God's love for which we long, we must first learn to restrain our pride which makes us imagine that we could somehow oblige God to love us. The love of God, like the love of each other, is therefore characterised by both longing and restraint.

According to Simone Weil, 'the extreme greatness of Christianity lies in the fact that it does not seek a supernatural remedy for suffering but a supernatural use for it'.[43] This supernatural use lies in the fact that affliction can make us aware of our vulnerability and so help to free us from the illusions of personal worthiness which prevent us from receiving divine love as a gift. Through affliction we can achieve what she calls 'spiritual nakedness' before God. In the *Gorgias*, Plato tells a myth of how souls judged after death are required to come before their judges naked so that the judges would not be deceived by outer appearances. According to Eric Springsted, Simone Weil's metaphor of 'spiritual nakedness' is an extension of this idea:

When nothing stands between us and God, our true selves can be joined to him and clothed in his goodness. We however, do not easily give up this veil, for our positions and prestige give us security in the world and a way to manage our daily bread. In affliction, though, the veil is torn away. If we continue to love in affliction and do not wish for our old costumes back, because God crosses the void to all who truly desire him, then there is an opportunity for a pure, undiluted

---

[42] Bultmann, *Essays*, 174.
[43] Simone Weil, *Gravity and Grace* (London 1972), 73.

contact of the soul and God. In that contact, when there is nothing between the soul and God, spiritual unity can be achieved and our deepest longings for good fulfilled.[44]

Loving God and loving other people can both involve suffering and affliction. In our love for finite persons, this affliction is often the result of the fact that we let each other down and are prone to become unfaithful in our love for each other. This does not apply to our love for God, since God is never unfaithful and never lets us down. However, in all our loves, both for God and for each other, our affliction is often the result of our lack of restraint through which we seek to coerce or oblige God and other people to love us, and thereby we systematically pervert the love for which we long. And we long because we *need* to be loved. Why this need?

9.4 NEED-LOVE

We need to be loved because our fellowship with others determines both our identity and our value as persons. This requires some explanation. Let us start with the concept of personal identity.

As we explained in section 1.1, every entity shares many characteristics with other entities and can therefore be classified as a member of many different classes of entities. However, every entity can also be identified by the specific configuration of characteristics which distinguishes it from all other entities. This distinct configuration constitutes its identity as an object. As human beings we are also bodily entities, and can therefore identify each other in the same way in terms of the configuration of physical characteristics and capacities, spatio-temporal locations, behavioural dispositions, character traits, etc. which distinguishes each of us from all other human beings. 'Who is Jack?' 'Jack is the friendly bald man who lives in the next street and walks past here every morning muttering to himself.' In this way we can identify Jack as an object, but not as a person. What makes me the person I am is not the characteristics which I happen to have, nor even the wishes and desires and

[44] Eric O. Springsted, *Simone Weil and the Suffering of Love* (Cambridge Mass. 1986), 46.

convictions which I happen to have, but rather the wishes and desires and convictions which I endorse and want to motivate my actions. My individuality as a person is bound up with my authenticity, with whether or not my actions and responses come from me, and whether or not I endorse as my own the convictions from which I act, the desires I pursue.[45] In this way being a person entails what Harry Frankfurt calls 'the capacity for reflective self-evaluation that is manifested in the formation of second-order desires',[46] i.e. desires as to which of my first-order desires I consider conducive to my good and therefore authentically want to be the effective motivation of my actions. This connects with the point we raised in section 9.2 that as a person I have the capacity for objective appraisal of my own wishes and will in the light of what I consider to be my own good. Roger Scruton points out that persons may set themselves to oppose their own desires. In that case their actions are not merely motivated by self-interest but by a conception of the good.[47] Such appraisal can lead one to endorse some of one's first-order desires and to repudiate others.

An individual human being 'transcends' his feelings, desires and the various features of his character ... [i.e. he] can himself be aware of them so that he can endorse or repudiate them and thus assume responsibility for what he is. They do not belong to him in the sense that the properties of a stone belongs to it ... Where a man repudiates an aspect of his character, say his greed ... he transcends it. He does not identify himself with it, he does not act from greed; but when he does he feels ashamed. When he endorses it too he transcends it ... He has made the greed his own; it is not something just given.[48]

When looked upon as an object, my identity is given in the distinct configuration of characteristics which I happen to have. As a person, however, my identity is given in the desires, character-traits, characteristics, etc. which I endorse in my

[45] Dilman, *Love and Human Separateness*, 131.
[46] Harry G. Frankfurt, *The Importance of What We Care About* (Cambridge 1988), 12. On page 16 he introduces the term 'second-order volitions' for those desires which I want to endorse as my 'effective desire or will', and states that 'it is having second-order volitions ... that I regard as essential to being a person'.
[47] Scruton, *Sexual Desire*, 42.
[48] Dilman, *Love and Human Separateness*, 132. Dilman is here expounding the view of Jean-Paul Sartre.

second-order volitions and for which I authentically assume responsibility. In terms of the distinction which we introduced in section 5.2, we might say that my identity as an object is given in my imperfect actuality, whereas my identity as a person resides in the perfect potentiality or individual *daimon* with which I choose to identify. As an object my identity is *given*; as a person I *choose* my identity. In this connection Dilman refers approvingly to Jean-Paul Sartre's rejection of the view that one's identity as an individual is given to one by other people. For Sartre the personal characteristics which define an individual's identity are not simply *given*. They do not exist '*en soi*', like the properties of a stone. Sartre insists that we have the power to fight and reject the identity which others attempt to foist on us. Acquiescing in it is sinking into 'bad faith'.[49] Allowing others to foist an identity on me means allowing them to treat me as an object rather than as a person.

True as this may be, it is not the whole truth. Indeed, my authentic choice is a *necessary* condition for determining my identity as a person. But it is not *sufficient*. I cannot just claim any identity I please. Since my existence as a person is not solipsistic, my identity claim can only be upheld to the extent that others endorse it and recognize me to be the person I claim to be. For this reason the need for recognition is not something perverse, but is appropriate for persons who have to live with others and in the sight of others. Behind our need for recognition is the knowledge of our dependence on the opinion of others, and on the others themselves.[50] My identity as a person is neither determined by myself alone, nor is it foisted upon me by others, but it is constituted by a consensus in which my claim is endorsed by others. Persons can interact intelligibly only on the basis of an agreement or consensus about who each of them is. Thus van de Vate points out that the cliché lunatic who claims to be Napoleon imposes impossible identity requirements on those who would interact with him as if he were sane. If they agree with him, then others will not agree with them, and their own identities are put at risk. Hence they think him mad.[51] Note

---

[49] Ibid., 69.   [50] Bultmann, *Essays*, 172.
[51] Van de Vate, *Romantic Love*, 23.

that my endorsement of your identity claim does not only help constitute your identity as a person, but it also determines my own identity as someone who is committed to treat you as the person with the identity which you claim. This is the same point which we raised in section 7.3 where we argued that in loving you I identify with you and thereby assume responsibility for remaining faithful to this identification. Not only is our identity as persons bestowed on us in the love which others have for us, but our own identity is equally determined by the love which we have for others.

However, your love for me does not only endorse my personal identity but, as we have shown in previous chapters, it also bestows intrinsic value on my person by looking on me as an irreplaceable individual. If you reject my fellowship, you reject me as a person and in so doing you threaten my ability to conceive of myself as intrinsically worthy, whereas in loving me you bestow a value on my person which I cannot give it myself. It means that my person, my individual *daimon*, not only matters to me but also to someone else apart from me, and that therefore receives a significance which it is beyond my power to bestow on it myself. Your love bestows value on me which I would otherwise not have. It does not merely recognize a value which I already have apart from this recognition. In this sense Nygren is correct in his observation that love *creates* value in the beloved, and does not merely recognize it. Since in this way both our identity and our value as persons is constituted by our relations of fellowship with others, we *need* to partake in such relationships. As persons we therefore *necessarily* long both to love and to be loved.

All this applies to fellowship with other people. For the believer this applies even more to the love of God. As we have argued, my identity as a person is constituted by those desires and character-traits of mine which I authentically endorse as being conducive to my good and therefore in accordance with my individual *daimon*. As a believer I seek my *ultimate* good in the love of God. Thus, as Augustine says, our ultimate happiness (*frui*) consists in being in the love of God. The identity which as a believer I endorse as my own is precisely that of a person who enjoys a relation of loving fellowship with God. For this identity I am dependent on the recognition of God. Hence as a believer I would not merely anchor my personal identity in the recognition of other people, but would ultimately need divine recognition in order to be the person I claim to be. Who am I? I am the person that mother loves, and that Jill loves. Indeed. But ultimately I am the person that God loves.[52] Furthermore, in loving me God makes my good his very own concern, and since my good is identical with my loving him, he desires my love. 'When God loves, he desires nothing but to be loved, since he loves us for no other reason than to be loved, for he knows that those who love him are blessed in their very love.'[53] In this way I know that my good and my love are of infinite value, because they are of value to God. In the words of John Lucas, 'to be esteemed by another secures one's own self-esteem, and gives body to one's sense of identity'.[54] To this the believer would want to add that to be esteemed by God secures one's own self-esteem *infinitely*, and gives *infinite* body to one's own sense of identity.

Clearly then, we long for the love of others because as persons we necessarily *need* to be loved. But can we say the same of God? Does God also *need* our love in the way we need his love? If, as we have argued, God *desires* our love, it would seem to follow that he also *needs* our love for this desire to be fulfilled. Thus as Murdoch Dahl points out, it is a constant theme of grass-roots Christian devotion that God *longs for* a response from his children and if he longs for it he must in some sense need it.[55] In the Christian theological tradition, however, this whole line of argument has often been rejected as contrary to the doctrine of divine aseity or self-sufficiency as this follows from the Platonic view of divine perfection which we discussed in section 7.8 and which, as pointed out in the previous section, is also the basis for the doctrine of divine impassibility. Thus if God's perfection means that he lacks nothing, he would indeed have no desires and no needs, and would not need our love. However, the kind

[52] Cf. John Lucas, *Freedom and Grace*, 60.
[53] St. Bernard, *Song of Songs*, Sermon 83. [54] Lucas, *Freedom and Grace*, 60.
[55] Dahl, *Daughter of Love*, 272

of God entailed by this view of divine aseity is not the kind of God who can relate in loving fellowship to persons beyond himself. On the contrary, it would be a narcissistic God who in solitary self-sufficiency eternally contemplates and loves himself. In this sense Plato is correct in claiming that divine perfection as conceived by him entails that the gods cannot love. Clearly then, part of the conceptual price of the model of love is that we give up the doctrine of divine aseity in this form. Keith Ward points out that we should not try to preserve an idea of divine self-sufficiency by denying that he depends upon any finite thing in any way, for that would entail a denial that the divine nature can be co-operative, self-giving love.[56]

On the other hand, the model of love does not require us to hold that there are no respects in which God is self-sufficient. In fact, the term 'self-sufficiency' is an incomplete symbol which requires us to specify in which respects something is self-sufficient and in which respects it is not. Here Paul Fiddes makes a useful distinction between 'self-sufficiency' and 'self-existence': although God is the ground of his own being, this does not necessarily entail that he must be unconditioned by anything else in every conceivable way. To affirm that God is 'self-sufficient' for the fact of his existence (or self-existent) does not necessarily mean that he is self-sufficient for the whole mode of his divine life.[57] Furthermore, the fact that God is dependent on us for being the kind of loving God he is, is not something which is foisted on him by some necessity inside or outside of him. He is as he is because that is the way he chooses to be. 'God does not "need" the world in the sense that there is some intrinsic necessity in his nature, binding his free choice ... but he does need the world in the sense that he has freely chosen to be in need.'[58] In brief, then, like our love, God's love needs to be reciprocated. God needs our love, because he is the loving God he has freely decided to be.

---

[56] Keith Ward, *Rational Theology and the Creativity of God* (Oxford 1982), 86.

[57] Paul S. Fiddes, *The Creative Suffering of God* (Oxford 1988), 66–7.

[58] Ibid., 74. Thus also: 'He is self-existent (*a se*) in the sense that he has absolute freedom to choose himself and his relationship to others. He is unconditioned only in the sense that he is free to choose whether to be conditioned or not', 68.

Defenders of the so-called social theory of the Trinity might reject this view and argue that God does not need persons beyond himself in order to be a God of love, for the three persons of the Trinity eternally love each other. God can have personal relations within himself. This view of the Trinity is unsatisfactory for both religious and theological reasons. From a religious point of view, a God who does not need to participate in loving fellowship with us, is unable to 'secure our self-esteem and give body to our sense of identity' in the sense which we explained above. From a theological point of view, this theory of the Trinity (like the view on the relation between the Father and the Son which we criticized in section 8.3) cannot do justice to the unity between the persons of the Trinity. As Keith Ward explains:

Some philosophers have tried to show that God could express self-giving love even without creation, by positing a sort of committee of gods loving each other ... Others have suggested that the Trinity is a sort of social reality, that there are three persons (centres of awareness) in one substance. But ... it is clear that a person is a substance, and that is one being ... not a society of persons. To admit many centres of awareness in God would split the divine being unacceptably ... The view is indistinguishable from a more robust polytheism, and must be rejected by thoroughgoing monotheists, such as Christians are supposed to be.[59]

A further objection which might be brought against the claim that God needs our love, is that it too easily interprets divine love on the model of human love. The sort of need-love which we described above is characteristic for finite human beings. God's love is different. It is pure gift-love or *agape*. 'This primal love is gift-love. In God there is no hunger that needs to be filled, only plenteousness that desires to give ... God, who needs nothing, loves into existence wholly superfluous creatures in order that he may love and perfect them.'[60] Furthermore, it might be objected that this analysis is also flawed as far as human love is concerned. Have we not merely turned human

---

[59] Ward, *Rational Theology*, 86. It is significant that a contemporary champion of this social theory of the Trinity like Jürgen Moltmann criticizes Karl Barth's view for being a form of 'Christian monotheism'. See Moltmann, *The Trinity and the Kingdom of God* (London 1981), 139–44.   [60] Lewis, *Four Loves*, 116.

love into a form of egocentric self-regard as opposed to selfless other-regard? Should human love not be like divine love in being unconditional giving rather than a desire for self-fulfilment? Helen Oppenheimer points out that for many Christians the answer to these questions appears obvious: Fulfilment must give way, and

its honourable recurrence in the Christian tradition is taken to be an aberration. Regard for self is just one insidious way in which selfishness, the great enemy, is manifested. What Christianity is really about is *agape*, that totally selfless love for which Christians had to find a name to distinguish it from all our human egoistic loves ... That is how God loves and so that is the sort of love we are to learn.[61]

Let us now turn our attention to this concept of gift-love and see how it is related to the need-love described above. Are these two loves really 'two fundamentally opposed types of religion and ethics' as we have seen Anders Nygren argue? Does unconditional giving in human love exclude the desire for self-fulfilment? And is it adequate to restrict God's love to gift-love and deny that he can have need-love as well? And is Nygren correct in his view that all need-love or *eros* is necessarily self-seeking?

9.5 GIFT-LOVE

In section 7.3 we argued that in a relation of fellowship or love I identify with you by serving your interests as being my own. This devotion to your good is unconditional in the sense that I do not serve your interests on condition that you serve mine in return. That is what distinguishes love from an agreement of rights and duties where I serve your interests in order to earn your services in return. I enter such agreements with you for the sake of the advantage which I can gain from it for myself. My aim is purely self-regarding whereas in love my aim is other-regarding since there I devote myself to serving your good which through identification I have made my own. In this sense love is indeed unconditional *agape* or gift-love rather than the desire for the fulfilment of one's own needs or interests.

[61] Oppenheimer, *Hope of Happiness*, 104.

Let us illustrate this distinction from the correspondence of Abelard and Heloise. There Heloise writes to Abelard: 'God knows I never sought anything in you except yourself; I wanted simply you, nothing of yours...It was not my own pleasures and wishes I sought to gratify, as you well know, but yours.'[62] And Abelard writes to her: 'My love, which brought us both to sin, should be called lust, not love. I took my fill of my wretched pleasures in you, and this was the sum total of my love.'[63] In the terms of the popular song, Heloise loved Abelard 'for himself alone', while he loved her 'for her golden hair and her eyes of blue'. According to Abelard we should love God in the way Heloise loved him and not in the way he loved her.

Since loving God for his sake meant loving him regardless of rewards, Abelard argued that to love God properly one had to renounce even the desire for beatitude. Like all his contemporaries, Abelard asserts that the perfect love of God is itself beatitude; yet he insists that God must not be loved *because of any desire* for beatitude. Loving God should enable us to renounce *everything* for his sake – including the search for goodness.[64]

Does this mean that loving God requires us to renounce the desire for beatitude and the search for goodness, that loving you for yourself alone requires me to be indifferent to your golden hair and your eyes of blue, that pure gift-love or *agape* requires us to foreswear all need-love or *eros*? This conclusion, which we saw Nygren defending, is defective in a number of ways.

First of all, as we have shown in previous chapters, pure giving without receiving is not love but mere beneficence. Not only does this treat the beloved as an object to be beneficently 'managed or handled or cured or trained', but it also denies the reciprocity which is a necessary condition if love is to be a relation of mutual fellowship. In the words of Macmurray which we quoted in section 7.2, 'If in my relation with you I insist on behaving generously toward you and refuse to accept your generosity in return, I make myself the giver and you the recipient...This is the worst kind of tyranny, and is shockingly unfair to you.'

[62] *Letters*, 113.   [63] Ibid., 153.
[64] Singer, *Nature of Love* I, 195. See also Gilson, *Mystic Theology*, 158–66.

Secondly, it is incoherent to demand that everyone should exclusively adopt an attitude of gift-love and foreswear all need-love. It is logically impossible for there to be only givers and no receivers. 'If any creatures are to be loved and cherished, then sooner or later we ourselves are likewise to be loved and cherished. What is sauce for the gander is sauce for the goose. To shut our eyes to this for ever would be inverted pride or faithlessness rather than Christian humility.'[65] If we were to foreswear all need-love it would also be logically impossible for God to bestow any gift-love on us. If beatitude consists in being in the love of God, we logically cannot love God and at the same time foreswear the desire for beatitude. Furthermore, Abelard's demand that we should love God in the way in which Heloise loved him would become logically impossible if God were unable to show need-love toward us. As we have shown in section 6.2, Nygren fails to show that although God can have no need-love, this does not entail that we are unable to give God anything. In the end he concludes that not we but God is the agent of our gift-love toward God. Instead of being the agents of *agape*, we are merely the pawns through which God bestows *agape* upon himself.

Thirdly, it is impossible to oppose need-love and gift-love in the way Nygren does, since in crucial respects they are identical: it is only by needing that we can give. As we have shown in the previous section, it is only through need-love, which desires your good as well as your love, that I can bestow value and identity on your person and your love and so 'secure your self-esteem and give body to your sense of identity'. The Beatle Paul McCartney expresses his desire still to be loved 'when I get older losing my hair, many years from now', in the words: 'Will you still need me, will you still feed me, when I'm sixty-four?' Obviously feeding is not enough; we also need to be needed. If I am not needed, I am nothing. To be loved and have literally nothing asked of one, and to be made to feel that there is no way in which one can ever give back anything of any value, is to be made into a pauper.[66] Nygren is correct in his claim that

---

[65] Oppenheimer, *Hope of Happiness*, 103.
[66] See Oppenheimer, *Incarnation and Immanence*, 185.

love creates value in its object, but mistaken in thinking that this creative function belongs to *agape* rather than to *eros*. This also applies to the love of God. Only by needing us can God bestow value on us and upon our love for him. If God does not need us, we become infinitely superfluous. Thus, as we quoted C. S. Lewis in the previous section, a 'God who needs nothing, loves into existence wholly *superfluous* creatures'. God can bestow value on us and on our love only if he needs us to bestow value on him. Without our bestowal he is not magnified in the way suggested by the opening line of the Magnificat: 'My soul doth magnify the Lord'. As Irving Singer explains:

If love glorifies its object by bestowing value, even treating it as perfect in relation to the lover, then perhaps the sanctified soul *can* give God something equal and comparable to what it receives. For in loving me, the Lord doth magnify my soul just as I magnify his. He is perfect and man is not, but God bestows value in loving man despite his imperfections. Man bestows value in recognizing the infinite goodness of God and delighting in it. They reciprocate within a community of bestowals.[67]

In response to these considerations, Nygren might seem to have one trump-card left: all forms of *eros* aim at self-realization and are therefore expressions of self-love which is contrary to the aims of the Christian faith. Christian faith requires us to cultivate self-denial rather than seeking to secure our own self-esteem. In various ways this response is inadequate. First of all, as we have shown in section 6.2, Nygren's rejection of the human desire for self-fulfilment turns Christianity into a form of quietism which seeks to renounce all human self-esteem. Is Nietzsche not correct in rejecting this kind of Christianity as morally corrupt since it requires us to achieve nonentity? Is not this demand both spiritually harmful and well nigh impossible to achieve? 'For most of us, the conscious attempt to put self last could make us at best difficult to live with and at worst eaten up with spiritual pride. We cannot forget ourselves on purpose.'[68] Furthermore, as we argued in section 9.1, our awareness of being irreplaceable individuals ourselves, is the necessary clue

---

[67] Singer, *Nature of Love* I, 215.   [68] Oppenheimer, *Hope of Happiness*, 102–3.

to knowing what it means to esteem others as irreplaceable as well. It follows that renouncing our own self-esteem could also prevent us from bestowing value on others. In this respect Max Scheler is correct in pointing out that one cannot give from emptiness. Gift-love is impossible if we seek to become non-entities who have nothing to give.

Secondly, renouncing our self-esteem entails a denial of the Christian gospel. The good news of the gospel is that God loves me in spite of myself, and that in loving me he bestows infinite value on my very existence. Seeking to renounce my self-esteem amounts to a rejection of this divine bestowal. 'It is impossible to eliminate love of self ... because God loves us, and we should cease to be like him if we ceased to love ourselves.'[69]

Thirdly, Nygren is mistaken in his claim that self-denial and humility entails the renunciation of our self-esteem. The search for self-denial and humility which is the first step in the *via mystica*, is not the abandonment of that self-esteem which is merely an affirmation of the fact that I am esteemed by God. Rather, Christian self-denial means abandoning the illusion that I can somehow earn God's esteem as a reward for my intrinsic goodness and can therefore anchor my self-esteem in my own merit rather than in the free gift-love of God. My value as a person is not something intrinsic to me which somehow merits the love of God. On the contrary, it is bestowed on me freely in the love of God. Thus, faith 'is the radical abandonment of self-glorification, of the desire for recognition by one's own strength and achievement. It is the knowledge that the recognition which makes one secure for oneself and in the presence of God can only be gifted.'[70] The humility of faith does not reject the gift but abandons the illusion that the gift has somehow been earned. 'My friend, who makes you so important? What do you possess that was not given you? And if you received it as a gift, why take the credit to yourself?' (1 Corinthians 4: 7).

Hence love does entail a desire for self-fulfilment. However, it knows that this self-fulfilment cannot be *achieved*; it can only be

---

[69] Gilson, *Mystical Theology*, 117.   [70] Bultmann, *Essays*, 171.

bestowed. For the believer such self-fulfilment is the beatitude which is bestowed on frail mortals in that reciprocal 'community of bestowals' which is the love of God:

> *When I look up at your heavens, the work of your fingers,*
> *at the moon and the stars you have set in place,*
> *what is a frail mortal, that you should be mindful of him,*
> *a human being, that you should take notice of him?*
> *Yet you have made him little less than a god,*
> *crowning his head with glory and honour.*
> *Lord our sovereign,*
> *how glorious is your name*
> *throughout the world.* (Psalm 8: 3–5, 9)

Index